AF614845

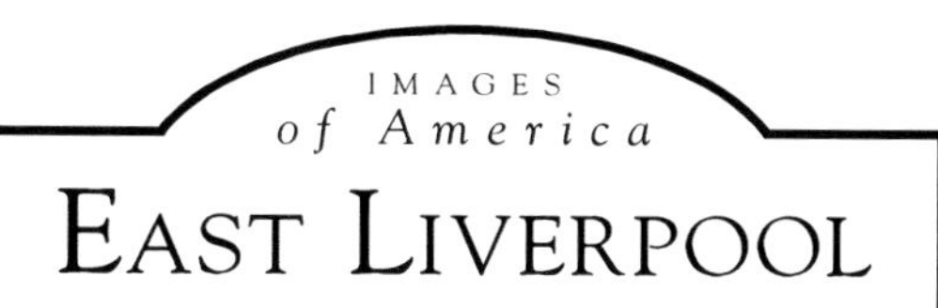
IMAGES
of America
EAST LIVERPOOL

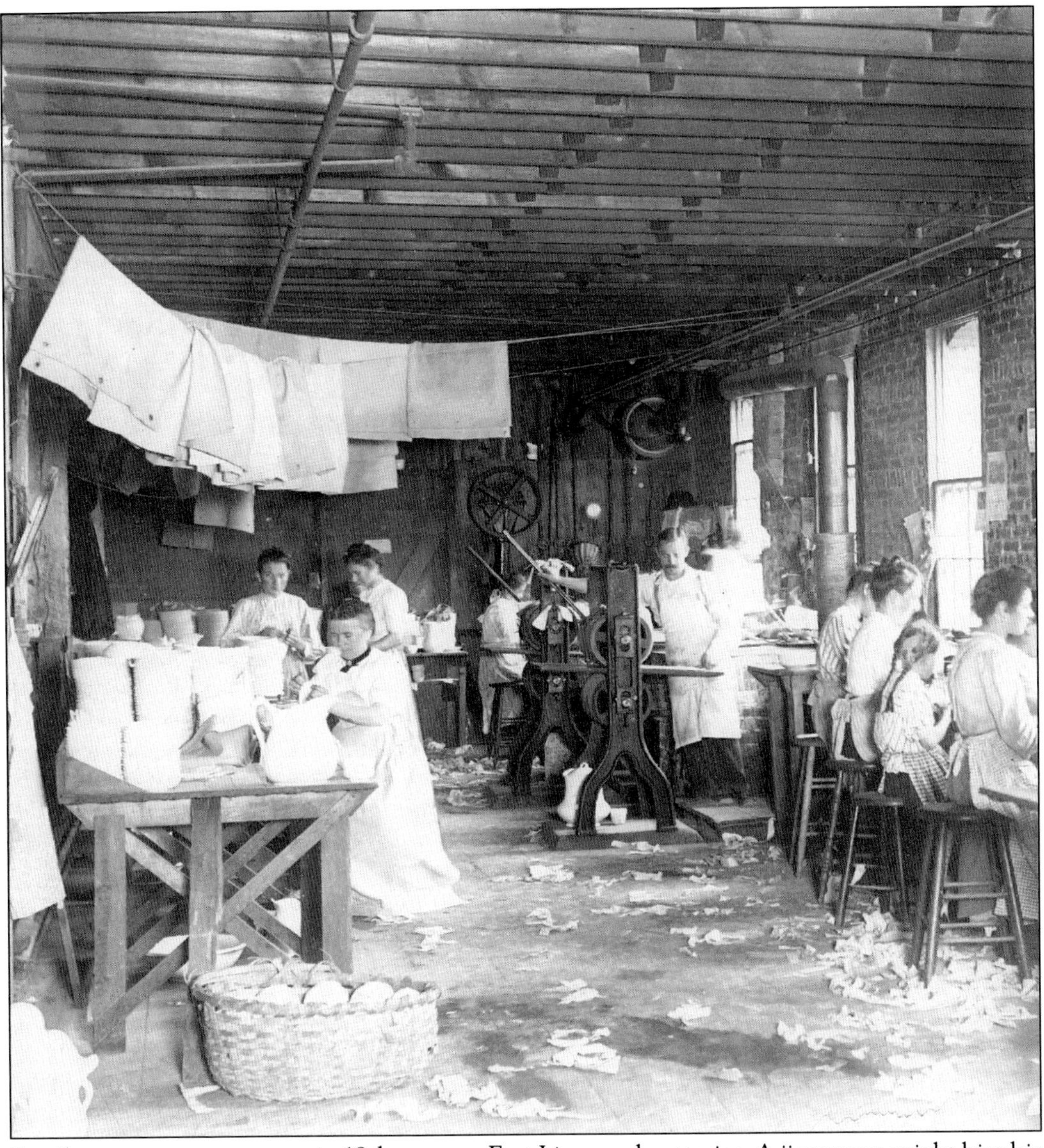

Family groups were common in 19th-century East Liverpool potteries. A jiggerman might hire his wife, his sons, his 10-year-old daughter, or even his mother to fill out a crew. This group worked at one of the four Knowles, Taylor & Knowles plants on Broadway and Bradshaw Streets between 1870 and 1929. (East Liverpool Historical Society.)

On the Cover: Sometime in the summer of 1910, this Brunt Knob Works crew gathered for a photograph after a hard day's work. Pictured from left to right are, from the back cover to the front, Steve Elliot, Floyd Starr, a Starr son, Grover Masters, another Starr son, Dorie Wallace, Frank Graver, and George Bailey; John Chapman, and Ott Christian are out of the frame on the right. A crew could produce between 35 and 50 dozen pieces of ware per day. (East Liverpool Historical Society.)

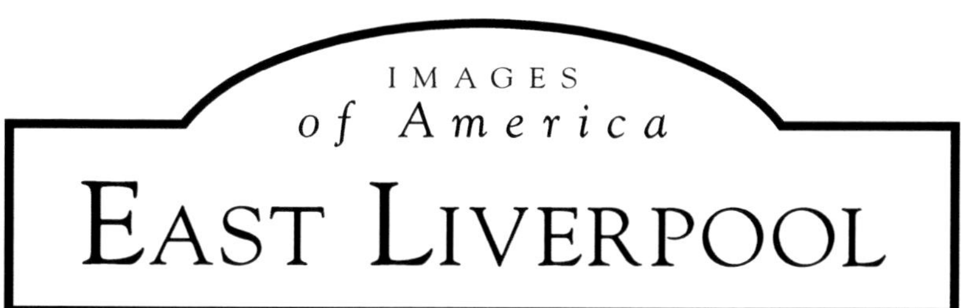

Cathy Hester Seckman

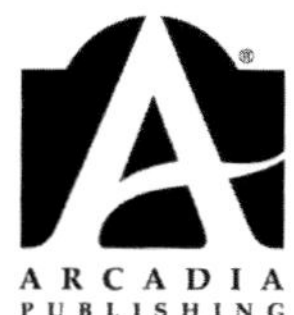

ISBN 978-1-4671-1374-8

Published by Arcadia Publishing
Charleston, South Carolina

Printed in the United States of America

Library of Congress Control Number: 2014958955

For all general information, please contact Arcadia Publishing:
Telephone 843-853-2070
Fax 843-853-0044
E-mail sales@arcadiapublishing.com
For customer service and orders:
Toll-Free 1-888-313-2665

Visit us on the Internet at www.arcadiapublishing.com

For Joan Witt and Glenn Waight, whose spirits are in this book

Contents

FOREWORD

The East Liverpool area, the nation's pottery capital since the late 19th century, has a rich heritage that continues to yield intriguing stories and interesting characters. As a journalist, author, bibliophile, and history buff, Cathy Hester Seckman is eminently qualified to write the newest book about the East Liverpool area. Along with the books *The City of Hills and Kilns* by William C. Gates Jr. and *East Liverpool, Ohio: Reflections of 200 Years*, compiled by members of the East Liverpool Historical Society, this book will further enhance our understanding of past East Liverpudlian people, places, and events.

It was an honor and a pleasure when she invited me to read her manuscript, offer suggestions, and write this foreword. As an area resident for most of my life, and as the director of the Museum of Ceramics, East Liverpool has long been important to me. I am a sixth-generation descendant of Jabez and Sarah Vodrey, English immigrants who became two of this area's pioneer potters in 1847. We Vodreys have loved the area ever since.

You, dear reader, will no doubt enjoy reading and rereading this book. I find that no matter what one's own burdens are, when considering 19th- and 20th-century joys and struggles he or she gains a deeper appreciation for the past and a more balanced perspective about the present and future. Readers can laugh at the foibles and be warned by the mistakes of those earlier East Liverpudlians who appear in these pages. Ultimately, we may each be heartened and even inspired by their sacrifices and altruism. So make yourself a cup of tea just as those immigrant English potters enjoyed, nestle into your favorite comfy chair, and prepare to do a bit of time travel, thanks to Cathy Hester Seckman.

—Sarah Webster Vodrey

ACKNOWLEDGMENTS

As with all books, this one could not have been published without a lot of help. My first thanks go to Mary Margaret Schley, former acquisitions editor at Arcadia Publishing, who thought an Images of America book about my hometown would be a fine idea. Thanks also go to my current Arcadia editor, Jesse Darland, for answers and encouragement.

I am deeply appreciative of East Liverpool's repositories of history: the Carnegie Public Library; the Lou Holtz/Upper Ohio Valley Hall of Fame and its staff; the Thompson House, administered by the East Liverpool Historical Society; and the East Liverpool High School Alumni Association, as well as Deanna Plemons and Frank C. Dawson. Special thanks go to Sarah Webster Vodrey, director of the Museum of Ceramics, and her staff. City attorney Tim Brookes, longtime president of the East Liverpool Historical Society, is also due a warm acknowledgment for his generous help. For providing information about city businesses, thanks go to Brian S. Allen at River Valley Health Partners (which Liverpudlians still know as "City Hospital"); Harold and Sarah Bricker of Bricker's Cafeteria and Delicatessen; Harry Comm, former owner of Hersche-Bloor Pharmacy, along with present owner Tony DeCaria; Keystone Printing; Amy Doak of Milligan's Hardware; Clyde McClellan of American Mug and Stein; and Jack Reynolds, longtime owner of Crook's Furniture. I am also indebted to Steve Huba at the *Review*, Megan Bennett and Salvation Army major Stella McGuire at the East Liverpool Salvation Army Citadel, and Stephen Hedges of the Ohio Public Library Information Network.

Many locals and out-of-towners allowed me to see, copy, and use their photographs, including Phyllis Conley, Liane Elliott-Gorby, Peter Hacker, Eddie Hedrick, Roxie Harsha, Inger Lloyd, Dawn Chapman, Pam Stewart Banfield, Rick Carter, Carolyn Wilson Nentwick, Vincent Maola Jr., Jill Winters, Richard W. Bangor, Donna Blazer McComas, Alonzo Spencer, Andrea and Larry Adkins, and Caryle Buck. Sincere apologies go to anyone who might have been inadvertently omitted.

East Liverpool touches on a deep and vast reservoir of city history, providing brief snapshots of life the way it was for our forebears. Anyone wishing for a more complete account is encouraged to read *The City of Hills and Kilns: Life and Work in East Liverpool, Ohio,* by William C. Gates Jr.; *The East Liverpool, Ohio, Pottery District: Identification of Manufacturers and Marks*, by William C. Gates Jr. and Dana E. Ormerod; and *East Liverpool, Ohio: Reflections of 200 Years*, by the East Liverpool Historical Society.

INTRODUCTION

Long before Thomas Bennett found clay deposits along the Ohio River in 1839 and opened East Liverpool's first commercially successful pottery, indigenous American Indians were using the clay they found near their homes to form pottery, pipes, and ceremonial objects. Clay objects made their lives easier and were useful for trade. When Europeans arrived on the scene in the middle of the 17th century, it did not take long for them to discover and tap the rich natural resources of the Ohio Valley.

The tiny settlement that would become East Liverpool had originally been named St. Clair in the early 1800s by its founder, Thomas Fawcett, in honor of the governor of the Northwest Territory, Arthur St. Clair. The first permanent residents, however, called it Fawcettstown. The name Liverpool was bestowed on the river settlement in 1817. In 1830, "East" was added to the town's name to distinguish it from another Liverpool, Ohio (which no longer exists), in Medina County. Though still small, East Liverpool was beginning to prosper as more families arrived and built houses, churches, and schools. Wharves, warehouses, and boat works were constructed to encourage river commerce; sawmills and gristmills began operation; and the first hotel appeared. Early potters were setting up shops and experimenting with local clays, but none survived very long.

It was not until Thomas Bennett appeared on the scene that East Liverpool could claim its first commercially successful pottery. Once Bennett fired his kiln, an industry was born. Clays and shales of the Pennsylvanian age and the Mississippian and Devonian ages supplied the materials that eventually made East Liverpool the "Pottery Capital of the World." Bennett soon sent for his brothers, and word began to spread in faraway England about opportunities in America. Labor unrest and economic conditions among potters in the Staffordshire district of England, many from Stoke-on-Trent, spurred skilled potters to consider immigration. New arrivals to East Liverpool wrote enthusiastic letters back home. Edward Tunnicliff, who arrived in East Liverpool in 1840, reported, "I am to have double price for dish making that they have in England." The earliest potters made Rockingham and yellow ware, but with the creative blending of clay, shale, flint, and other raw materials, plus modernized firing processes, East Liverpool plants eventually produced white ware, creamware, and semivitreous china.

By 1850, six potteries were in regular operation; 10 were recorded on an 1853 map. In 1854, some 11 potteries used 125,000 bushels of coal to produce 170,000 dozen pieces of ware with 387 employees. The early manufacturers, including William Brunt, Benjamin Harker, Isaac Knowles, Jabez Vodrey, and John Wyllie, were known to have close working relationships, frequently borrowing formulas and materials from each other and offering technical advice. By the time of the Civil War, East Liverpool had established itself as a town with one major industry. In the last half of the 19th century, dozens of potteries opened, closed, reopened with new names, then merged or closed again. Pottery owners changed partners with some regularity. Between 1851 and 1872, for instance, five potteries were founded: Douds and Barnes, Douds and Sebring, Douds and Moore, Douds and Welch, and Douds and Foutts. Mr. Douds might have been difficult to work with, one assumes.

The town's single-industry reputation caused some concern in the early 20th century. The editor of the *Review* stated in 1911 that East Liverpool's industrial community needed to be diversified since economic downturns and labor troubles in potteries caused needless hardship to residents. Entrepreneurs tried steelmaking, tile making, glassmaking, and other industries with varying degrees of success. The chamber of commerce was not enthusiastic about encouraging new businesses. In the 1920s, the chamber decided it was better to, according to the book *The City of Hills and Kilns*, "conserve the industries that we already have in our city than to bring plants here that would not prove a benefit to the community." One local businessman thought it "unwise" to draw employees away from the potteries to work in new businesses. Still, the standard of living was improving, streets were being paved, and the town prospered with a growing retail district and increasing population. There were 353 retail stores in town in 1929. The pottery industry was not so healthy. New technology and new marketing demands that were too expensive for small firms, plus cheap imports from Asia after World War I, contributed to a drop in the number of East Liverpool potteries. Another cause for the decline was a lack of price adjustments to reflect increased manufacturing costs. Only the largest and most modern plants, many of them located outside of town, survived. By the end of the Depression, East Liverpool was no longer the bustling hub of the pottery industry. The numbers of active potters in the city dropped steadily, and by the mid-1950s there were more steelworkers in town—many employed upriver in Midland, Pennsylvania—than there were potters. Between 1953 and 1963, employment in area potteries dropped from 6,101 to 3,075. In 1970, the number dropped to 1,026; in 1983, after the closing of Chester's Anchor Hocking plant (formerly Taylor, Smith & Taylor), it dropped to 937, with only 567 of those actually residing in East Liverpool.

Today, two potteries remain in town: Hall China Company in East End, now owned by Homer Laughlin China Company, and American Mug & Stein on Dresden Avenue. The city is also home to Commercial Decal and Mason Color Works, two of the biggest suppliers to the pottery industry in the country, and W.C. Bunting Company, which has dominated the pottery-decorating business. Bunting suffered a devastating fire in November 2014 but, at present, is still operating (with assistance from American Mug & Stein). Much-needed employment is provided by a hazardous-waste incinerator, Kent State University's local branch, and the ever-expanding City Hospital, now known as River Valley Health Partners. Smaller firms and the service sector also provide jobs, but many Liverpudlians travel out of town every day for work. The retail sector, struggling for years under the onslaught of suburban shopping centers, continues to decline.

In recent years, good news has arrived in the form of the East Liverpool High School Alumni Association, which revived local pride and optimism, and the Lou Holtz/Upper Ohio Valley Hall of Fame and Museum. As of this writing, plans are moving forward for a school of trades to open downtown, and rumors of a new revitalization effort are flying. Whatever its problems are today, East Liverpool is always conscious of its illustrious past and hopeful of a return of prosperity and self-esteem.

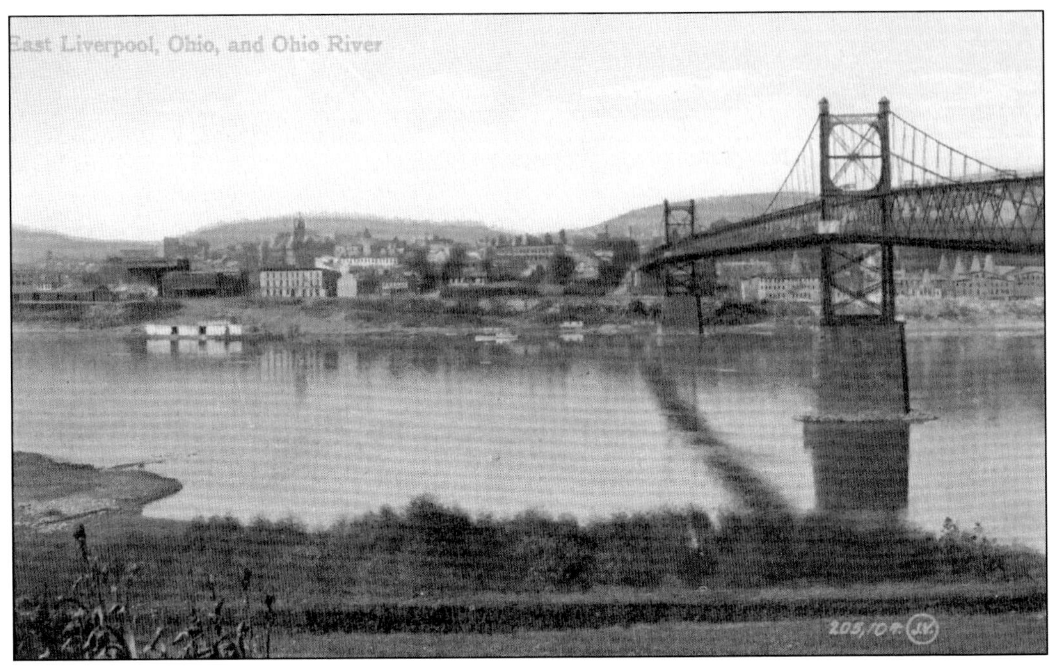

Above, pottery kilns dot the landscape in this early postcard view of East Liverpool taken from across the Ohio River. Under the old Chester Bridge is the C.C. Thompson Pottery. The hills behind the city are still undeveloped. Below, power poles are already in place along Fourth Street at the dawn of the 20th century, and early streetcars jostle with horses and buggies for space along the narrow street. At left is the Ceramic Theatre, built in 1912. (Above, Museum of Ceramics; below, Inger Lloyd.)

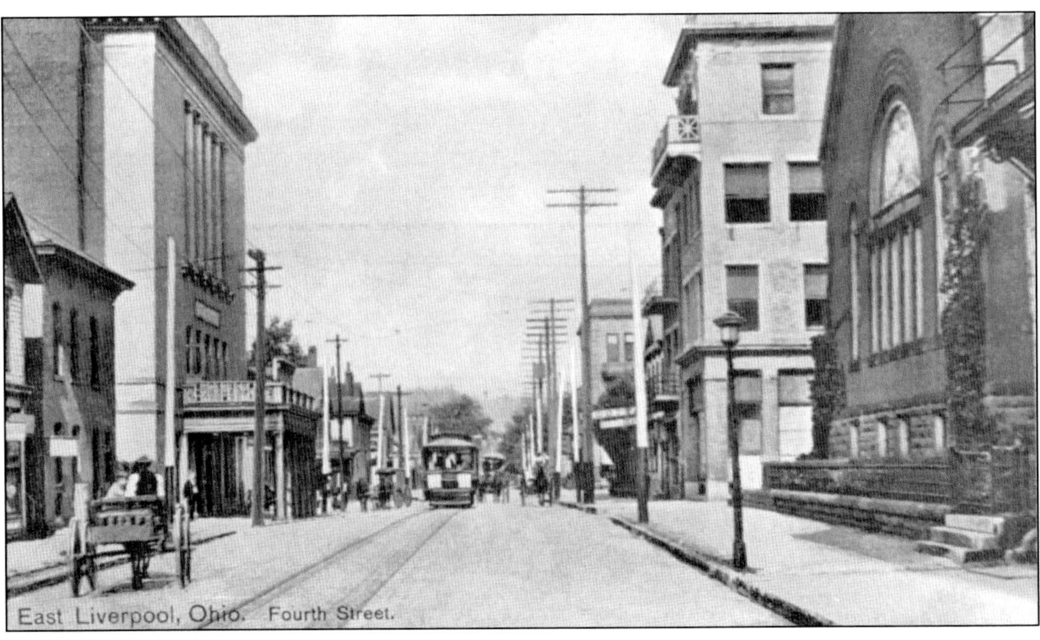

One

At the Beginning Point

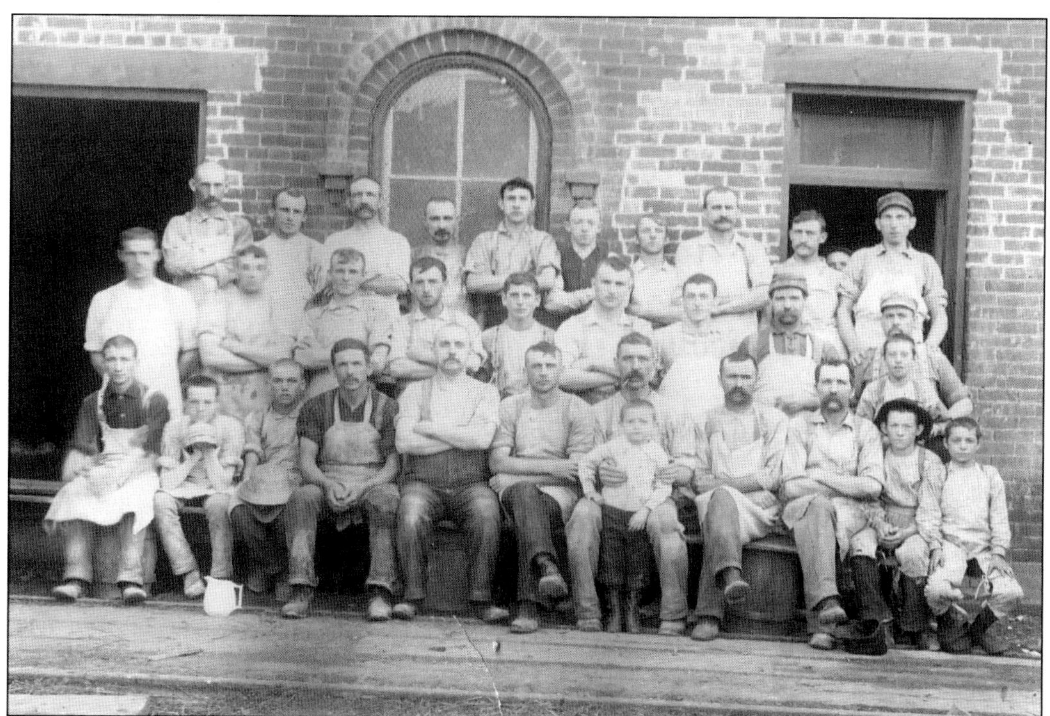

These stern-faced men and boys worked at the Brunt, Bloor, Martin & Company's Dresden Pottery at the turn of the 19th century. A crew leader, or jiggerman, hired his own batter-out (who placed prepared clay in the molds), mold runner, finisher, and clay carrier and paid them from his wages. He would often hire his wife and children for less-technical jobs so that more money would stay in the family. (East Liverpool Historical Society.)

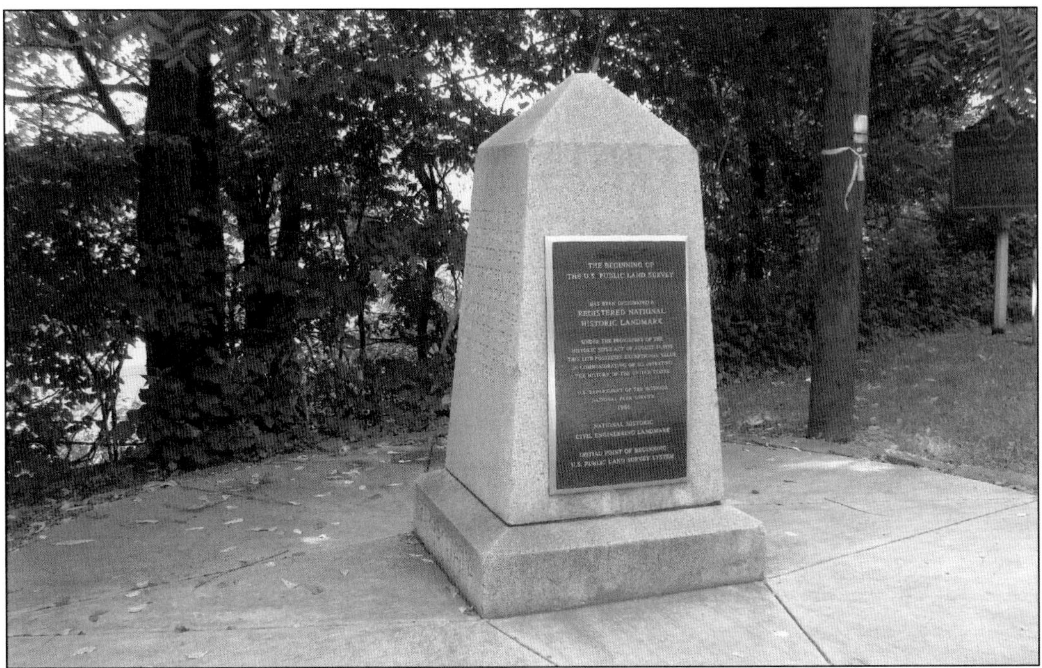

Thomas Hutchins, geographer of the United States, chose a spot 1,112 feet from this commemorative obelisk on the east side of East Liverpool as the beginning point of the US Public Land Survey in 1785. Born around 1730 in New Jersey, Hutchins began his career as an engineer in the British army. After he switched allegiance to the United States, he was appointed its first geographer in 1781. A few years later, he began his survey of the Northwest Territory by establishing the Point of Beginning. He had been commissioned by Thomas Jefferson to survey the recently acquired Northwest Territory in six-mile-square townships. Nearly every survey of land to the west of this spot in East Liverpool, except in Texas, begins from this point. (Both author's collection.)

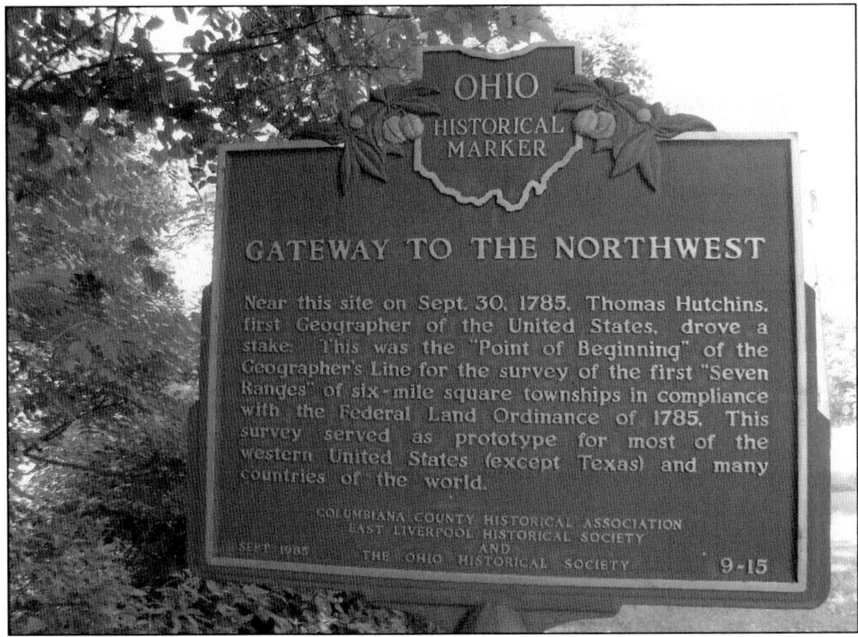

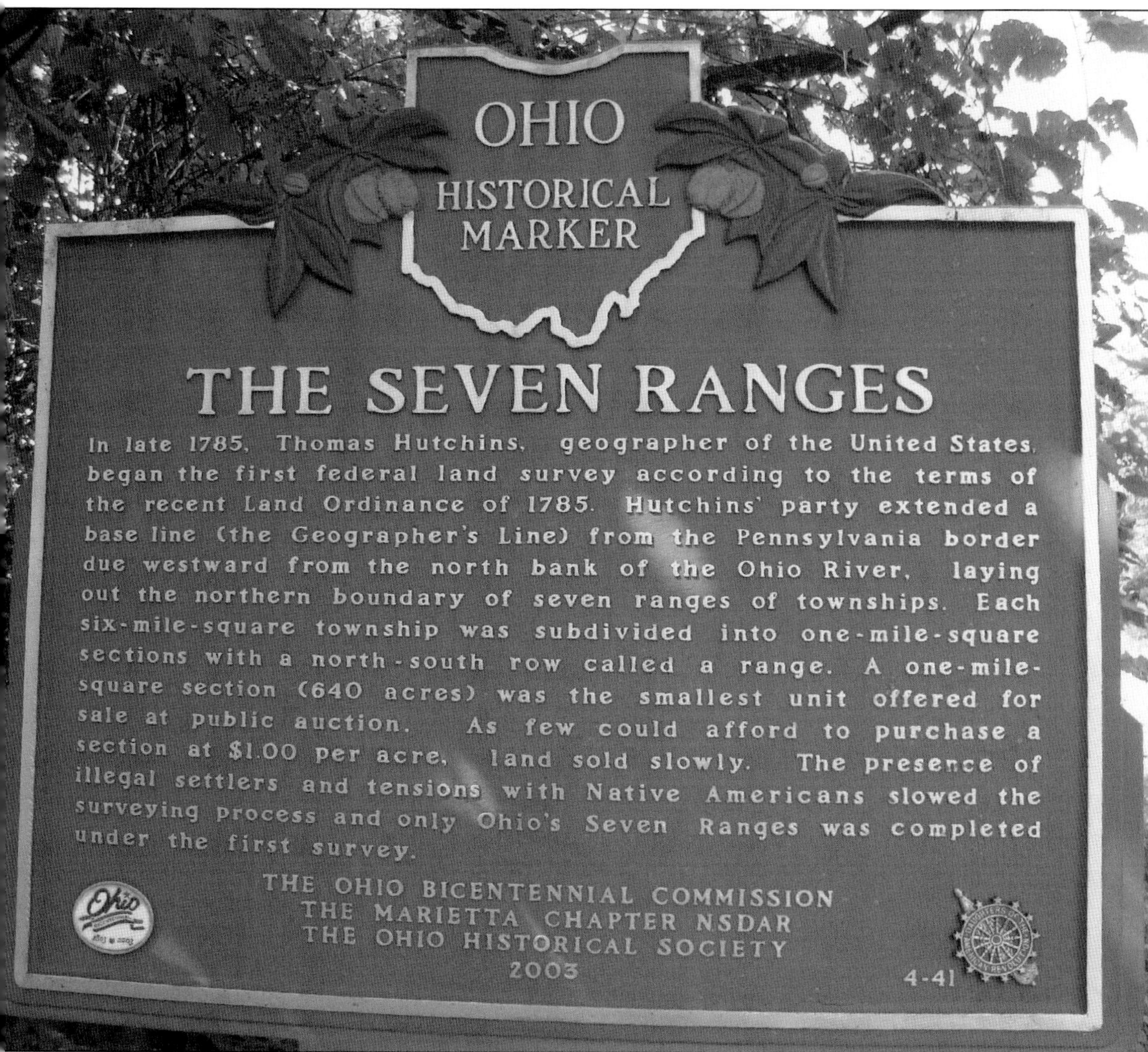

After establishing his beginning point, Hutchins used it to survey the Seven Ranges tract, the first in the Northwest Territory. The tract's north-south line was Ellicott's Line at the western boundary of Pennsylvania. The east-west line (Geographer's Line or Base Line) started at the Point of Beginning, where the Pennsylvania boundary met the Ohio River. The tract included all or part of seven Ohio counties. One-seventh of the Seven Ranges tract was earmarked for Continental army veterans, several numbered sections in each township were reserved by the government, and the rest were sold to the public, beginning in 1787 in New York City, Philadelphia, Pittsburgh, and at the Steubenville Land Office south of East Liverpool, which opened in 1801. The federal government had expected land sales to pay off its debts from the Revolution, but sales were slow and complicated by both illegal settlers and already established Native Americans. (Author's collection.)

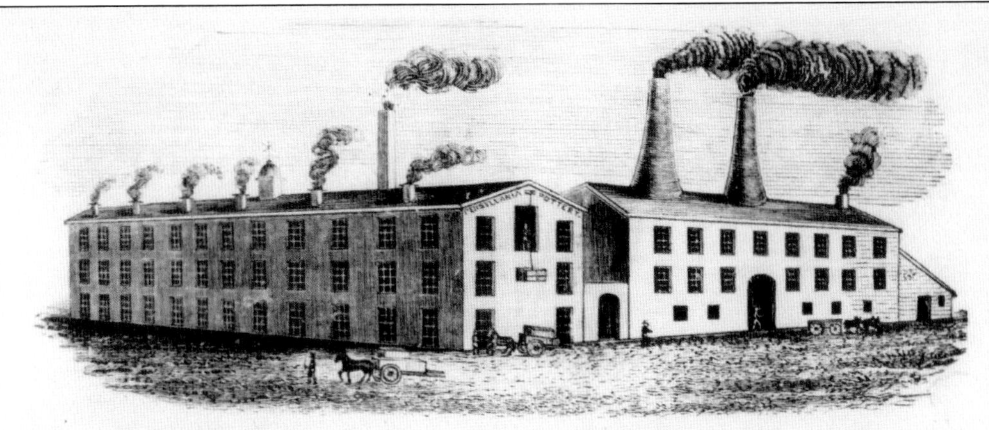

James Bennett, father of the area pottery industry, began an apprenticeship as a potter in Derbyshire, England, in the early 1800s. After immigrating in 1835, he worked in New Jersey and Indiana. A chance encounter on his hunt for a new home for his family caused him to stop in East Liverpool to inspect clay deposits. The town had been founded in 1800 by Irish Quaker farmers Thomas and Isabella Fawcett. By 1839, Bennett had established a one-kiln pottery here. He sent for his brothers Edwin, Daniel, and William in 1841. They formed the Bennett & Brothers Pottery Company, which operated until 1844. At that time, the Bennetts sold out to the Croxall family and moved near Pittsburgh. Bennett died at 50 from complications of "potter's lung," or "potter's asthma," now known as silicosis. (Both Museum of Ceramics.)

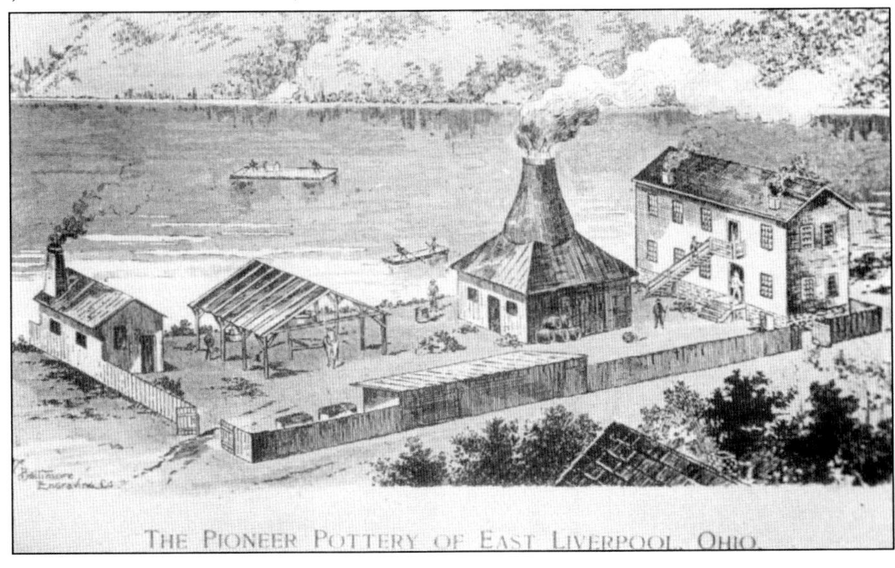

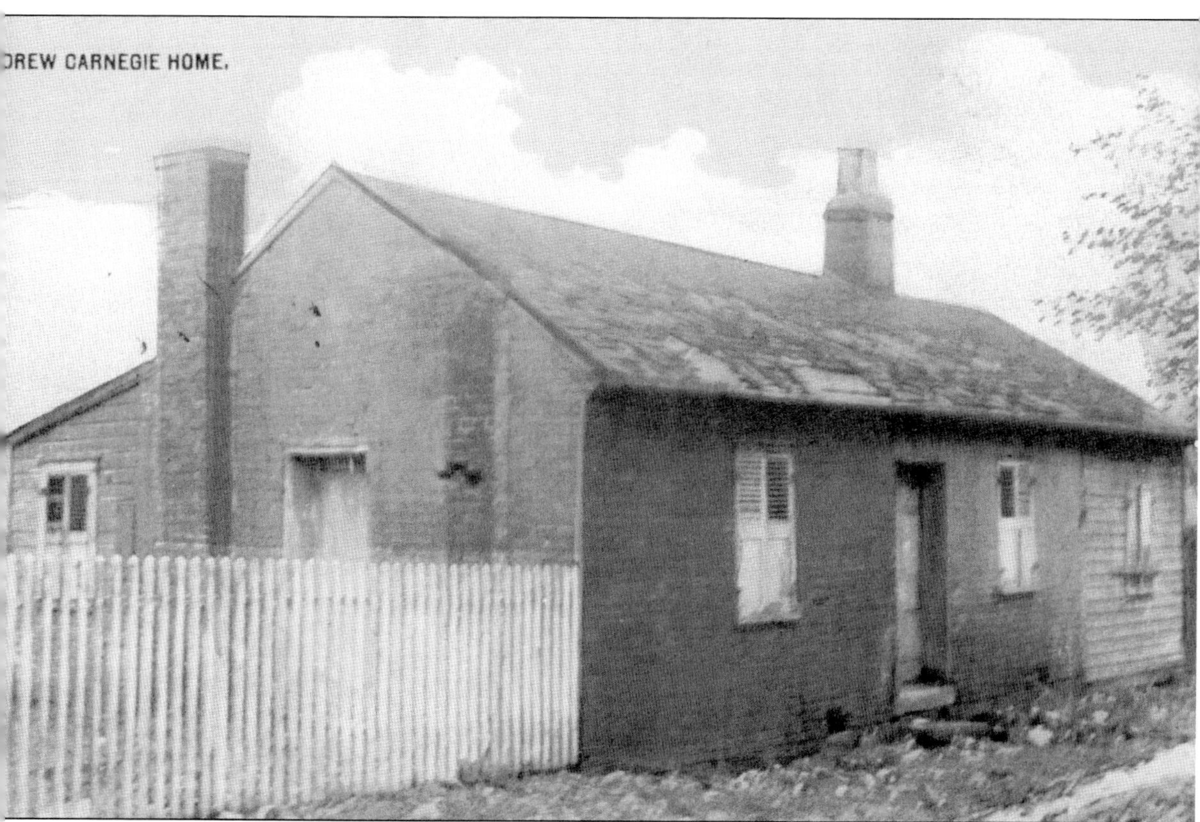

A 1¢ postcard proudly depicts an East Liverpool connection of 19th-century steel magnate and philanthropist Andrew Carnegie. According to a note on the back of the postcard, this two-room brick home on West Second Street, valued at about $300, was owned by Carnegie's uncle William Morris in 1847. In his autobiography, Carnegie states that he visited the Morrises at least once on a summer vacation while he was working as a telegraph messenger boy in Pittsburgh. The autobiography also records a visit Carnegie's mother made to East Liverpool a few years later, when she mortgaged their home with a city bank so her son could buy shares in the Adams Express Telegraph Company. Carnegie may have been reminded of his local connections years later when he was prompted by East Liverpool business leaders to donate a library to the city. In July 1899, he provided $50,000 for construction and $3,000 a year for maintenance and operations. (Inger Lloyd.)

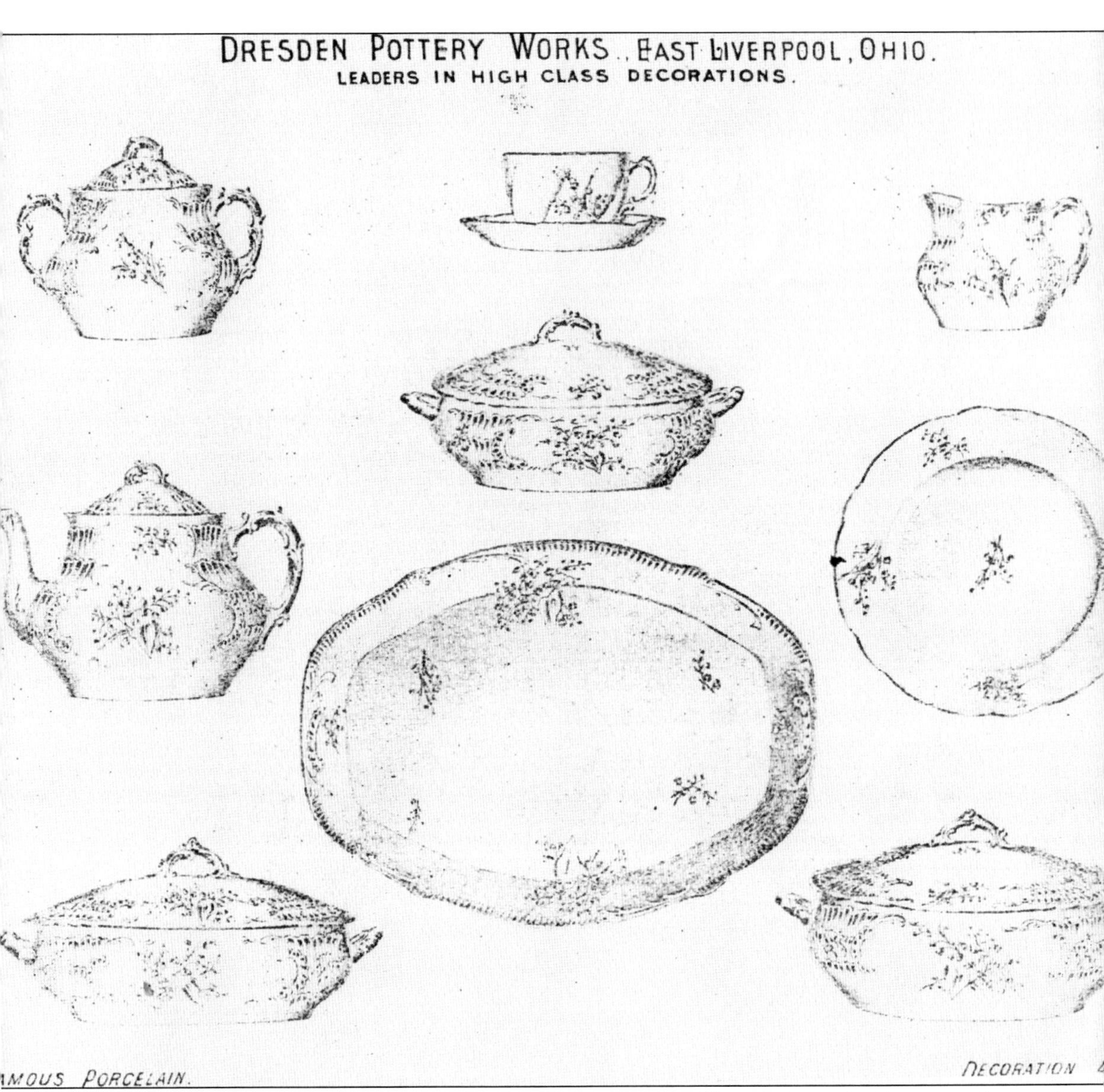

The 1896 catalog of the Dresden Street pottery of Brunt, Bloor, Martin & Company featured "high class decorations" on its Dresden porcelain dinner service. Built in 1876, the plant produced 781 casks of white ware in its initial year of operation. Those first-year figures might have been higher except for a roof fire caused by heat from a kiln. East Liverpool potteries were especially vulnerable to fire and flood in the early years. Products from the pottery were displayed at the Centennial Exposition in Philadelphia that year and won awards. By 1880, output had increased to 3,000 casks per year, thanks to a demand for white ware, and the owners hosted a "first annual" picnic for workers and their families. The five-kiln plant became the Potters Cooperative Company when it was purchased for $40,000 by a group of potters in 1882, with assistance from the Knights of Labor. It was renamed the Dresden Pottery in 1925. (East Liverpool Historical Society.)

Two

One Town, One Industry

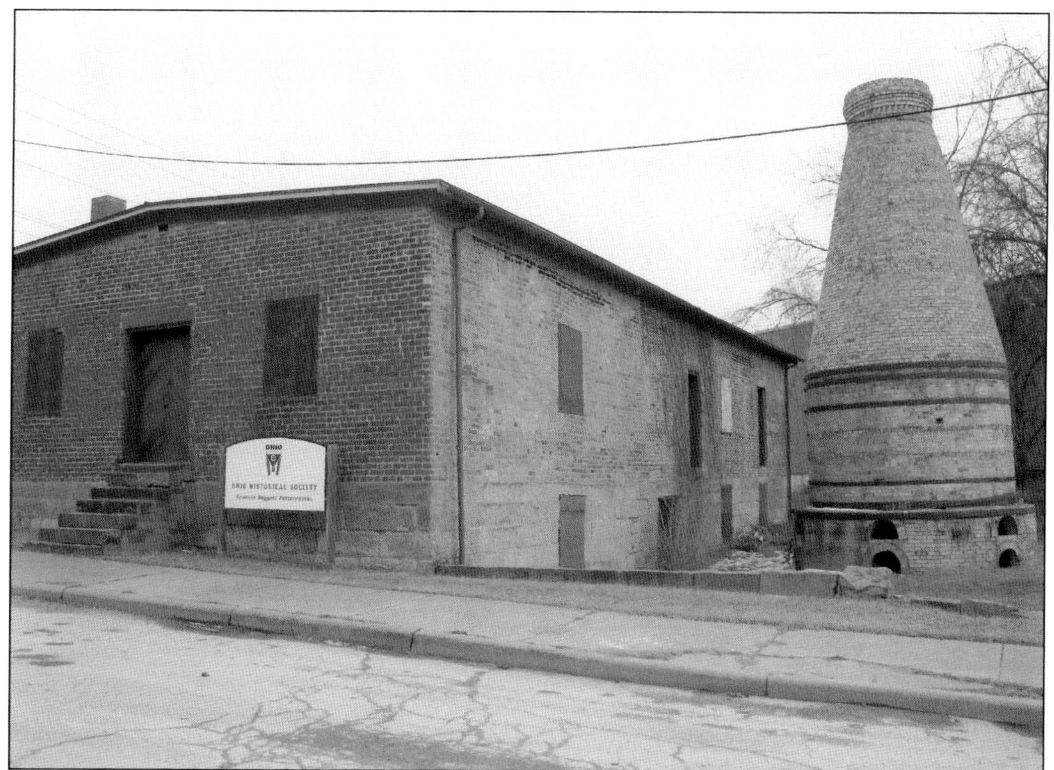

These are the oldest pottery structures in East Liverpool, located at Second and Market Streets. The building and bottle kiln are in the National Register of Historic Places. John Goodwin produced pottery here in 1843, followed in 1853 by the Baggott Brothers. Roof and building repairs and exhibit planning were paid for by a state appropriation of $105,000 in the 1970s; the roof was replaced in 2006. (Author's collection.)

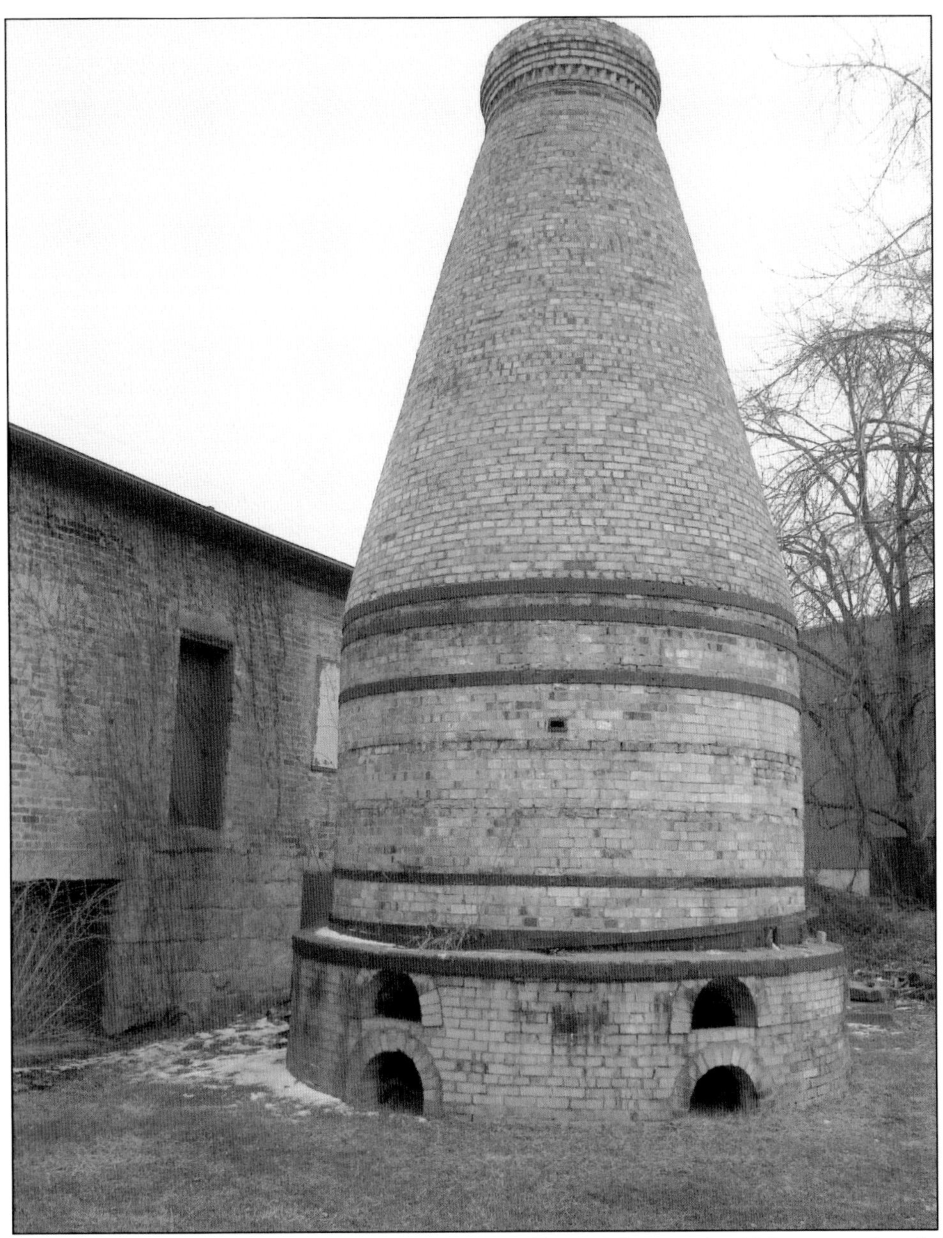

A brick bottle kiln is an iconic image for East Liverpudlians. The city shield features a bottle kiln, as do other local shields and flags. The East Liverpool High School Potters use a kiln with a face and legs as their mascot, Potter Pete. This kiln, adjacent to the Goodwin-Baggott building, is typical of the style. By city ordinance passed in 1846 for fire prevention, a kiln was to be 35 feet high and more than 100 feet from nearby houses or businesses. Either wood or coal could have been used to heat the first kilns, but natural gas, available locally, was the fuel of choice by the late 18th century. Ware was placed in fireproof sagger containers and loaded into kilns. Pieces of ware were separated from each other by kiln furniture called pins and spurs. The first firing was about 48 hours, then a 48-hour cooling period followed. Depending on type, some ware required more than one firing. Each individual kiln could be fired, if all went well, two or three times a week. (Author's collection.)

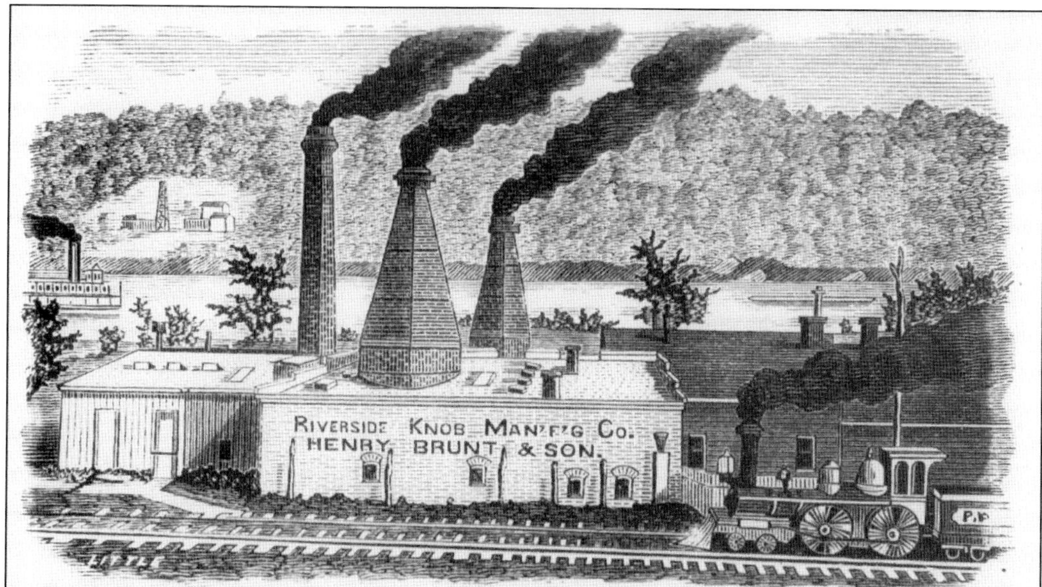

William Brunt Sr. and his brother-in-law William Bloor Sr. built the Brunt Pottery in 1849 on Market Street. After experimenting with doorknob and furniture-knob production, the plant was making knobs by 1850. The name was changed to Riverside Knob Works by 1856. Metal doorknobs eventually claimed more of the market, but because of a metal shortage during World War II, the plant made as many as 80,000 ceramic knobs per day. Imperfect knobs discarded in riverside dumps were sometimes used in a lunchtime throwing game similar to horseshoes. Ceramic doorknobs made a nostalgic comeback of sorts in the 1980s when area businesses began selling packaged doorknob games made with original, then later, replica ceramic knobs by Homer Laughlin China Company. The National Doorknob Tossing Championships are held each summer at the Tri-State Pottery Festival. (Both Museum of Ceramics.)

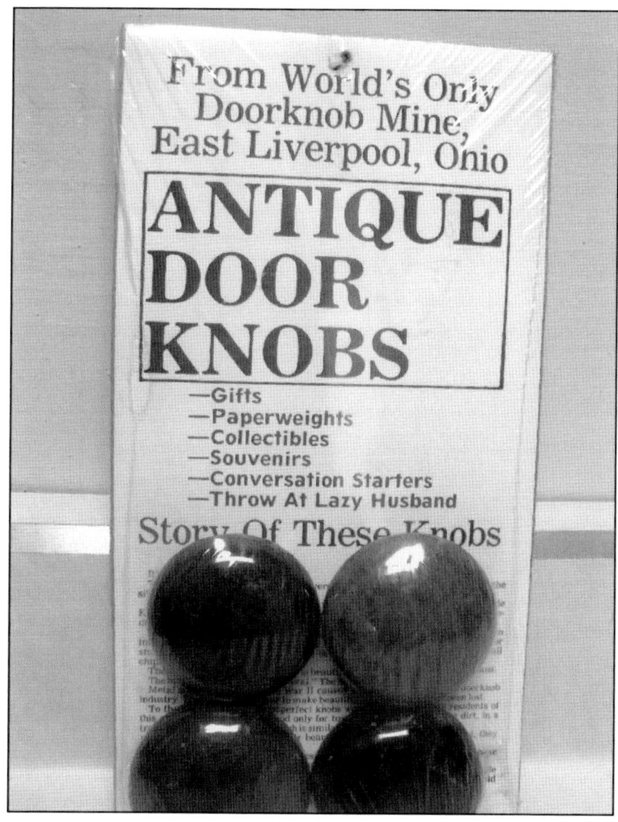

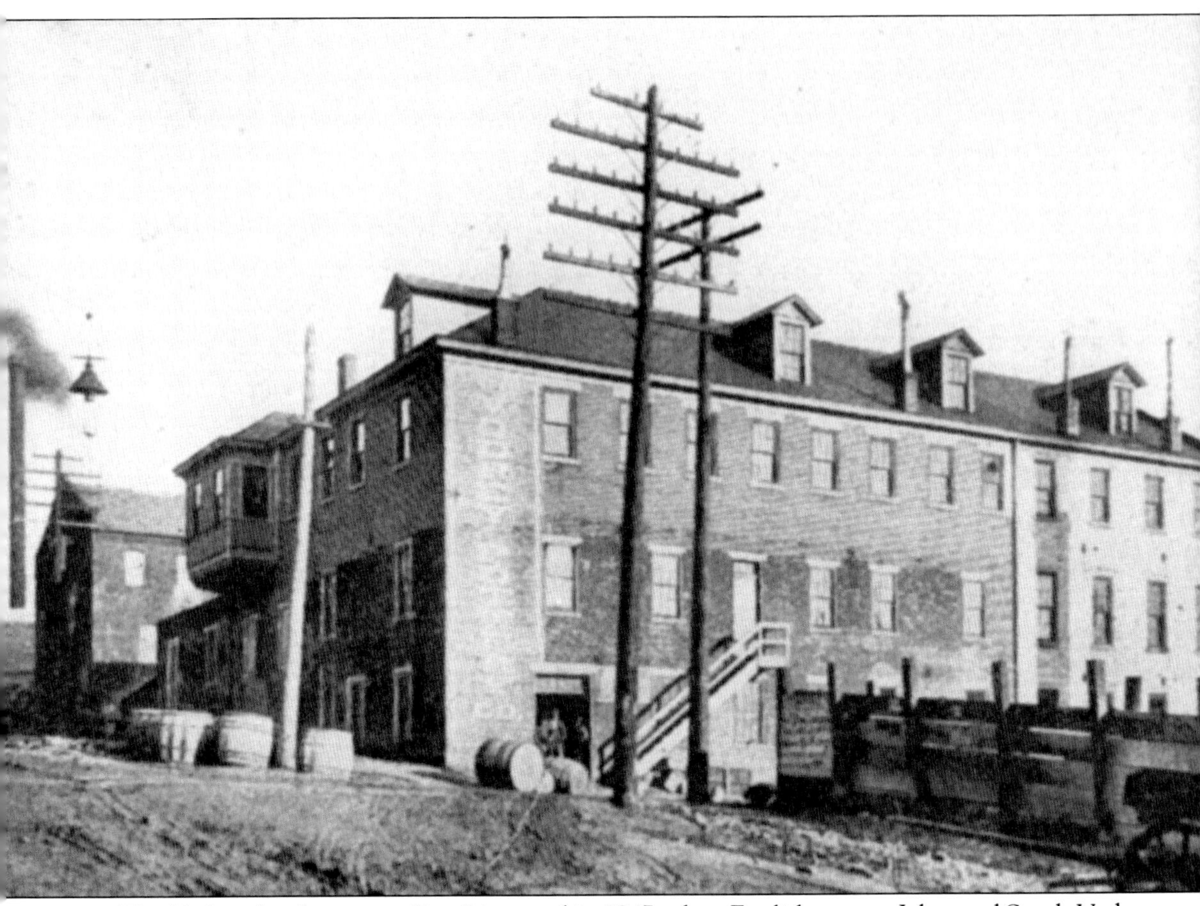

The Vodrey family came to East Liverpool in 1847, when English potters Jabez and Sarah Vodrey moved from Troy, Indiana. With their first partners, they operated the Phoenix Pottery on Fourth Street. Sons James, John, and William opened the Palissy Works (Vodrey & Brother Pottery) at Fourth and College Streets in 1857, using the partially burned remains of the community's first Catholic church. The pottery produced yellow ware, Rockingham, and ironstone, having six kilns and 225 employees by the end of the 19th century. The Vodrey Pottery Company closed in 1928, and most of the buildings were razed in the 1930s. Memorial Auditorium, once part of the city high school and now owned by Kent State University's East Liverpool branch, was built on the site in the 1940s. The fifth-, sixth-, and seventh-generation descendants of Jabez and Sarah Vodrey continue to live, work, and contribute to the educational and cultural life of the area. (Museum of Ceramics.)

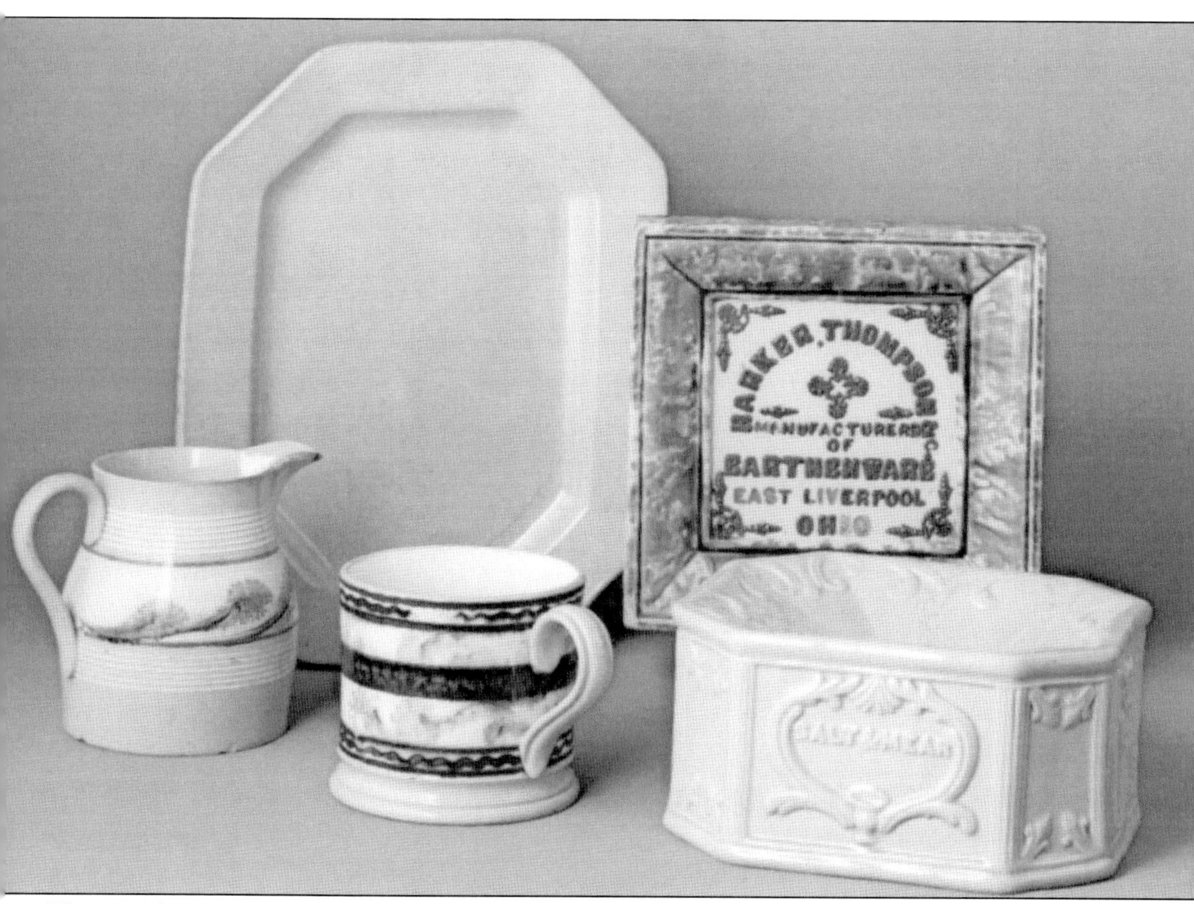

These 19th-century examples from the burgeoning pottery industry of East Liverpool are a Bennett & Brothers platter, 1840–1844; a ceramic Harker Thompson "business card," 1851–1854; a pitcher attributed to McNicol, Burton & Company, around 1873; a frog mug attributed to the Vodrey Brothers Pottery, around 1860; and a molded Salt & Mear cuspidor, 1842–1850. Pottery companies of the era opened and closed with some regularity, and familiar names were added and deleted as business partners fell out or gave up and as brothers or sons entered and left the pottery industry. The Harker name, for instance, was used by eight different pottery enterprises between 1840 and 1972. Harker Thompson, which operated from 1851 to 1854, sold Rockingham and yellow ware across the country. It was delivered by steamer and railroad, packed in casks. "Good casks," as one contract with a Detroit distributor specified, "with eight hoops . . . not over five percent broken." (East Liverpool Historical Society.)

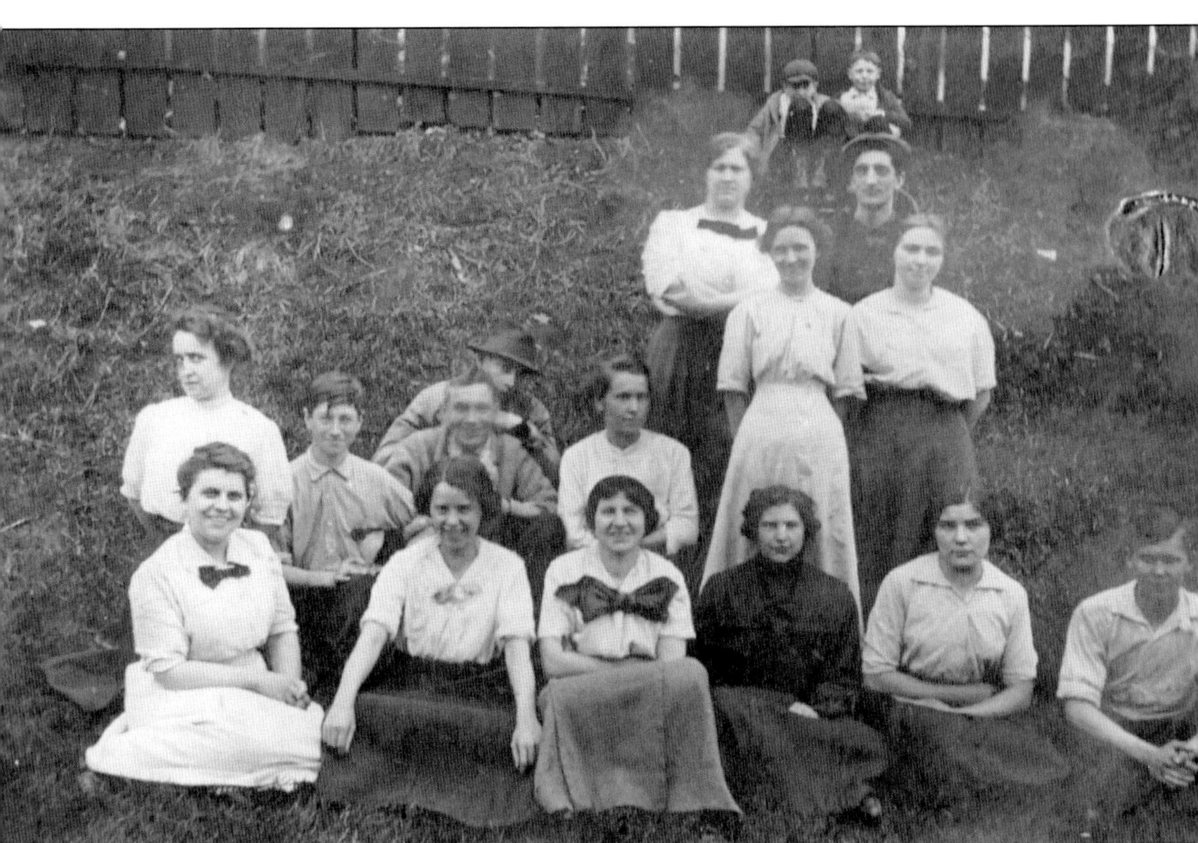

According to *The City of Hills and Kilns*, a potter of the Cartwright family was working in East Liverpool by the 1840s, when Thomas Cartwright was engaged by Harker's "as a turner of yellow ware and to do all the turning for one thrower to average 160 doz. of ware per week . . . at the rate of one dollar per score of twenty dozen." The Croxall and Cartwright Pottery was in business from 1856 to 1888. This Cartwright crew, possibly on a company-sponsored outing, includes, from left to right, (first row) Elizabeth Stamm, Mable Foster, Evelyn Watson, Bessie Funk, Dora Moffet, and Delbert Tittle; (second row) Flo Carter, Gordon Skelton, Ben Grimes, Lola Plummer, ? Wilkinson (standing), and Nina Green (standing); (third row) Stewart Hutchinson (sitting), Edna Orr, and Fred Tucker. The two boys sitting in front of the fence are not identified. (Frank C. Dawson.)

Confederate general John Hunt Morgan gave residents a scare when he had the audacity to raid above the Ohio River. It was the summer of 1863, and Morgan's forces were engaged in what would be the northernmost incursion of Confederate forces. The newly married Morgan, age 38, had brought nearly 2,000 soldiers through Indiana and Ohio to distract Union forces. Commanding general Braxton Bragg had refused permission for Confederate forces to cross the river, but Morgan entered Indiana on July 8, burned his boats, and was in Ohio by July 13. Harassed by Union forces, by late July Morgan was down to 475 horsemen and was headed toward East Liverpool, probably to try a crossing at Babb's Island or Smith's Ferry. (Both East Liverpool Historical Society.)

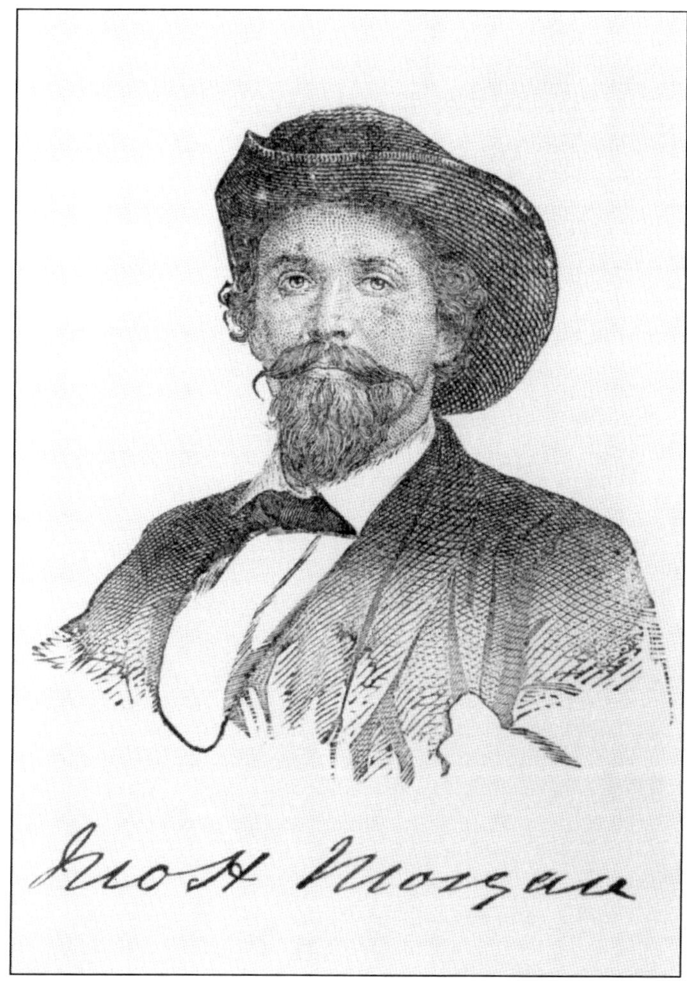

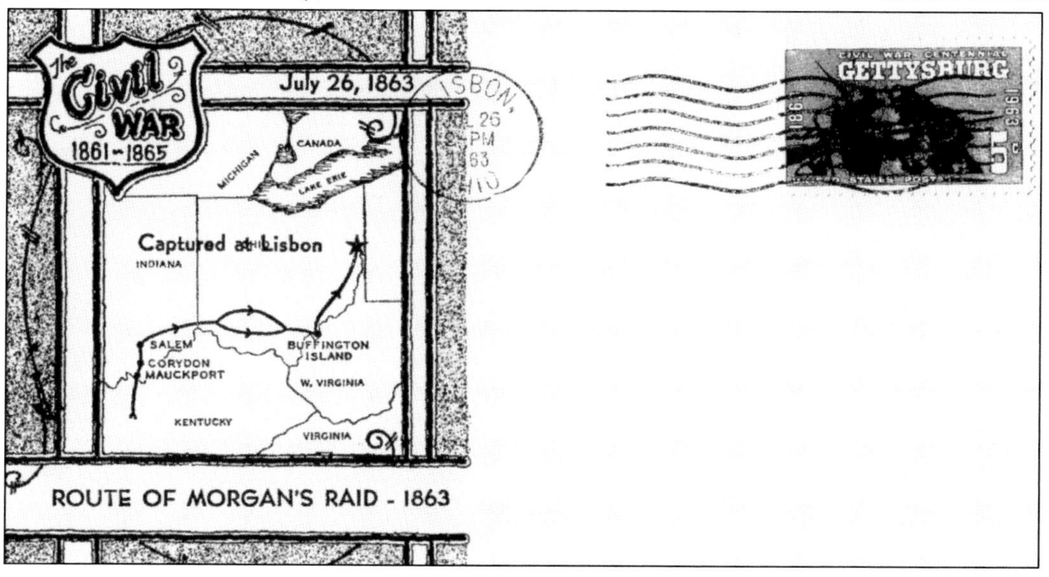

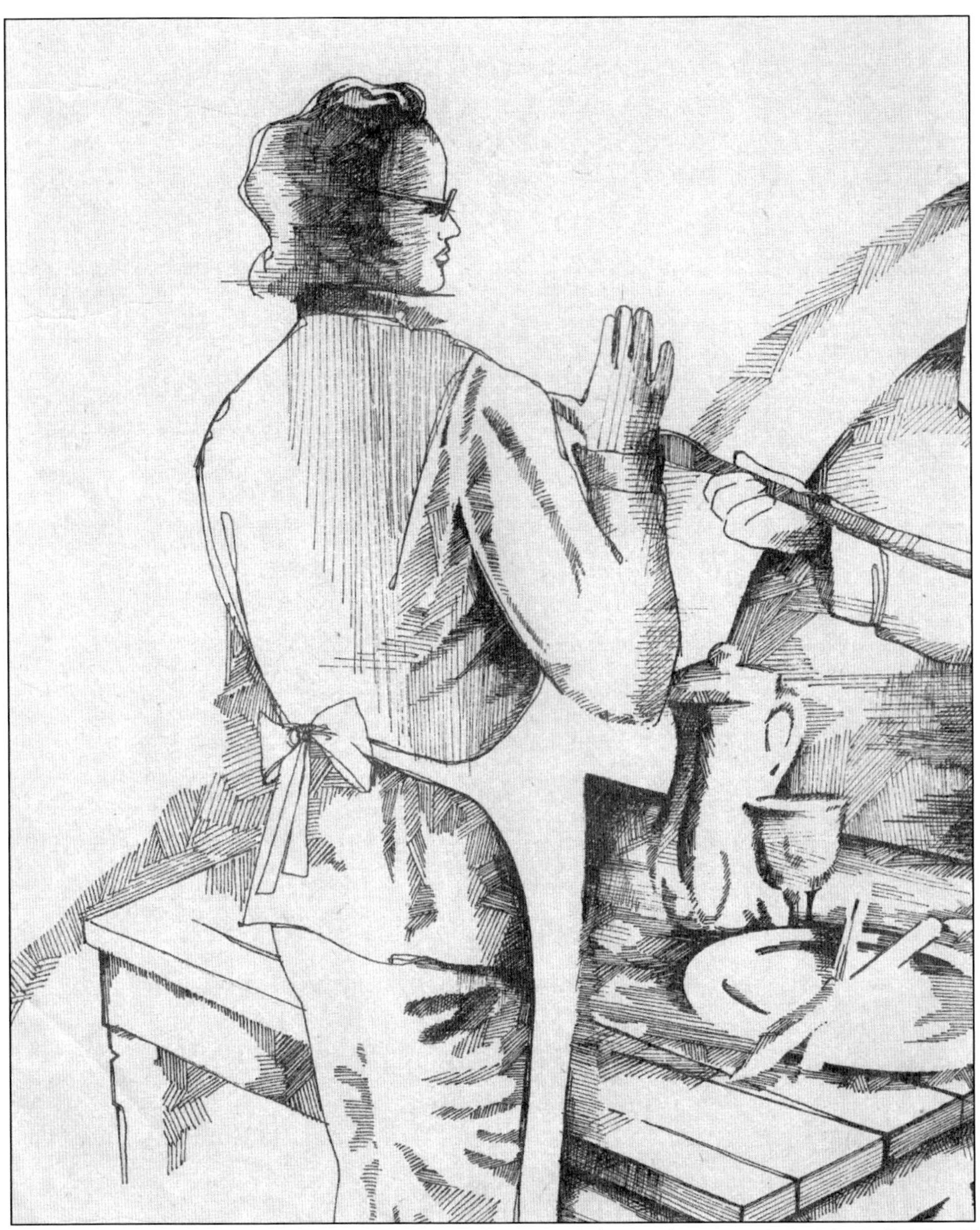

East Liverpool prepared frenziedly for the arrival of Confederate forces on July 26, 1863. The East Liverpool Home Guard, 49 men and a boy under Capt. James Gaston, was mustered on Broadway. A regiment of Pennsylvania troops arrived by train and formed up on a hillside. Across the river, men led by Squire William Pusey waited at Rock Springs with squirrel rifles and pitchforks. Maj. Gen. William T. Brookes was ready in Wellsville, just to the south. Surrounded and out of options, Morgan and the remaining 355 men raised a white flag at West Point, 10 miles northwest of East Liverpool. Pictured is a rendering of Morgan's surrender. The Confederates were brought into Wellsville by train later that day, and so ended Morgan's Raid. East Liverpool learned of the surrender by telegraph. That evening, women of the city fed nearly 500 Federal troops at Third and Market Streets. The trunk of the tree under which Morgan surrendered was kept for many years in the history room of Carnegie Public Library. (East Liverpool Historical Society.)

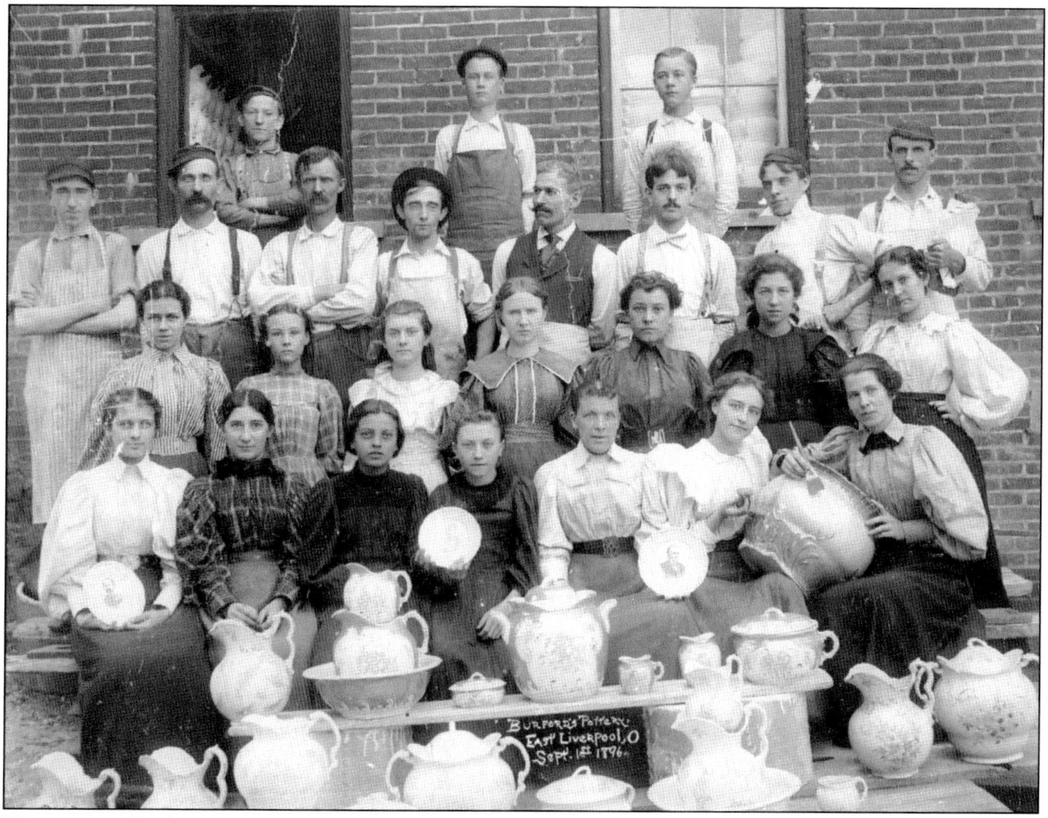

Women worked in city potteries as early as the 1840s on their jiggerman husbands' crews. Others worked in decorating shops, as these Burford Pottery workers seen above did in 1896. They also performed menial jobs in warehouses or walked on a type of treadmill to power machinery. In 1894, female potters were earning about $225 per year, while male potters earned about $500. Above, Annie Eardley is in the first row, fifth from left, holding a McKinley plate. Her daughters are first and second from the left in the same row, and her son George, who died at age 25, is second from right in the third row. Annie, according to her grandson Dr. Jack Eardley, worked as a potter until she was 92, retiring from the Homer Laughlin China Company. A smaller Burford crew is pictured below. (Both Museum of Ceramics.)

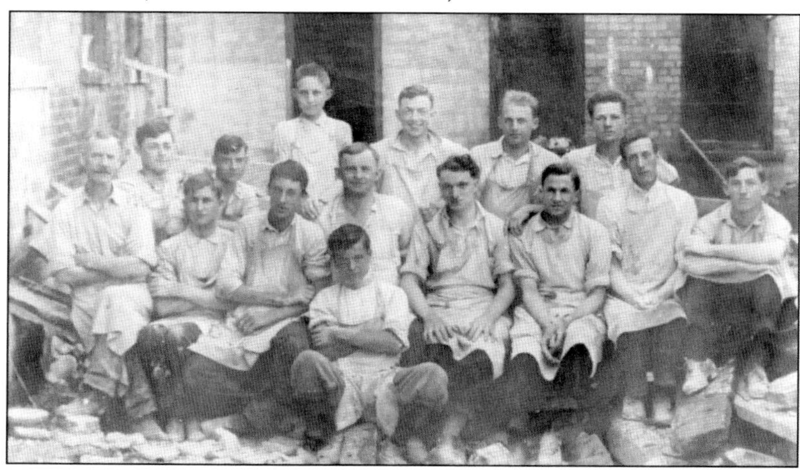

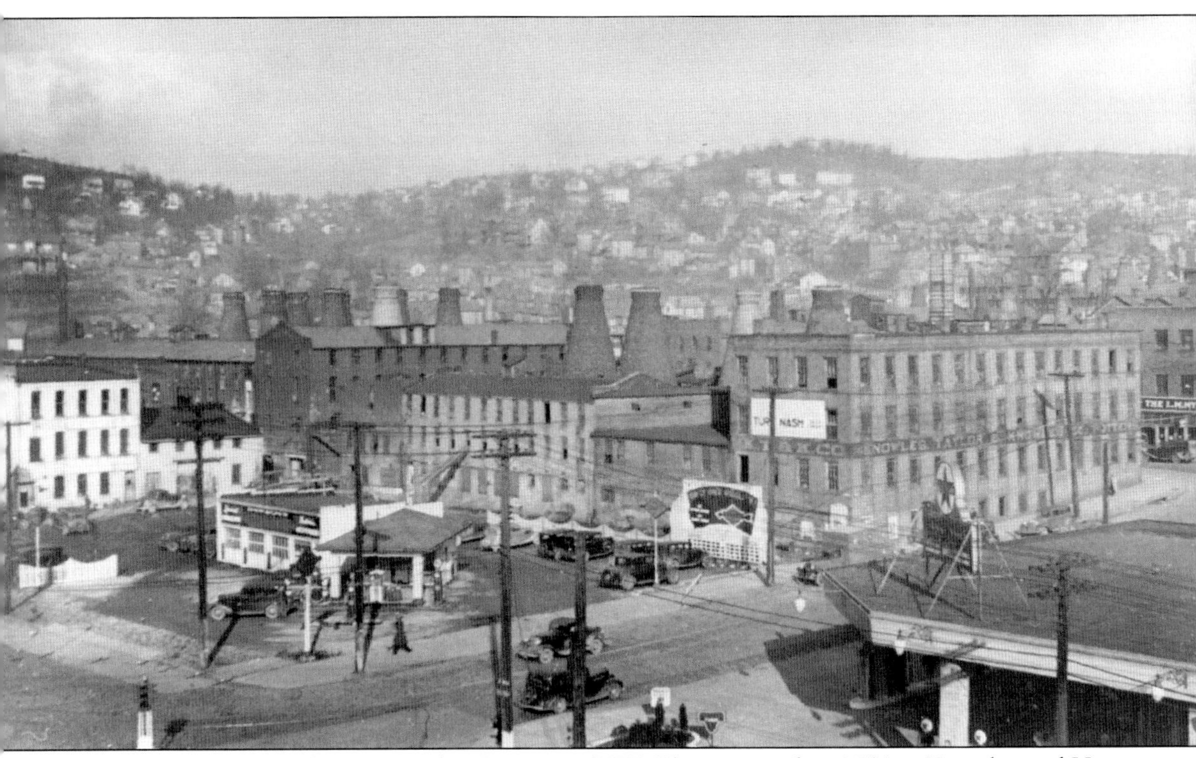

The Knowles, Taylor & Knowles Company (KT&K) originated in 1854 as Knowles and Harvey and was producing white ware under the name KT&K at its uptown plant by 1873. Isaac Knowles, a founder, is credited with inventing a refinement of the "pull down," or jigger, which replaced hand throwing. Isaac Harvey, Knowles's original partner, was followed by Knowles's son-in-law (Col. John N. Taylor) and son (Homer S. Knowles). KT&K interests, operating as Potter's Supply Company, also manufactured kiln furniture for local potteries. Other businesses of the Knowles and Taylor families were Knowles, Taylor & Anderson Brick and Sewer Pipe Works, the Edwin M. Knowles China Company, and Taylor, Smith & Taylor Pottery Company. In 1893, KT&K won recognition at the world's fair with its new line, Lotus Ware. Popular as it was, Lotus Ware lost money for KT&K because it was so delicate that a significant portion broke in the kilns or packing rooms. KT&K, by then merged with the American Chinaware Corp., declared bankruptcy in 1931, and the plants were razed in 1935. (Museum of Ceramics.)

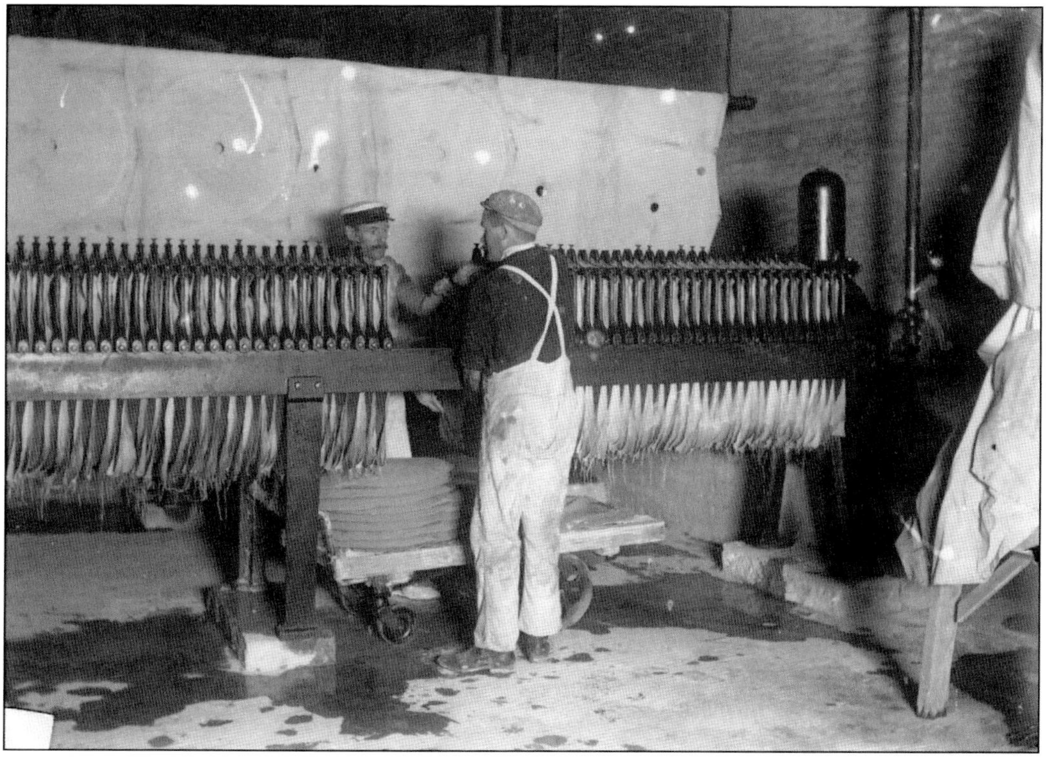

KT&K was the first local pottery to use natural gas from its own well, the first to use an in-house decorating crew, and the first to open a sample room. Though the plant was considered advanced for its time, workers still did plenty of lifting and toting, working in dusty and damp rooms, in constant danger from fire. KT&K was badly damaged by a fire in 1889. In the photograph above, clay rounds that had been mixed in a blunger from dry clay, flint, feldspar, and water were placed in a filter press to remove excess liquid. Next, the prepared clay was mixed again in a pug mill before being placed in molds by the jiggerman. A runner took the molds to a drying room, then ware was placed in saggers, seen below, for kiln firing. (Both Museum of Ceramics.)

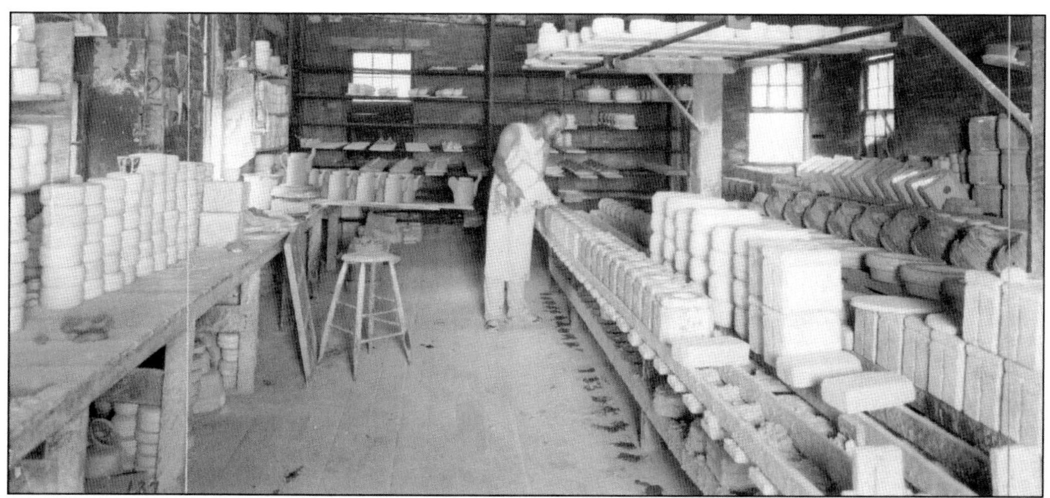

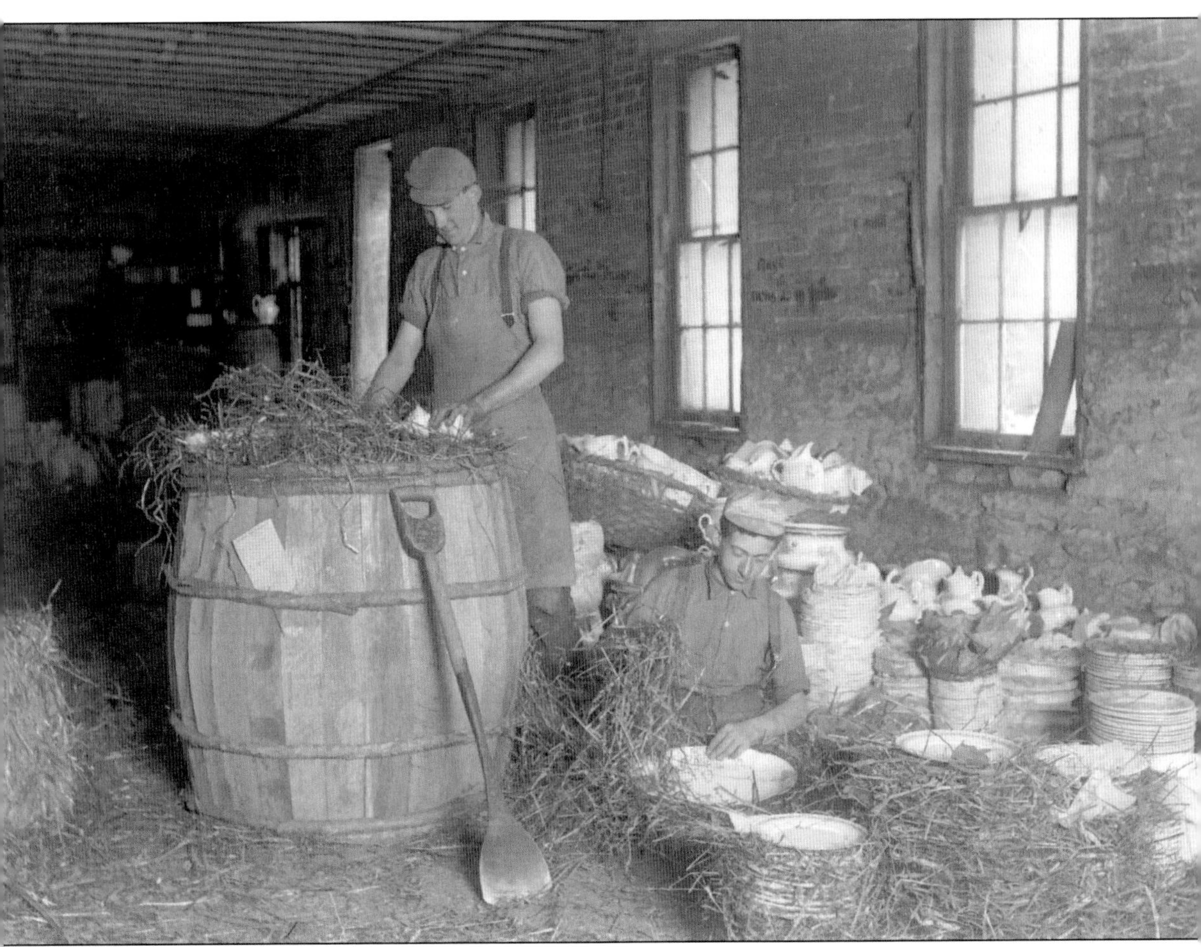

The last step for finished ware was the packinghouse. Workers at this unidentified plant cushioned the ware in fat, straw-filled barrels for transport out of the pottery by road, rail, and river. Straw packing supposedly kept the ware from breaking or chipping en route, but five-percent breakage per barrel was considered acceptable. A busy pottery could ship out 3,000 barrels a year. The barrels were built by hand of beveled wooden staves bound by wooden or metal hoops, with a flat top and bottom that could be fastened shut. A close look at this photograph shows wooden hoops, which suggests it is a very early picture. Coopers made the barrels, and hoopers made the hoops. Since at least one barrel-making shop was in West Virginia, East Liverpudlians to this day may affectionately refer to friends across the river as "Hoopies." (Museum of Ceramics.)

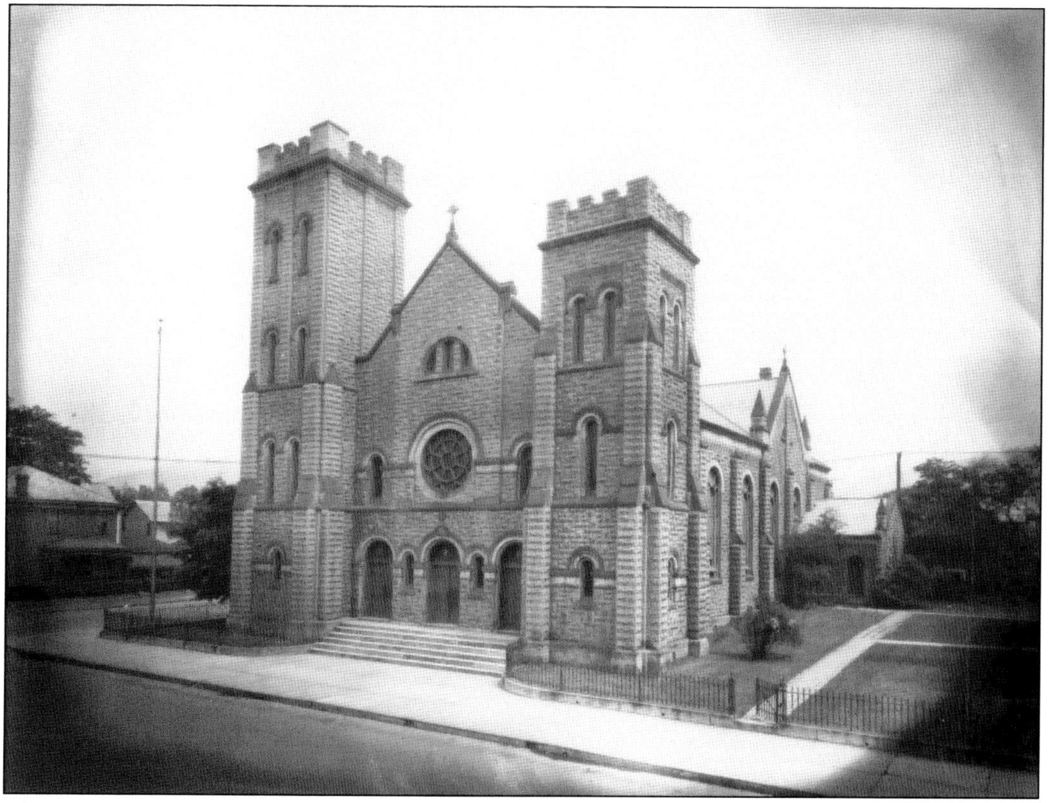

The town's first Catholic church was built in 1837 at College and Robinson Streets, but it burned on Palm Sunday in 1845. St. Aloysius Catholic Church, a wooden structure, was built in 1851–1852 on Jefferson Street at West Fifth Street. The present structure, now named Holy Trinity Parish, was erected on the same site in 1887, fronting on West Fifth. (Museum of Ceramics.)

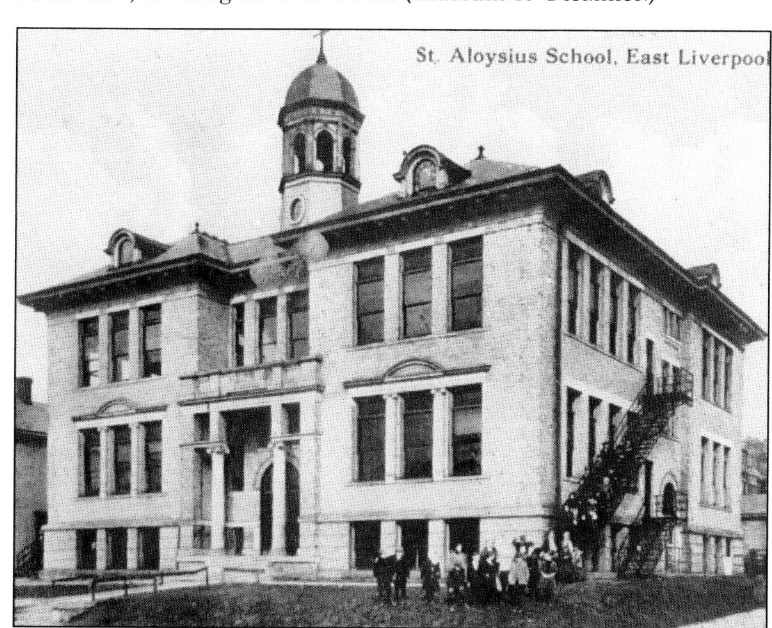

The building housing the original St. Aloysius School was constructed in 1876 as a rectory and later converted to school use. This new eight-room brick school was erected on the site in 1903. Some years later, an addition was added at the front to provide more classrooms, a modern cafeteria, and a gymnasium. The pre-K-8 school was closed in 2015 after enrollment dropped to 49. (Museum of Ceramics.)

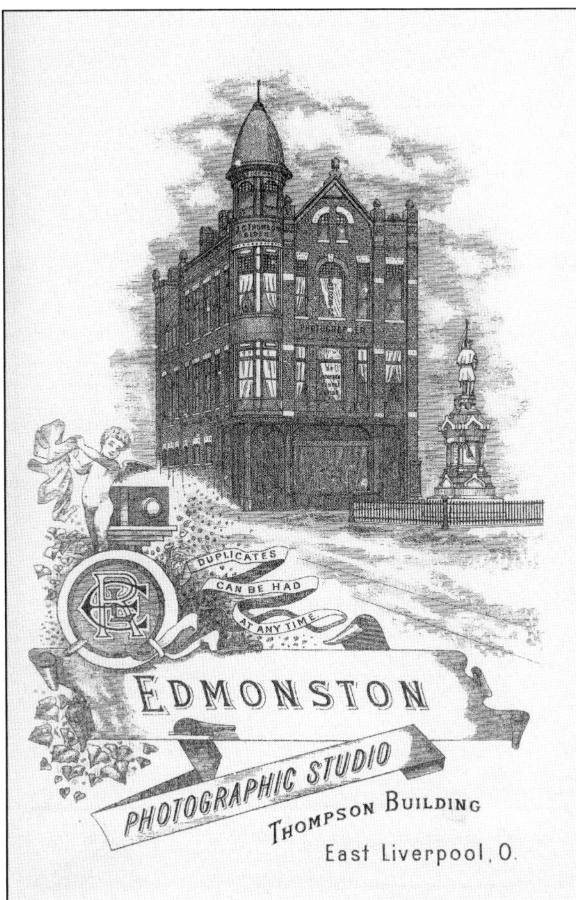

The Thompson name is found multiple times in East Liverpool history. Possibly the first to come to town was John Thompson, in 1816. William Thompson was part of a committee to bring a rail line to town in the 1830s. Josiah Thompson speculated in real estate as early as 1853, and by 1868 he was the richest man in town. That year, he founded the C.C. Thompson Pottery Company (which became the nation's largest) with his son Cassius Clay Thompson. The Thompson Building (at left), on a corner of the Diamond, and Thompson Hotel at Third Street and Broadway (below), were two of Josiah's enterprises. At different times, the Thompson Building housed the Ogilvie Clothing Store and the town's first public library. Despite several fires over the years, part of the building is still in use. (Both East Liverpool Historical Society.)

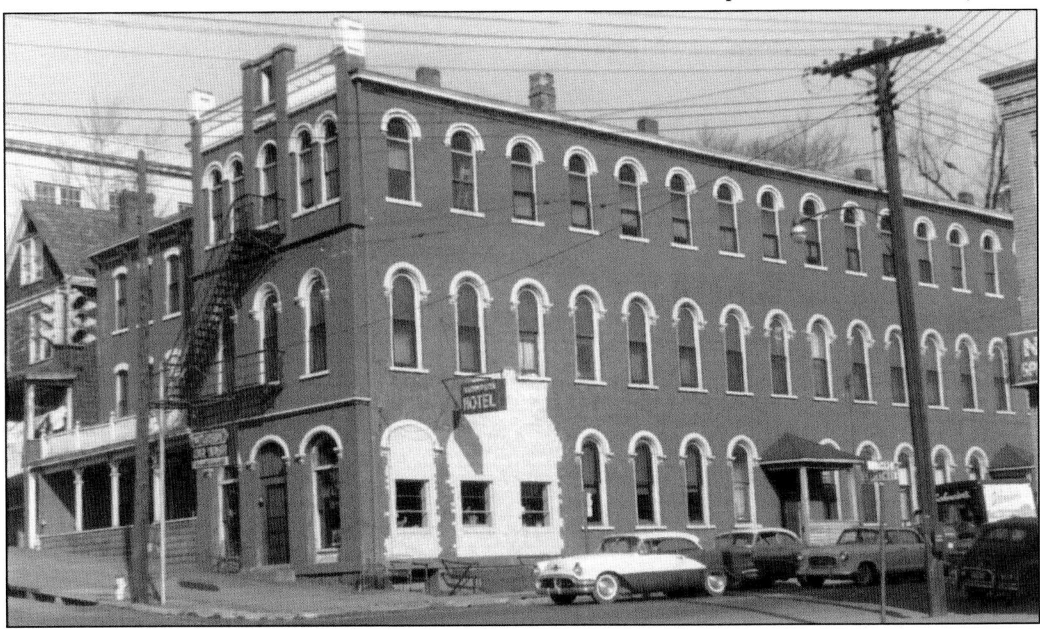

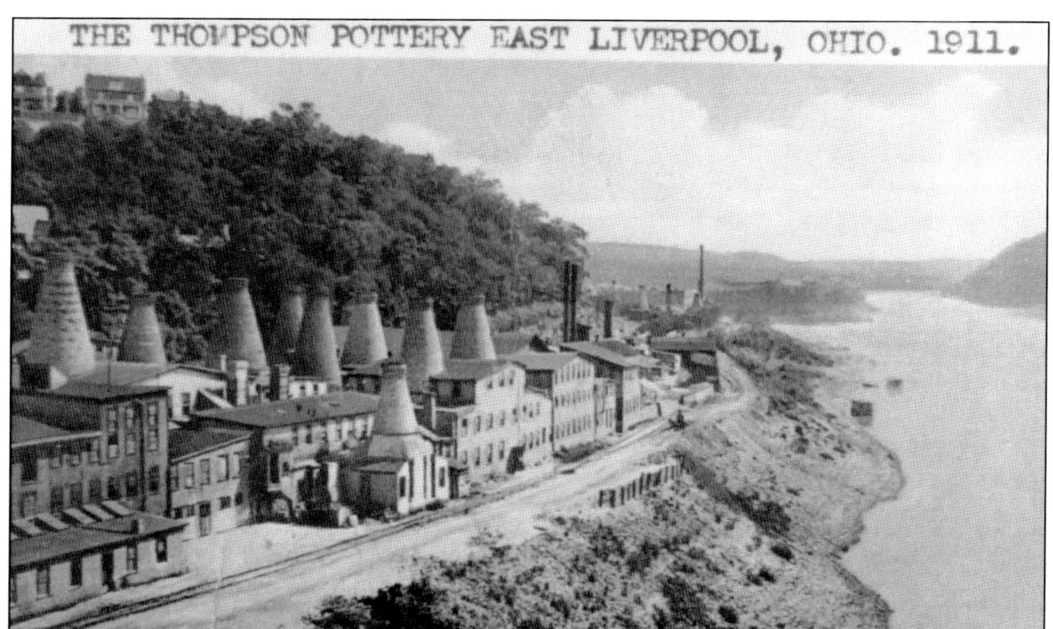

By 1911, the C.C. Thompson Pottery sprawled a long way down the Ohio River's banks, where floods regularly threatened. In 1907, the plant lost ware from eight kilns and closed for several days. Though two continuous tunnel kilns were installed in 1931, the pottery began to flounder in the 1930s, and at one point it paid employees in script to be redeemed "when cash is available." The pottery operated until 1938, when George C. Thompson called a halt due to "poor business and trade conditions," and 300 potters lost their jobs. The patent drawing shown was taken out by C.C. Thompson in 1885. The machine was to be used for forming, finishing, or turning both pottery and glassware. (Both East Liverpool Historical Society.)

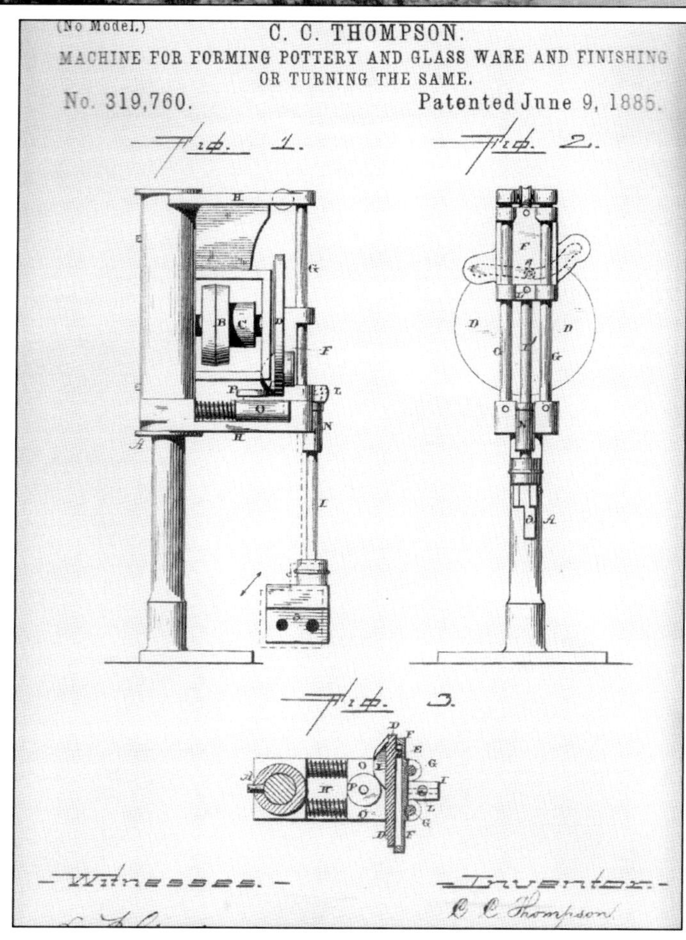

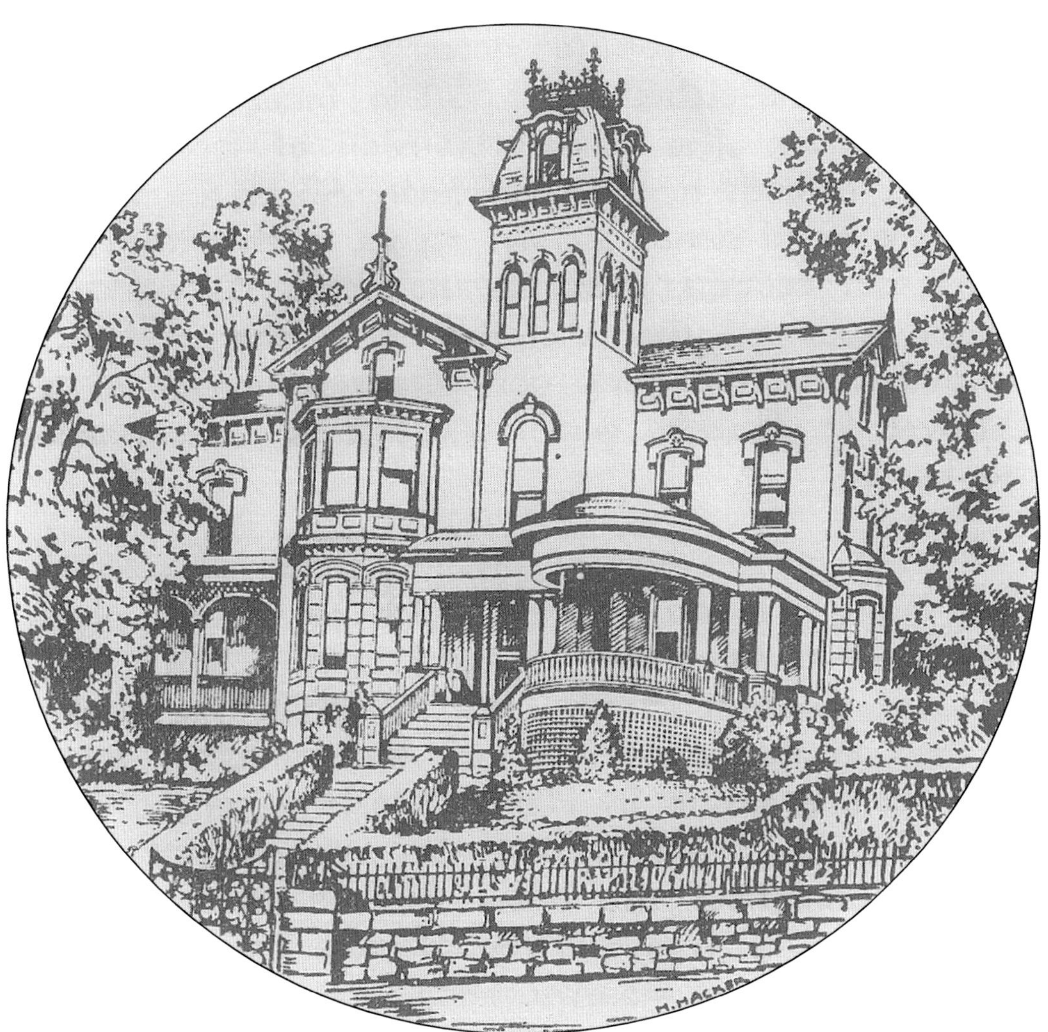

One of the most iconic buildings in East Liverpool is rendered here by prominent local artist Hans Hacker. The Thompson House, a late-Victorian form of Italianate architecture, was built at East Third and Walnut Streets in 1876 by Cassius Clark and Aria Martin Thompson, owners of the nearby C.C. Thompson Pottery. Its most distinguishing feature is the three-story tower at the front of the house, topped with an ornate wrought-iron railing. The veranda and a modern bathroom extension were built in 1900. The house was added to the National Register of Historic Places in 1971, and that designation saved it from being razed to accommodate a freeway extension. Dale Thompson, son of the builders, and his wife, Dorothy, were the last residents of the house, and in 1978 it passed to the East Liverpool Historical Society. The society undertook a major renovation and painting of the 15-room house in 1988. Regular programs and tours are offered by the society at the house. (East Liverpool Historical Society.)

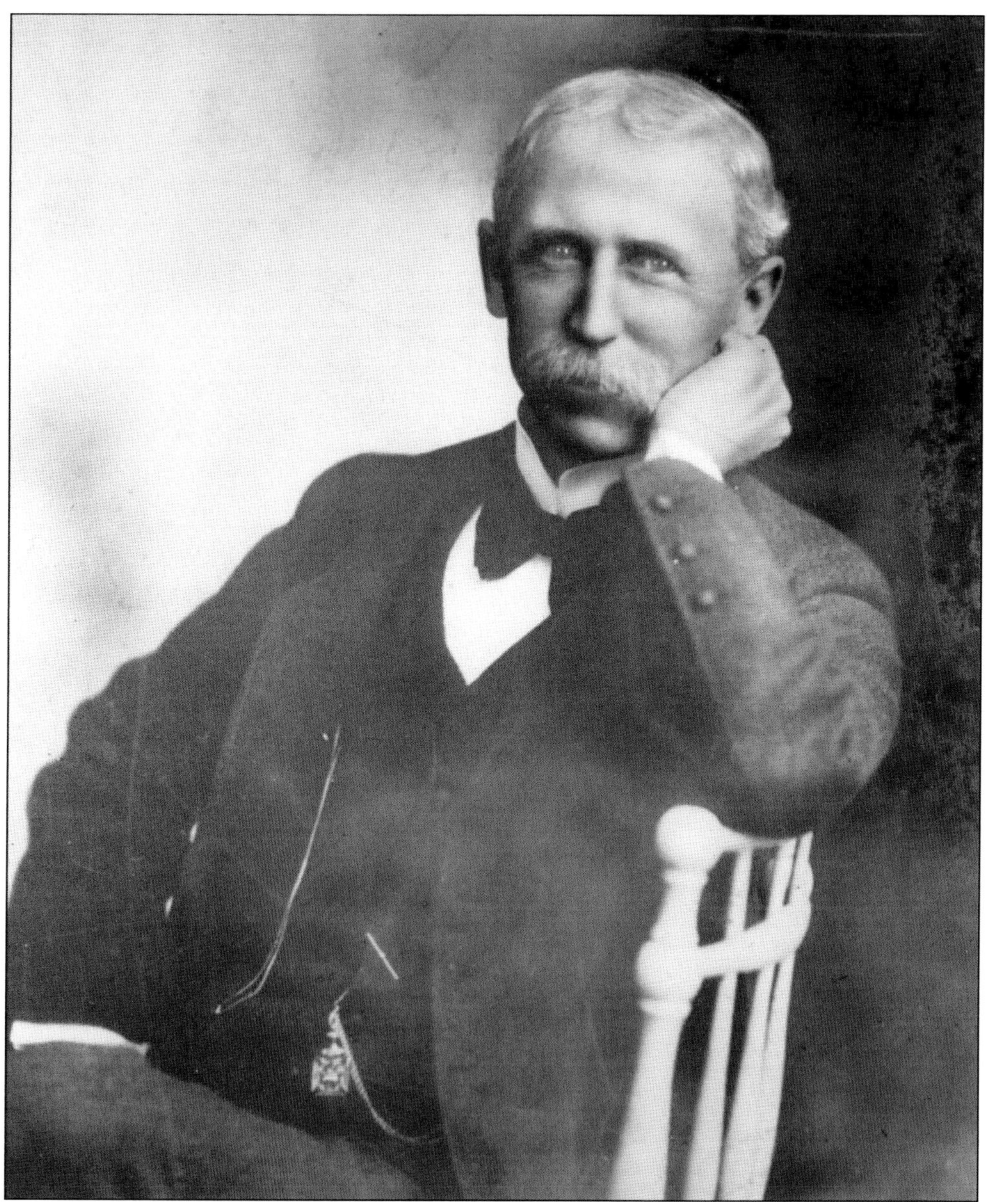

William Lamartine Thompson, son of Josiah and Sarah Thompson, made his mark in music at the close of the 19th century. After graduating from city schools, he studied at Mount Union College and the New York Conservatory of Music, completing his education in Europe. In his day, he was among the best-known composers of spiritual, secular, and patriotic music. His most famous piece, "Softly and Tenderly, Jesus is Calling," is still included in hymnbooks. He was the proprietor of W.L. Thompson and Company, a successful four-story emporium at Fourth and Washington Streets that sold music and instruments. He owned music-publishing companies in East Liverpool and Chicago and had interests in banking and pottery manufacture. He helped establish the city's first public reading room. After Andrew Carnegie donated funds for a library in 1902, Thompson served on its board. He was one of the founders of the city historical society. Thompson died in New York in 1911 after becoming ill while sailing home after a European vacation. (Museum of Ceramics.)

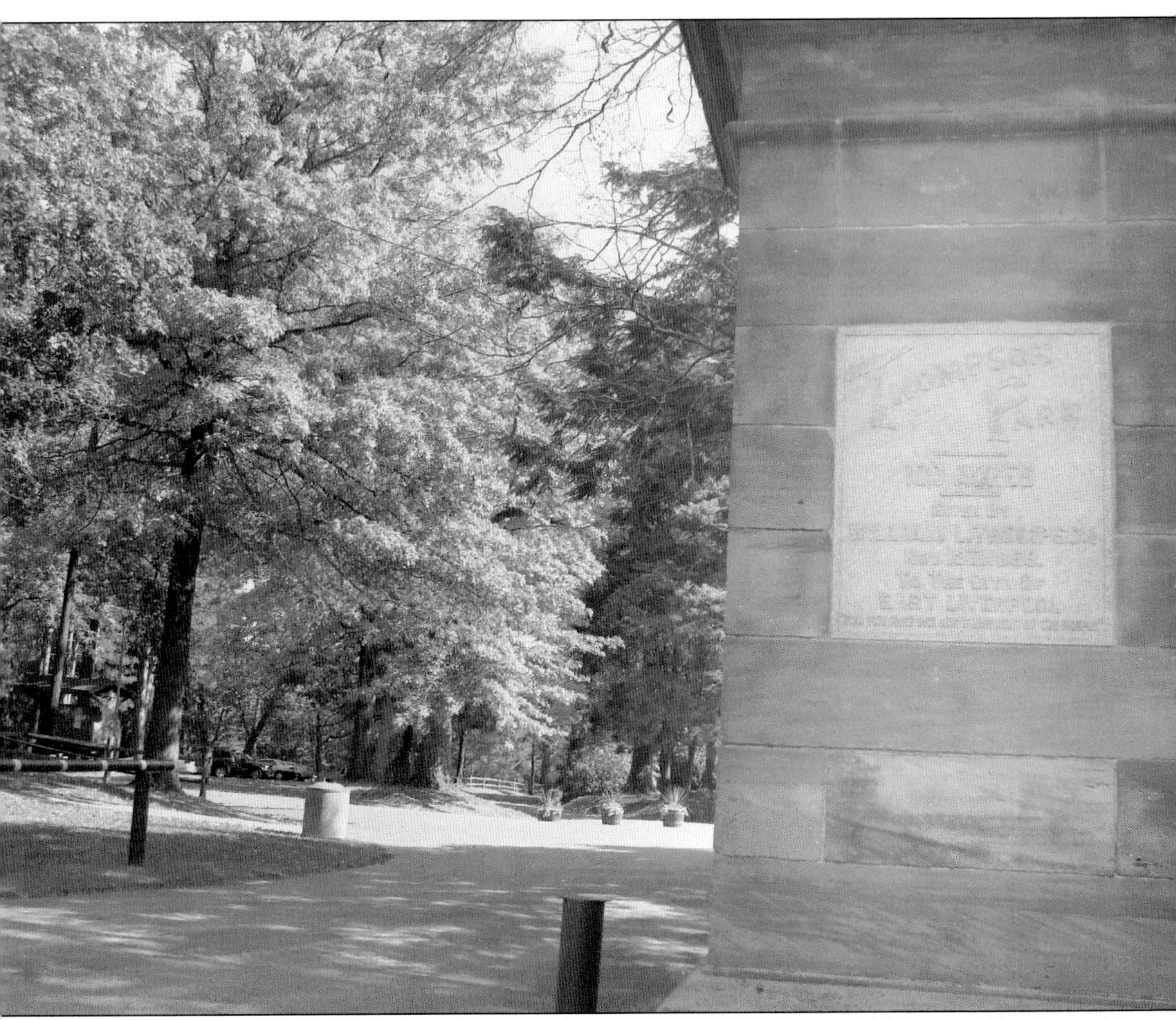

"For the free use and enjoyment of the people," Will Thompson donated 100 acres of land near his home to establish Thompson Park in 1899. His stipulations were that the city must spend $2,000 to install a drive through the park and $600 yearly for beautification. In addition, no alcohol or intoxication were to be allowed, and no sports or gambling would be permitted on Sundays. The park was officially opened in the spring of 1900 and has had regular additions over the years. There are hiking trails through the woods, and walkers use the upper-loop road for morning exercise. Tennis courts are available, as well as ball fields and picnic pavilions. A band shell at the park once hosted regular concerts. A public pool was built at the park by the WPA in 1939 and has been upgraded several times. A disc golf course was a recent addition. (Museum of Ceramics.)

Three

Town and Industry Flourish

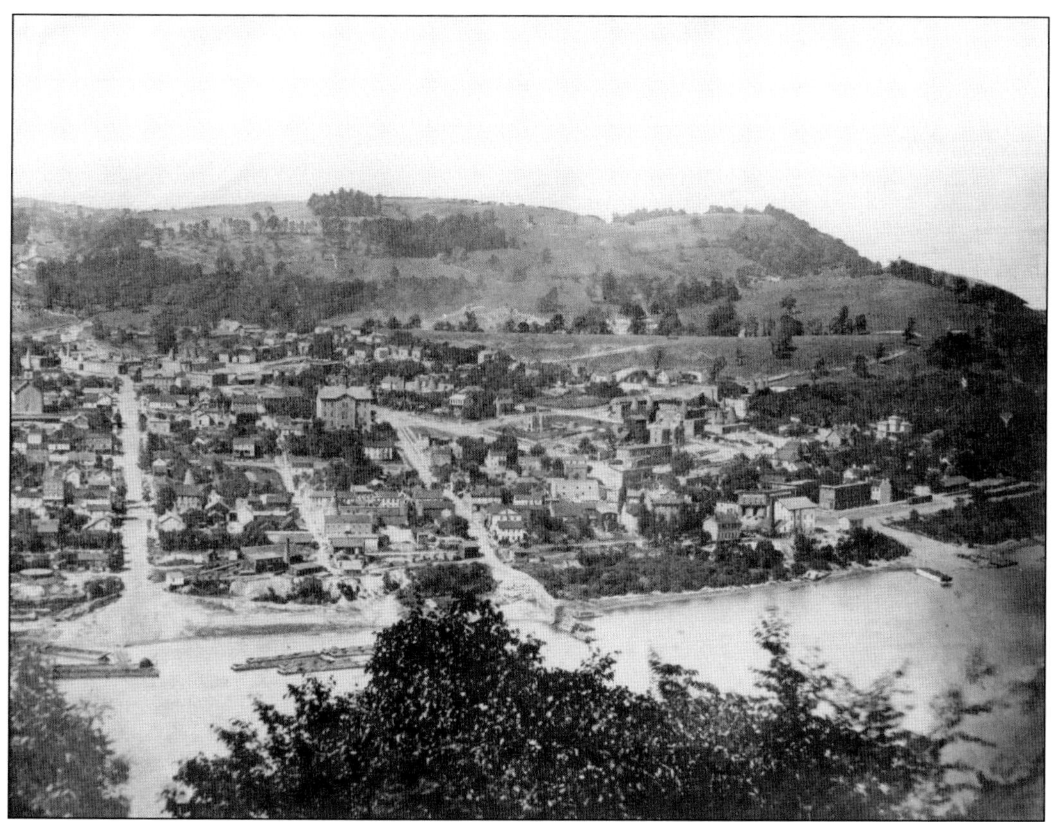

Taken from the heights of Chester, West Virginia, across the river, this early photograph of East Liverpool is centered by three-story Union School, which places the photograph sometime after 1871. A few kilns at early potteries are visible. The streets are still unpaved, and the surrounding hills are still in their natural state. (East Liverpool Historical Society.)

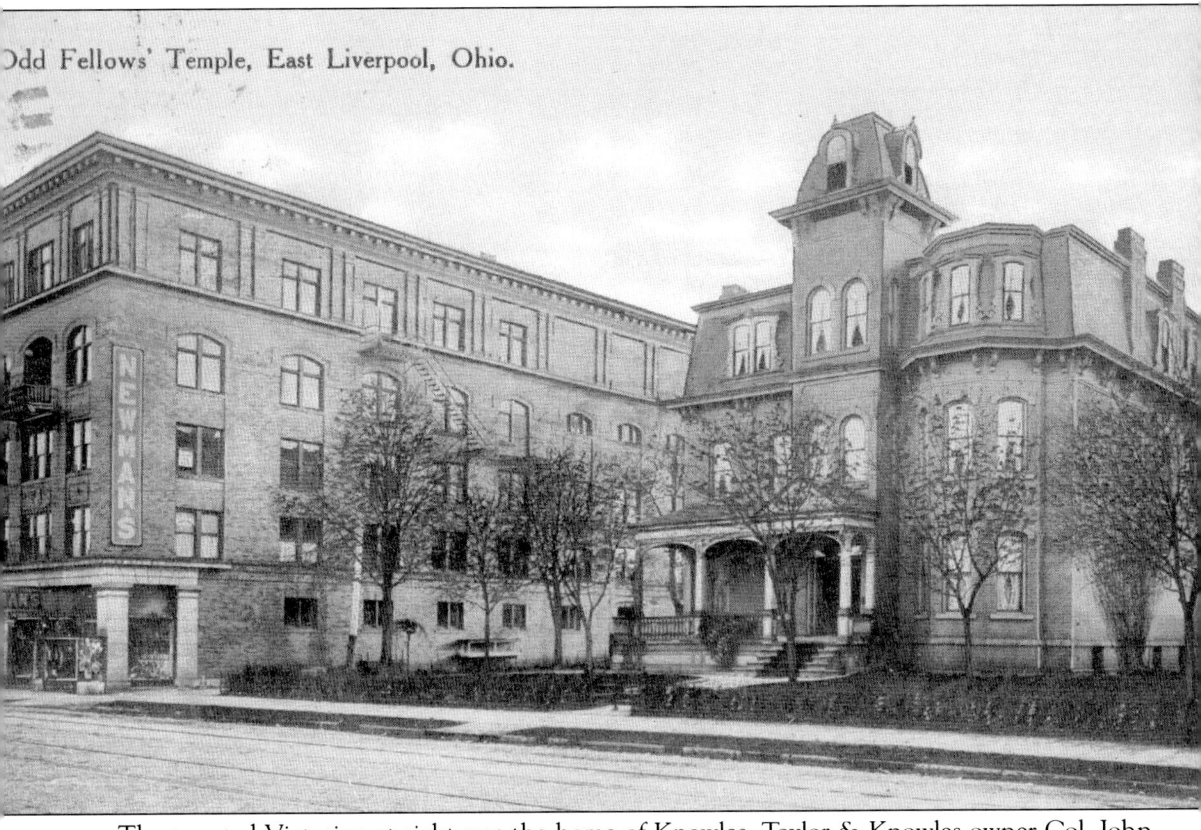

The turreted Victorian at right was the home of Knowles, Taylor & Knowles owner Col. John N. Taylor at the end of the 19th century and was typical of the opulent homes built by business leaders. The house no longer exists, and the site on West Sixth Street is the present home of city hall. The imposing five-story International Order of Odd Fellows hall at left was built in 1907 and was added to the National Register of Historic Places in 1985. At one time, the city chapter was the sixth-largest IOOF chapter of the 700 in the United States. Fraternal organizations flourished in East Liverpool at the turn of the century. Joining the Odd Fellows were the Knights of Columbus, Knights of the Golden Eagle, Knights of Pythias, Knights of the Tented Maccabees, Fraternal Order of Eagles, Order of Owls, Order of Orioles, Benevolent Protective Order of Elks, Loyal Order of Moose, and Masons. Today, the IOOF building has been converted to apartments. (East Liverpool Historical Society.)

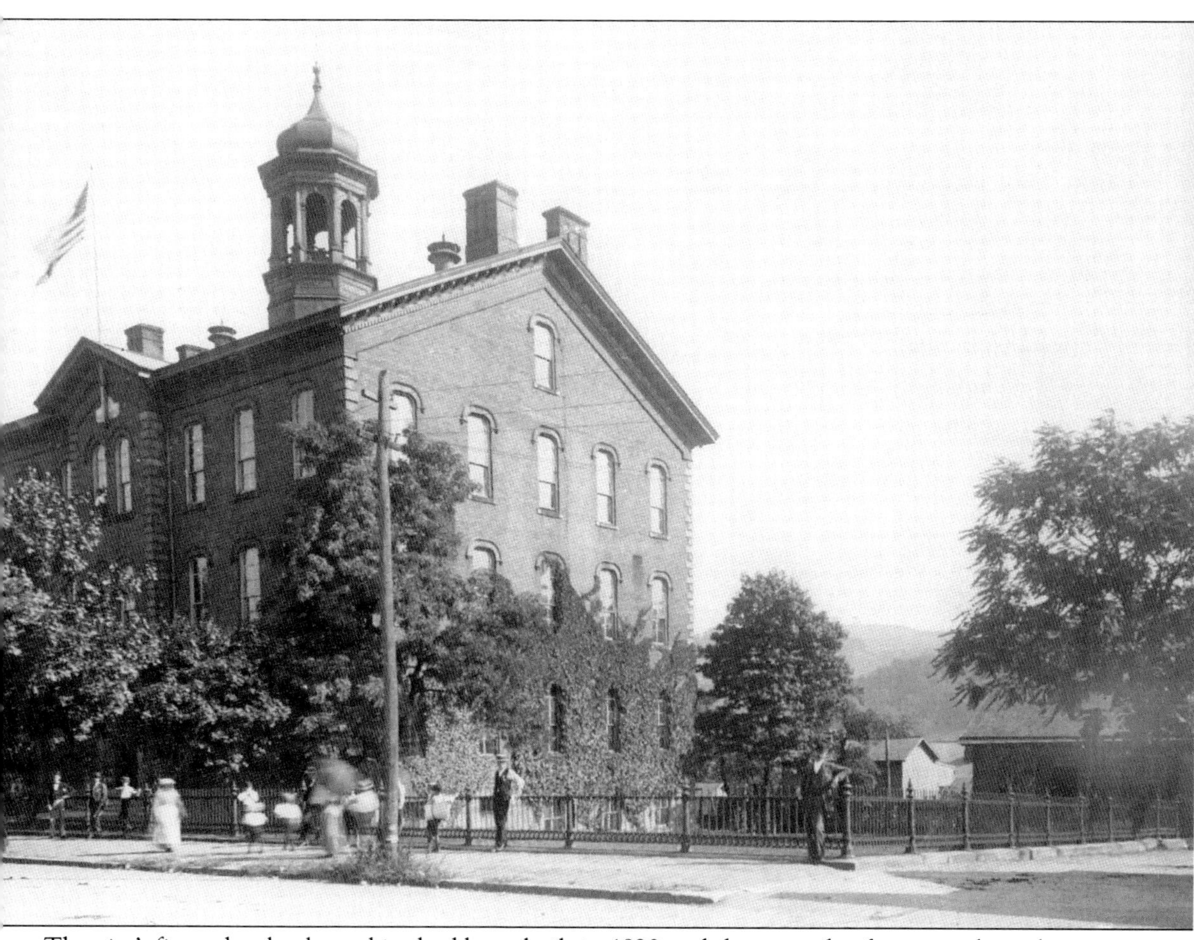

The city's first school, a log cabin, had been built in 1820 and the second, a four-room log cabin, in 1825 at Fourth and Union Streets. After the Civil War, the city's population increased, and more schools were needed. A two-story brick building succeeded the second cabin in 1849. That school was replaced by this three-story building in October 1871. Besides this building, pictured in 1892, three others were scattered around town. Some 564 students were enrolled in the four schoolhouses. On the elementary level, students learned the alphabet, pronunciation, and reading. The Union School building was replaced in 1895, when what is known as Central School was constructed. Central School served as the city's high school until it was replaced by a new complex on Maine Boulevard. Today, the original Fourth Street location is occupied by the East Liverpool High School Alumni Association clock tower and museum. (Museum of Ceramics.)

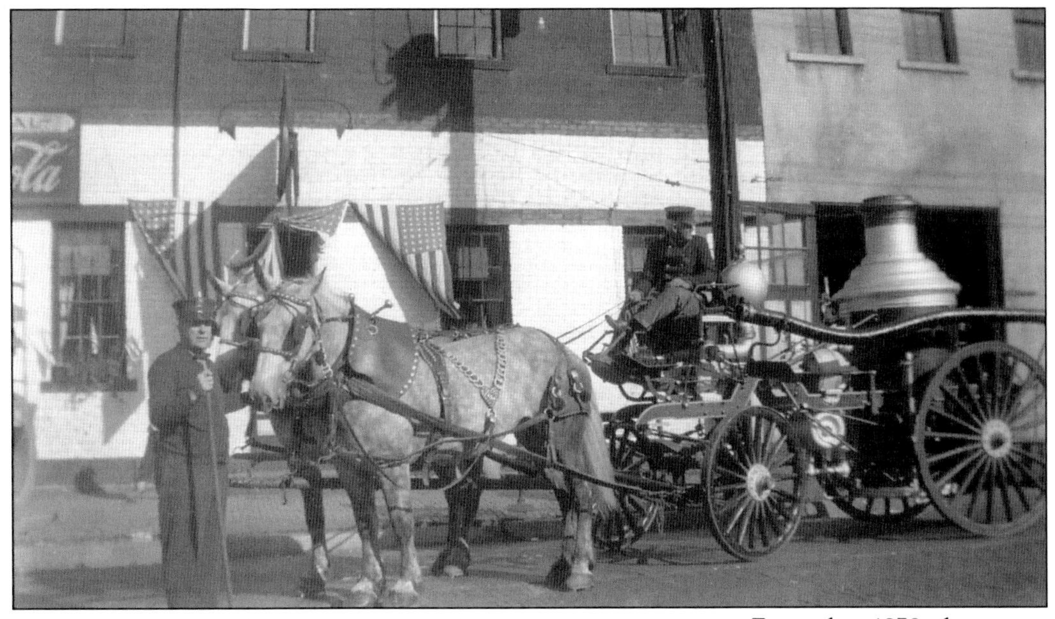

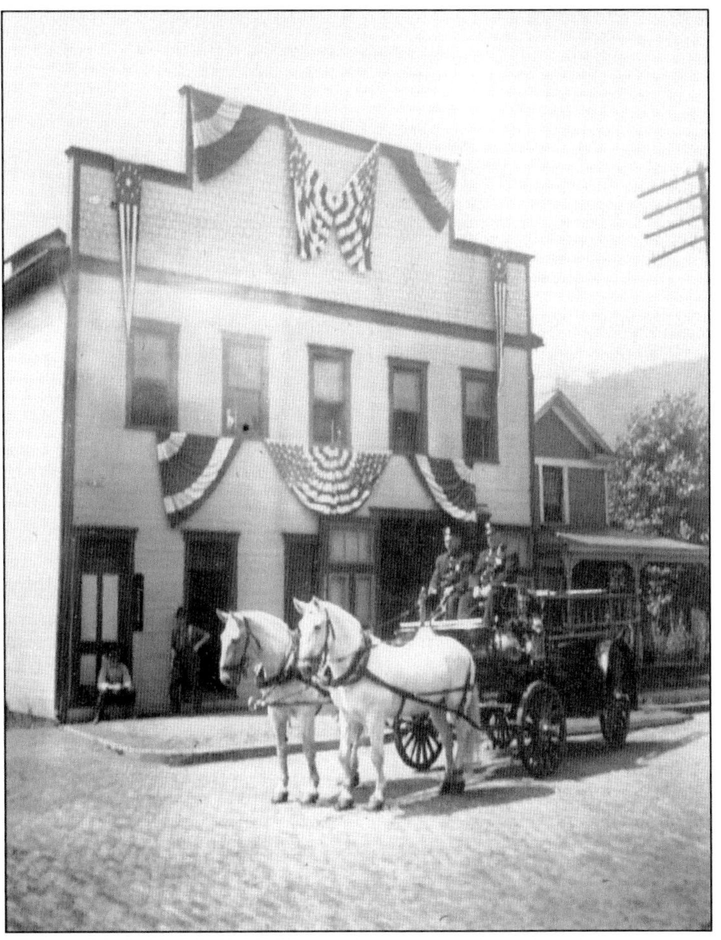

Formed in 1878, the original volunteer city fire department was named the Crockery City Fire Department. The first crew boasted 52 members and a bucket wagon that was pulled by hand, or with street department horses when they were not busy elsewhere. The first hose and a reel were purchased in 1879, and by 1886 the department had its own horses. In 1887, an additional station was built in the East End. Paid firefighters were on the job by 1893. In 1914, the department made history by being the first in the nation to change from horse-drawn to motorized equipment all at one time. The photograph above was taken at the old central station in 1911. The photograph at left features Tom and Jerry, as this matched pair of horses was named. (Both Museum of Ceramics.)

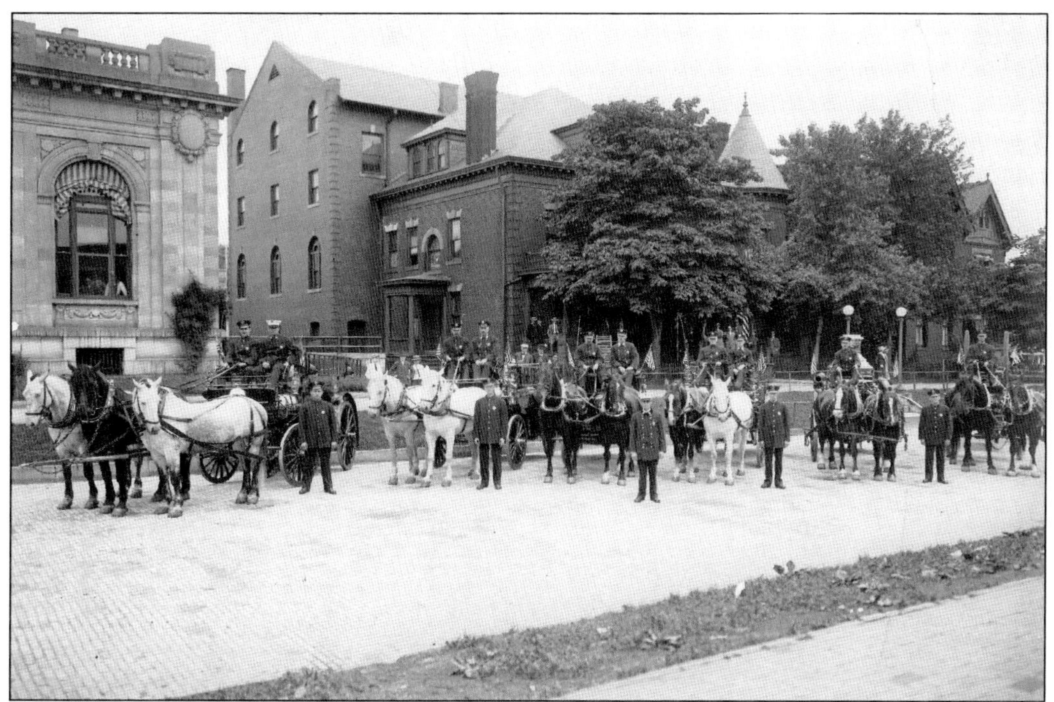

Above, city firefighters pose their full complement of six teams and a glittering array of apparatus in front of city hall. Below, this fire completely destroyed Frank Stewart's feed store at the corner of Sixth and Washington Streets on March 31, 1881. The kilns and buildings in the background belong to either the Knowles, Taylor & Knowles Pottery or the McNicol, Burton & Company. In 1898, firefighters responded to 63 calls that caused losses of nearly $100,000. Some city potteries installed sprinkler systems in 1902 because of an insurance-rate hike of 25 percent. Rates were increased by 50 percent in 1925, and in the next several years the city upgraded its water pipes and hydrants, added more firefighters, and built a new main fire station on Broadway. (Both East Liverpool Historical Society.)

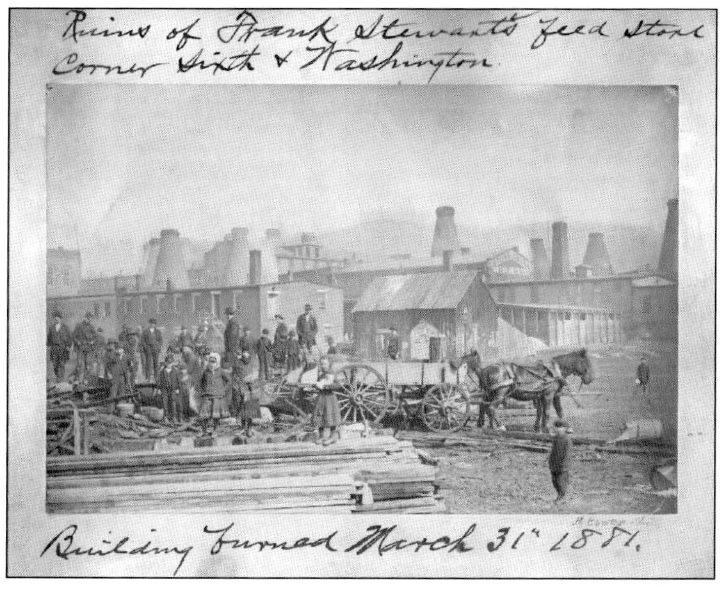

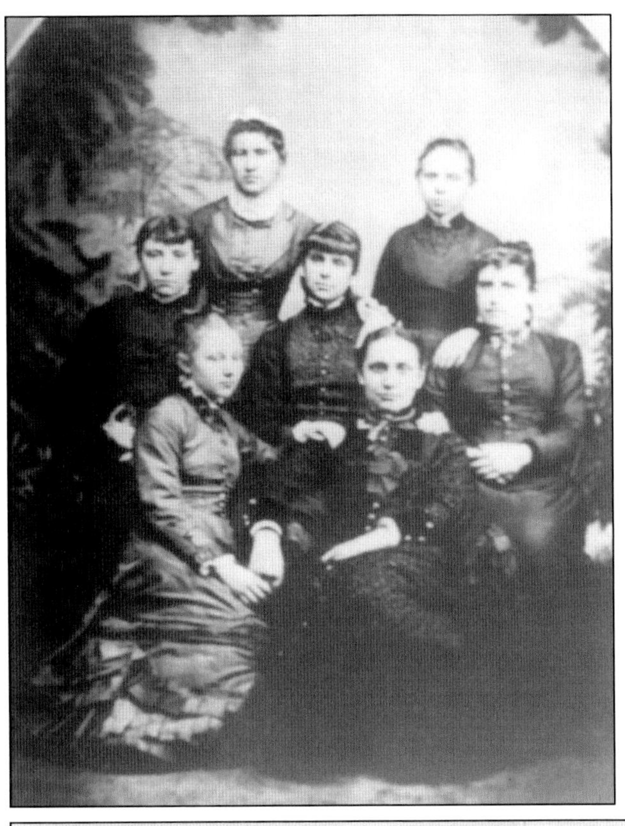

The seven women pictured at left are identified only as 1880 graduates of East Liverpool High School (ELHS). At that time, enrollment in the city school district was 1,068, but daily attendance only averaged 625 pupils. A year later, enrollment was 1,234, with average attendance at 802 per day. The graduating class of 1881 included eight women and one man. The program below shows that each graduate was given the opportunity to speak; seven women presented essays, while the lone male gave an oration. The valedictory address was offered by Rebecca A. Hart. In the early years of East Liverpool, it was especially common for boys to leave school early for work in a pottery since they could be paid less money for routine work. (Both Museum of Ceramics.)

COMMENCEMENT EXERCISES
OF THE
EAST LIVERPOOL HIGH SCHOOL,
IN THE
M. E. CHURCH,
FRIDAY EVENING, MAY 27, 1881,
AT 7:30 O'CLOCK.

BOARD OF EDUCATION.

J. M. KELLY, PRES. — H. R. HILL, SEC'Y.
W. H. VODREY, TREASURER.
N. A. FREDERICK, — WM. CARTWRIGHT,
J. N. TAYLOR.

R. N. FEARON, Superintendent.
E. B. HUSTON, Teacher.

Class of 1881.

Jennie E. Murphy, — Nannie J. Azdell,
Jennie E. George, — Rebecca A. Hart,
Alice P. Shepherd, — Ella M. Ashbaugh,
Carletta J. Harrison, — Margery McKay,
John C. Oliver.

Order of Exercises.

PRAYER.

MUSIC.

ESSAY—Salutatory—Nobility of Silent Work.............. CARLETTA J. HARRISON.

ESSAY—Every Man's Life a Web of His Own Weaving.... JENNIE E. GEORGE.

ESSAY—The Casket and It's Jewel.....NANNIE J. AZDELL

MUSIC.

ESSAY—What Lies Beyond!............MARGERY MCKAY

ESSAY—Earth's Battle Fields..........ELLA M. ASHBAUGH

ESSAY—Our Watch-words ....JENNIE E. MURPHY

MUSIC.

ESSAY—Under the Cloud.............ALICE P. SHEPHERD

ORATION—Progress of Mankind..........JOHN C. OLIVER

ESSAY—Valedictory—Voices of the Winds.................. REBECCA A. HART.

MUSIC.

Address to Class..................REV. J. WILLIAMS, D.D.

Presentation of Diplomas.

MUSIC.

BENEDICTION.

D. B. Martin, Printer.

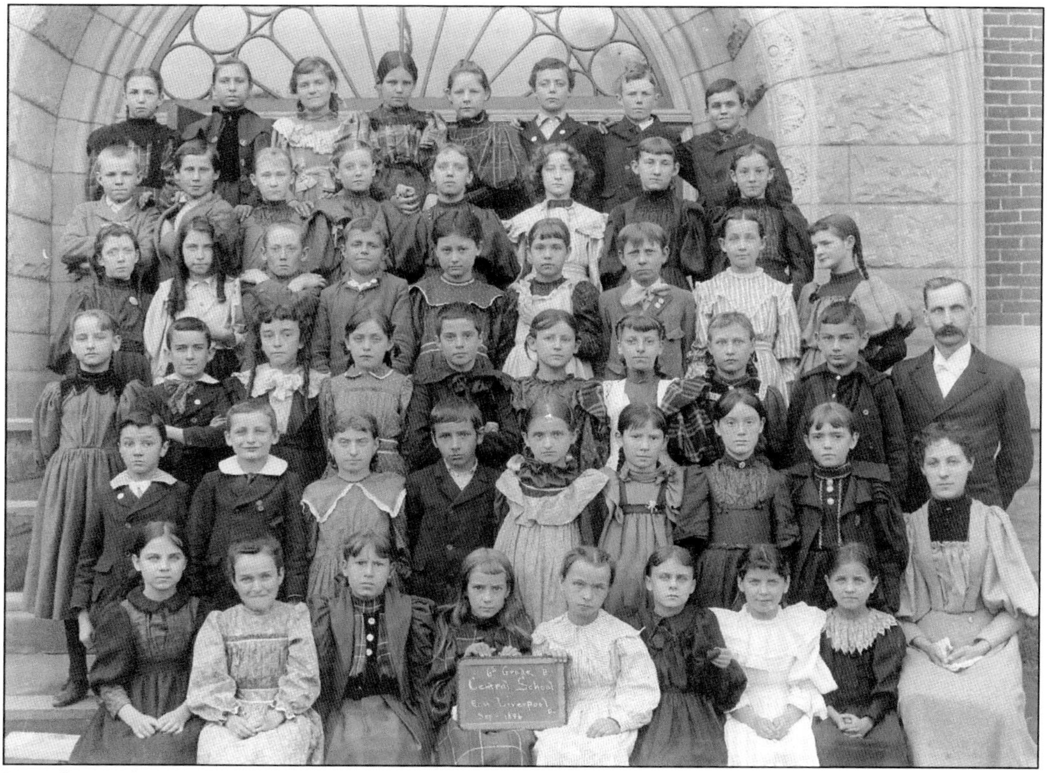

Even by sixth grade, city school classes were overwhelmingly female. Some of the boys of the 1896 class above look like they are more than ready to be done with school and out earning money in a pottery. The senior class of 1897, seen below, poses with dramatic flair behind their teachers on the steps of Central School. The young men of this class, having stayed long enough to earn high school diplomas, may have been headed to college. Because of healthy population growth, a ninth school building had been erected in the city in 1893, and in 1897 three suburban elementary schools were added. By 1900, there were three schools in the East End, including the two-story Horace Mann School. (Both Museum of Ceramics.)

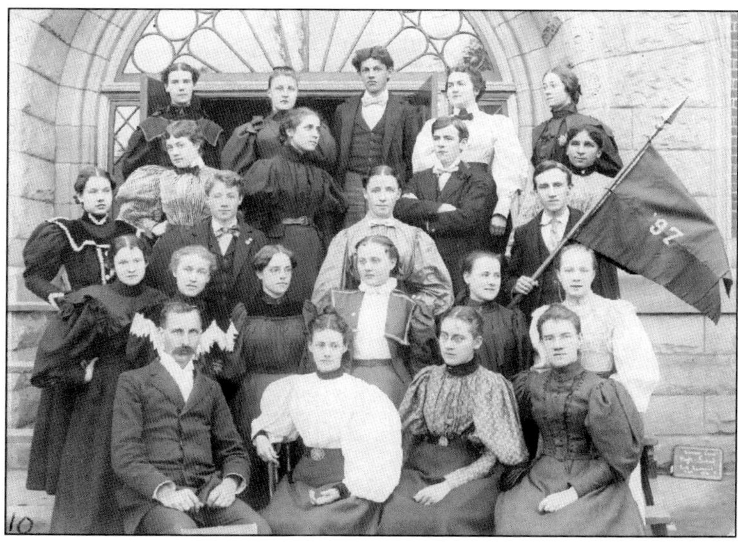

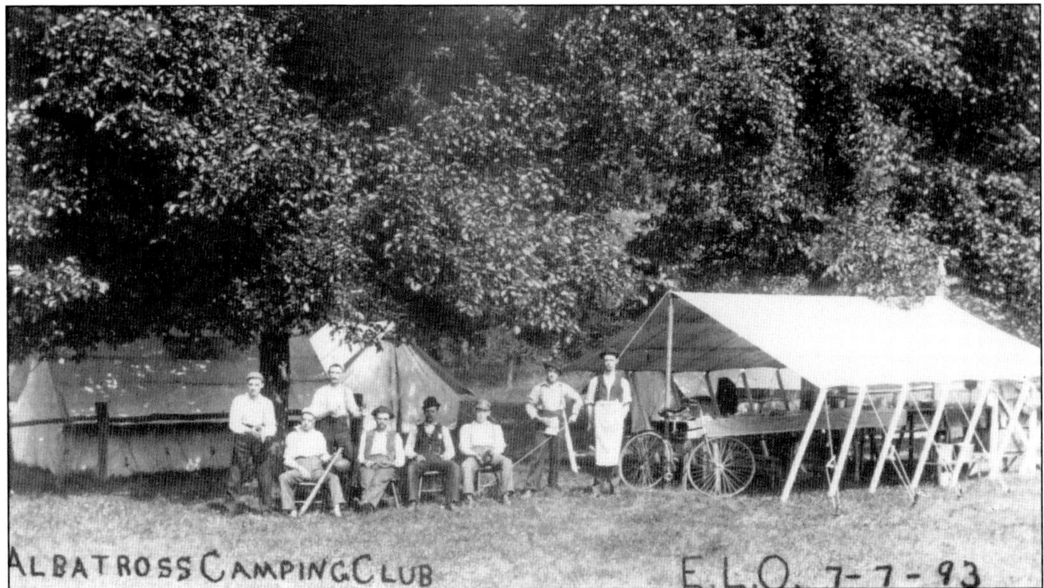

Outdoor clubs for the hardy have surfaced once in a while in East Liverpool history. The Albatross Camping Club, pictured above, set up this campsite in July 1893. Even earlier than that, the Forest and Stream Camping Club adventured in wilderness areas. The photograph below was captured in 1882 to memorialize their time on Little Beaver Creek, near the site of the surrender of Confederate general John Hunt Morgan. From left to right are Capt. Will Hill, J.W. Curry, Frank Croxall, W.W. Harker, George W. Thomas, Ed Bell, Meridian Hill, A.H. Clark, A.W. Thomas, James Ackley, George B. Harvey, T.H. Arbuckle, H.N. Harker, R.W. Taylor, and Ed McHenry. The small boy is Charles R. Thomas, and the cook standing behind the group is Sidney Grimm. (Above, Frank C. Dawson; below, Museum of Ceramics.)

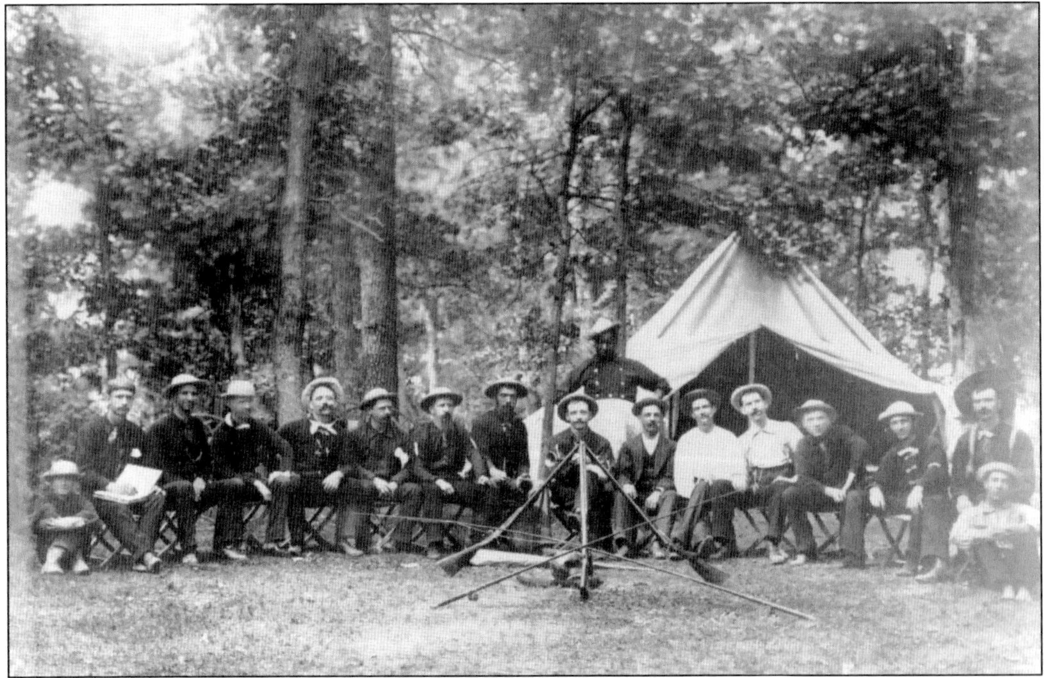

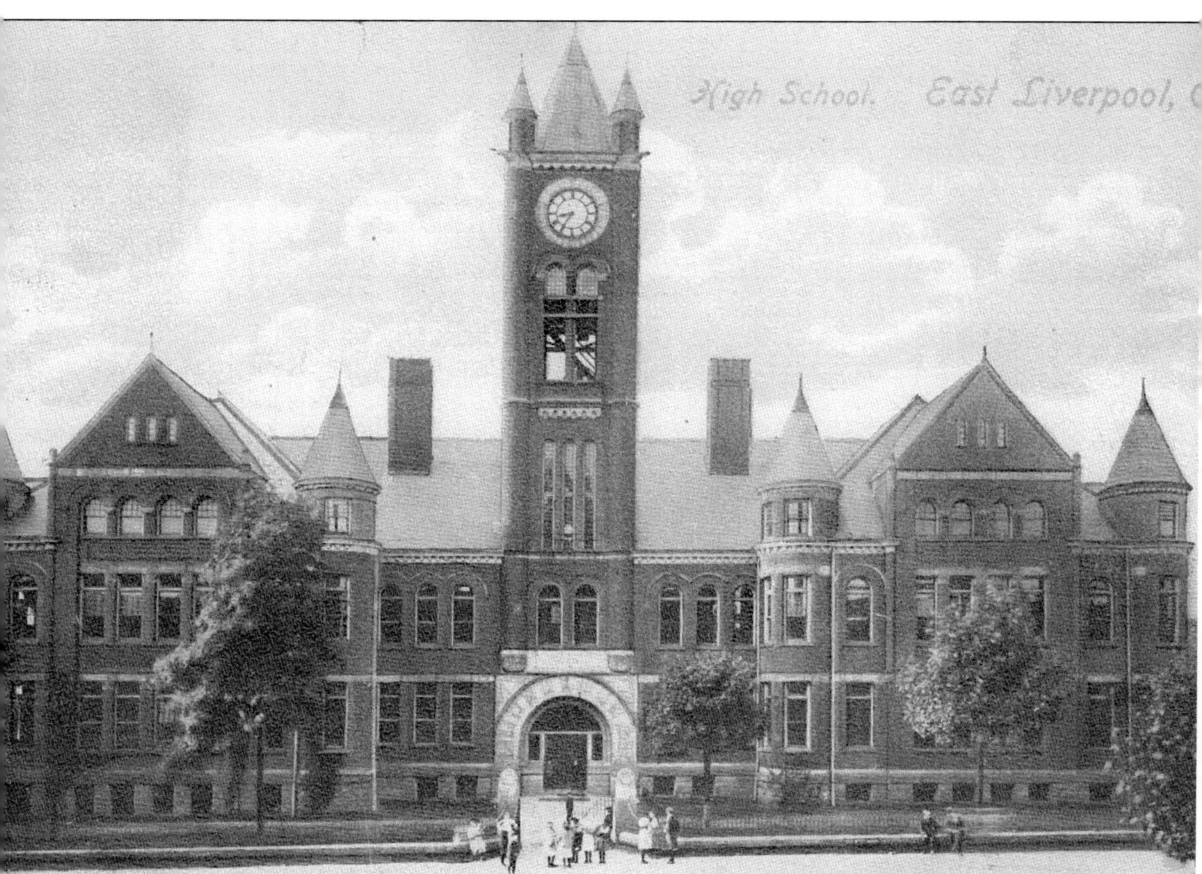

Between 1895 and 1968, East Liverpool's high school students attended Central School, the crowning achievement of city education for its time. Sprawling Romanesque architecture and an 80-foot-tall clock tower highlighted the city's pride and growth. The stone and red-brick building added 20 classrooms to the city's capacity and could accommodate 1,000 students. By 1900, the system boasted 12 buildings and 60 classrooms for 2,771 elementary students and 173 in higher grades. (East Liverpool Historical Society.)

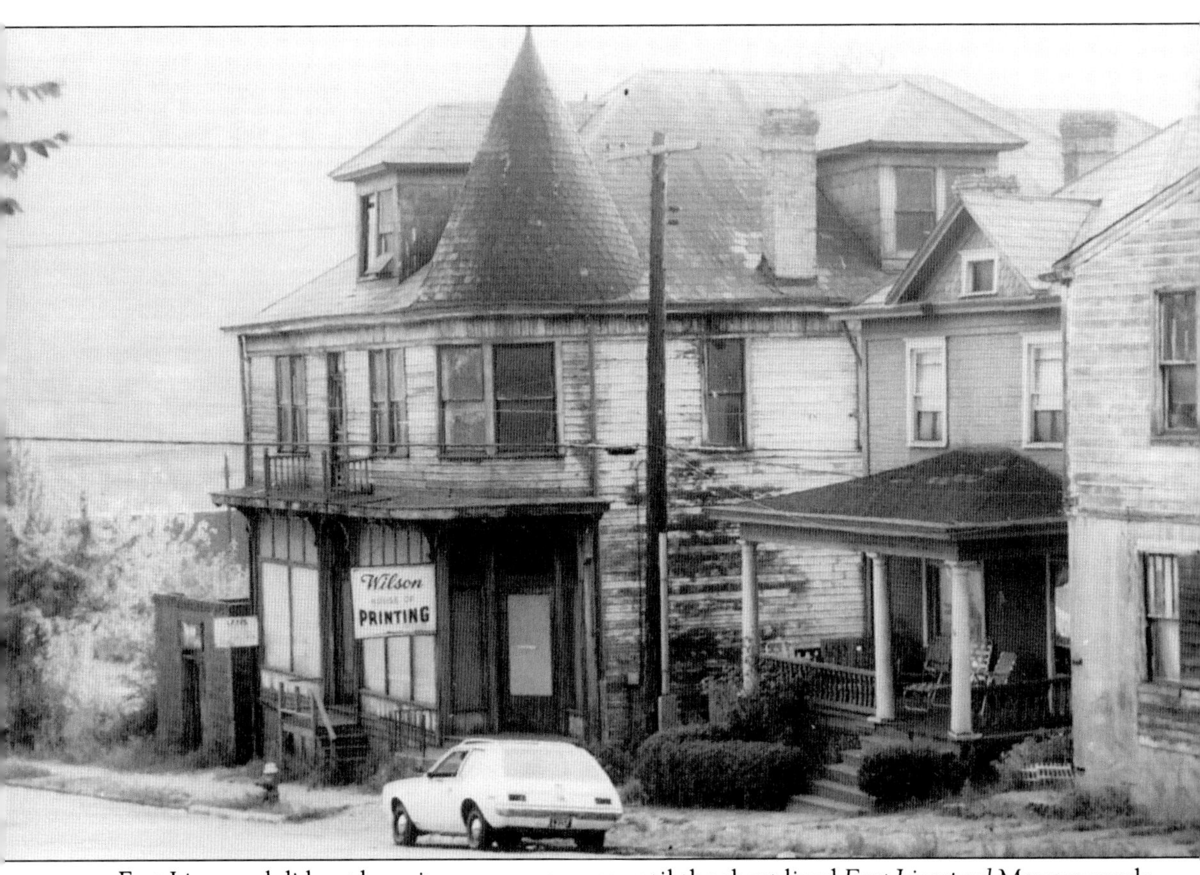

East Liverpool did not have its own newspaper until the short-lived *East Liverpool Mercury* made its debut in May 1861. The paper's finances were so straitened by early 1862 that proprietors J.W. Harris and George J. Luckey announced, "Flour, potatoes, apples, coal . . . and pretty much anything and everything else" would be accepted as payment for a subscription. The last issue was published later that year, but other newspapers followed. This structure at 213 Market Street, shown in its declining years, was built by Jere H. Simms, editor of the *East Liverpool Tribune*, in 1900. In September 1902, the building became the home of the *Morning Tribune*. The *East Liverpool Messenger* was produced there from 1915 to the late 1930s, and Simms also operated a printing business there. The building and businesses were sold to Alex Wilson, a 35-year employee, in 1924. Richard Wilson, his son, took over Wilson Printing in 1946 and operated it until 1972. The building was demolished in 1983 for a highway project. (Inger Lloyd.)

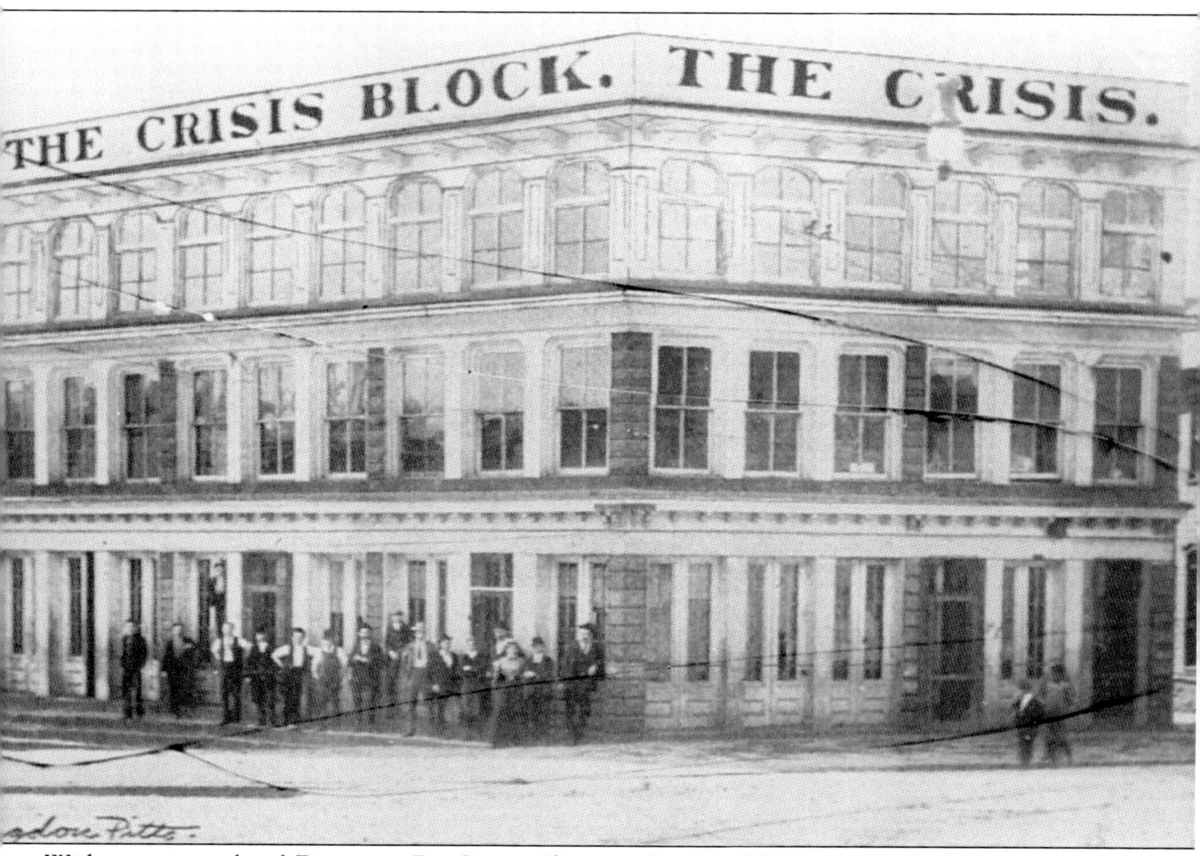

With prominent local Democrat Dr. George Ikirt as editor, and James C. Deidrick, Democrat Central Committee secretary, as business manager, the *East Liverpool Crisis* was launched on October 4, 1884. Its nameplate boasted the declaration, "Democratic In All Things—Neutral in Nothing." The inaugural editorial declared that the paper's "political complexion will be such that it will not be necessary to peruse its columns with a microscope to ascertain its creed." The paper began daily publication on March 28, 1887, and cost a penny. Also that year, the *Crisis* became the first paper in the county to receive daily telegraph news service. Deidrick became editor at 21 after Ikirt's retirement and provided much news fodder himself when he was put on trial in 1893 for shooting a neighbor in a family dispute. When he was sentenced to 30 days in jail, he blamed political infighting for the verdict. In 1904, the *Crisis* merged with the *News-Review* to become the *News-Review and Crisis*, but by 1905 the paper's name reverted to *The News-Review*. (East Liverpool Historical Society.)

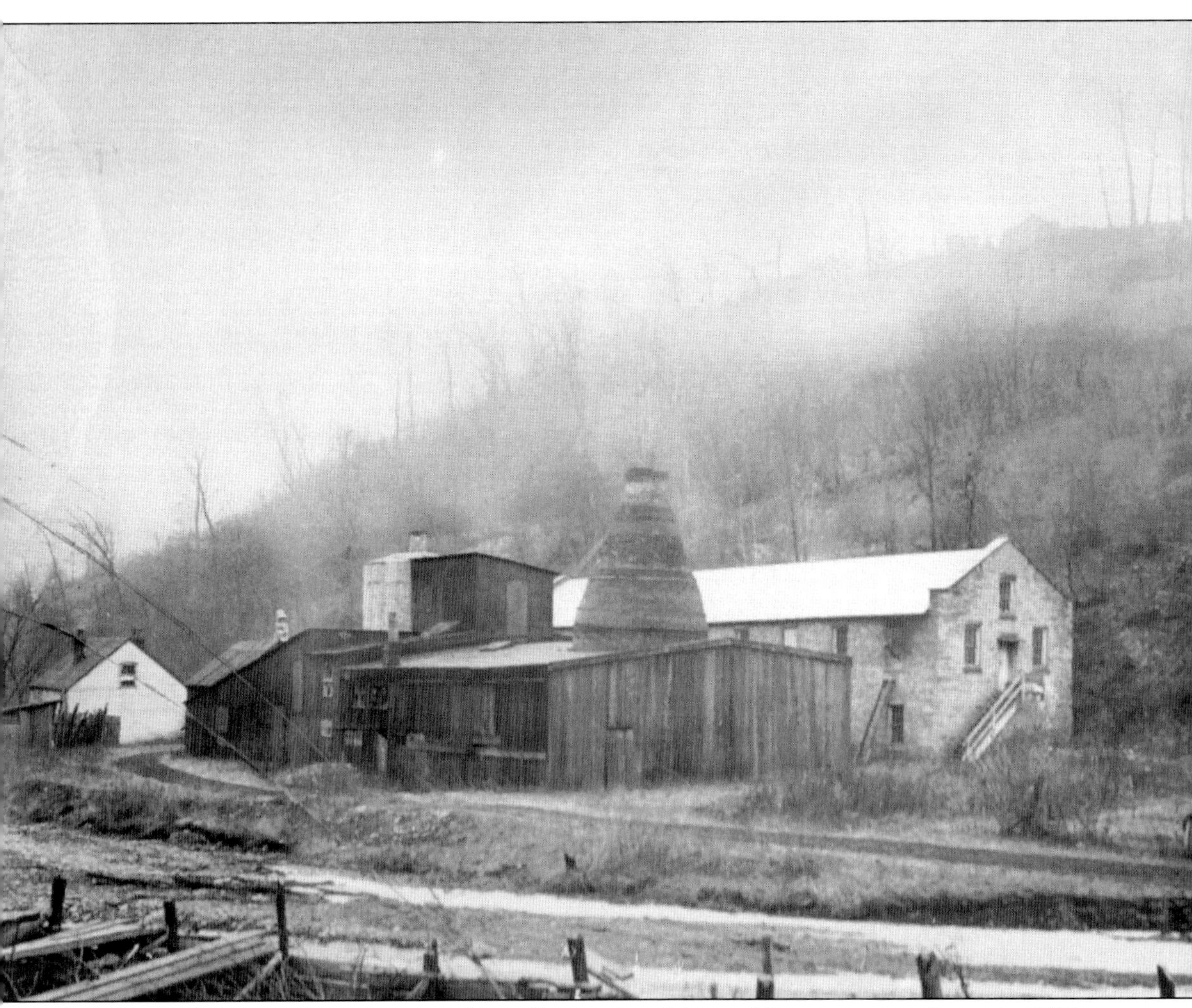

Typical of many of East Liverpool's small potteries, this one-kiln enterprise, shown in 1898, never developed into a large concern, possibly because of its overly frugal business practices. Its proprietors, McDevitt and Moore, also owned other potteries. One longtime potter described the primitive conditions in the California Hollow pottery, stating that the wedgers, who cut and kneaded clay, worked in a "damp hole." Later, when a pug mill was installed to prepare clay, fees were assessed to the workers for its use. Workers were required to provide their own candles, hand tools, and sponges. Working conditions in many 19th-century potteries were dirty and oppressively hot, and the labor was repetitious and backbreaking. Occupational diseases common in pottery workers included silicosis, pneumonia, bronchitis, and "potter's paralysis" from lead poisoning acquired in glaze-dipping and decorating departments. Workers also suffered from exhaustion, working long hours while business was good to compensate for weeks of layoffs when business was slow. (East Liverpool Historical Society.)

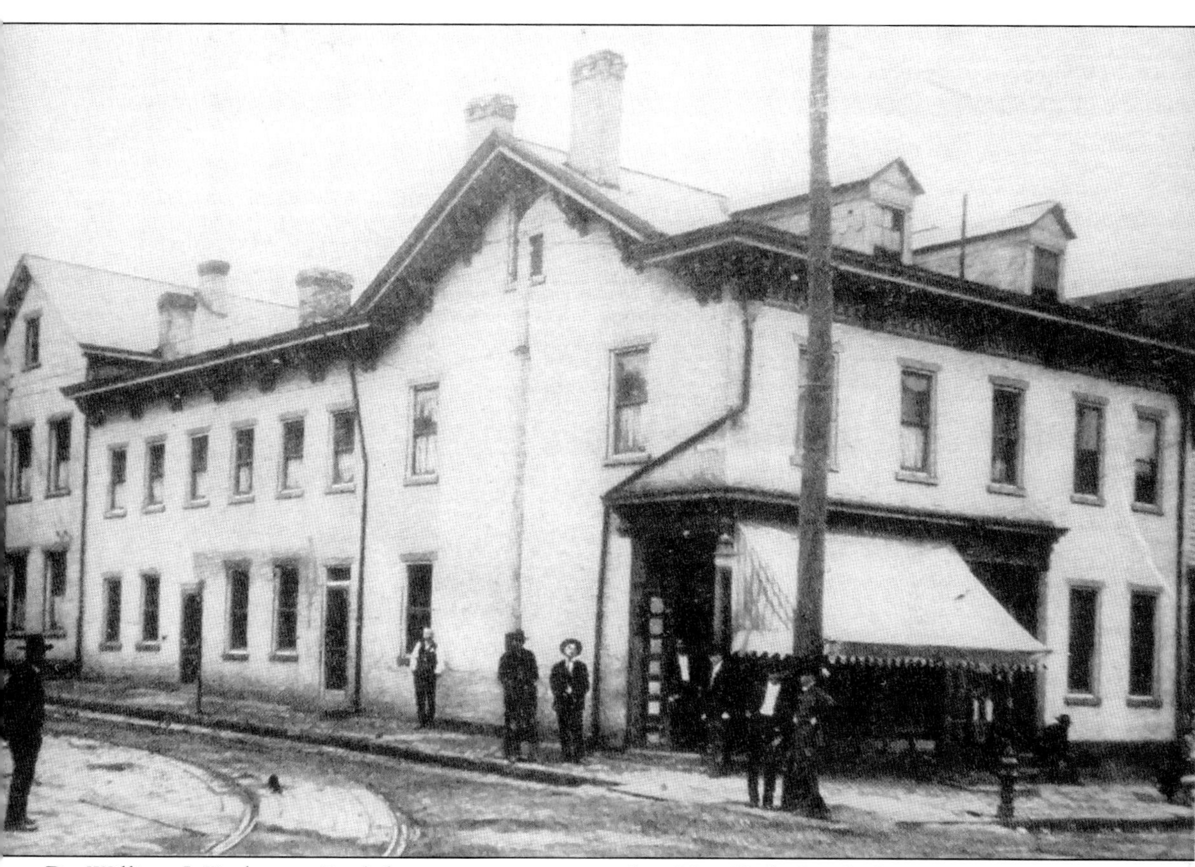

Dr. William J. Taylor, an English immigrant, practiced in New York City before moving to East Liverpool and opening the city's first private hospital and Red Cross training school for nurses at Second and Union Streets at the turn of the 20th century. Dates for the hospital's opening vary in historical records, either as 1892, 1894, or 1902. The original building, which included four wards with 12 cots and an operating room, was said to be "fitted with every modern appliance," as well as "every other known appliance used in electro-therapeutics." A nine-room addition was built the following year in response to urgent demand. Taylor was known as one of the best surgeons, with one of the best hospitals, in eastern Ohio. Besides taking care of townspeople and training nurses, Taylor provided free medical attention to city firefighters and police officers. By 1905, he was the official city physician and was operating a free dispensary for the poor. The hospital continued until the early 1920s. (Inger Lloyd.)

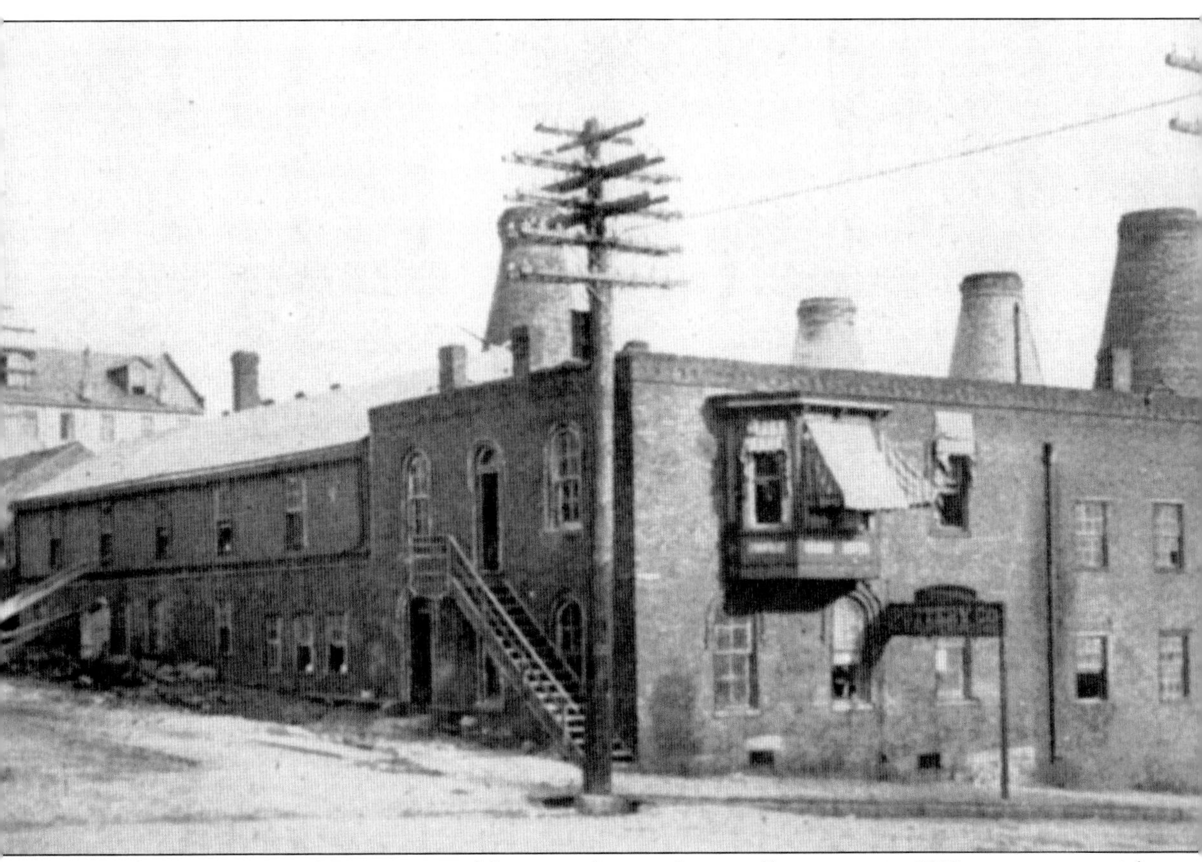

The East Liverpool Pottery joined forces with six other small potteries in 1901 to compete with larger operations. The resulting East Liverpool Potteries Company included the Globe Pottery Company, the East Liverpool Pottery, the East End Pottery Company, Wallace & Chetwynd, and the George C. Murphy Pottery Company, as well as the United States Pottery Company in Wellsville. The new corporation boasted 31 kilns to handle large orders. Each plant owned company stock and was operated individually with a single general manager overseeing all. An office and showroom were established in the former Potter's National Bank Building at Fourth Street and Broadway. After initial success, the merger broke down in July 1903, though the Globe Pottery Company and the United States Pottery Company continued until 1907 under the name East Liverpool Potteries Company. This former East Liverpool Pottery plant was then purchased by Robert T. Hall, who founded Hall China Company there. Hall China continues to operate today as a subsidiary of the Homer Laughlin China Company. (East Liverpool Historical Society.)

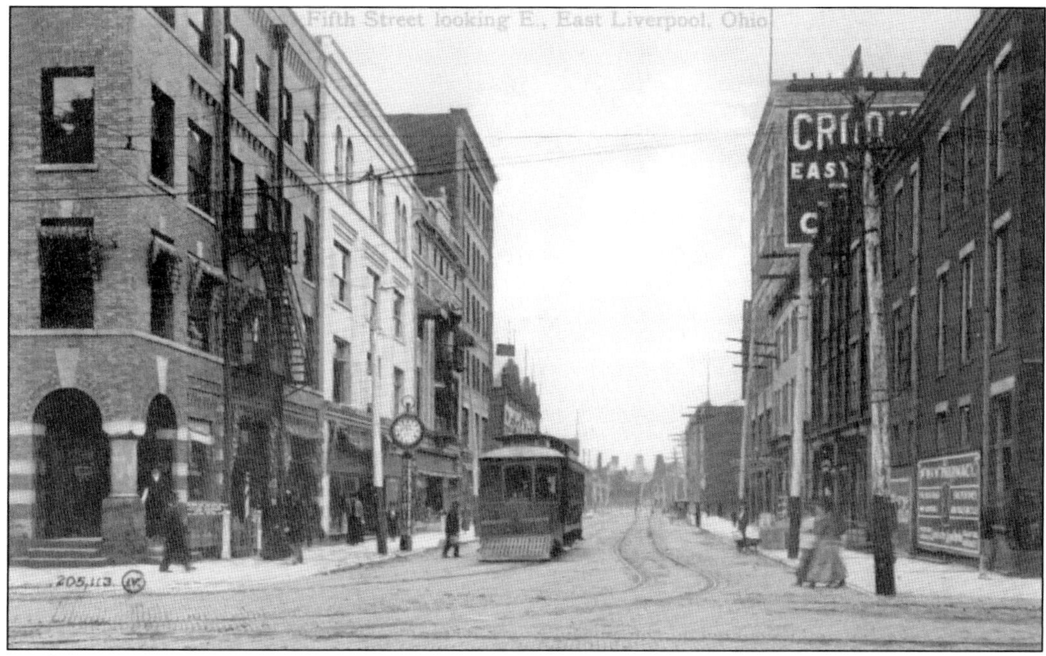

Looking east on Fifth Street, a row of bottle kilns is visible at the far end on the spot where the Museum of Ceramics is located today. The John Wyllie & Son Pottery operated near there from 1874 until near the end of the century. Trolley car service had been available in town since 1891. At right is the seven-story Crook Building. Frank Crook and his partner had opened their first retail furniture business, Crook & McGraw, in 1884. By 1893, the business was incorporated as the Crook Furniture Company, which opened in this building in 1905. Phyllis Crook died without an heir in 1978, and Jack and Lynda Reynolds purchased the business from a bank trust. They operated Brook's Furniture another 23 years, closing it in 2000. (Above, Inger Lloyd; below, Museum of Ceramics.)

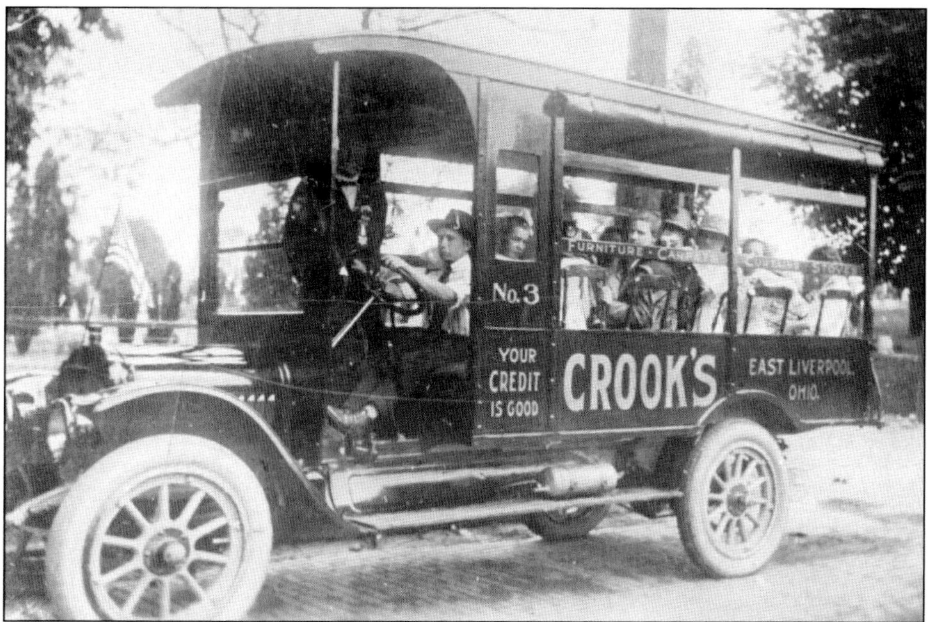

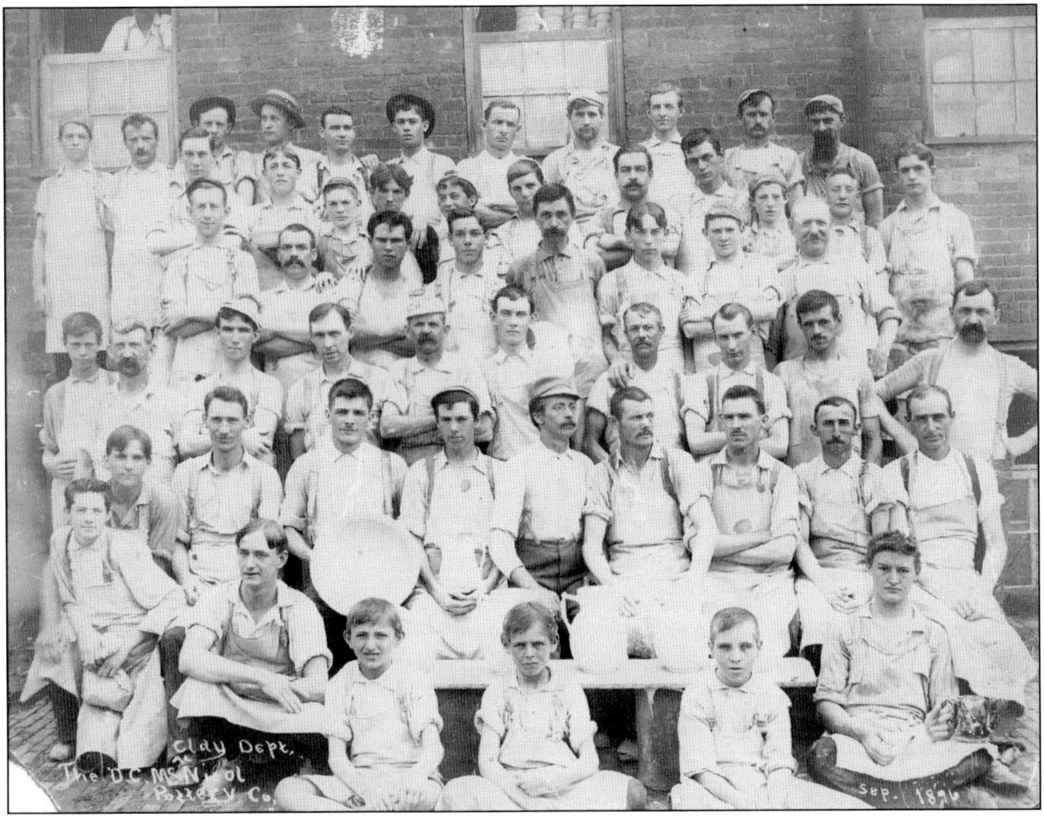

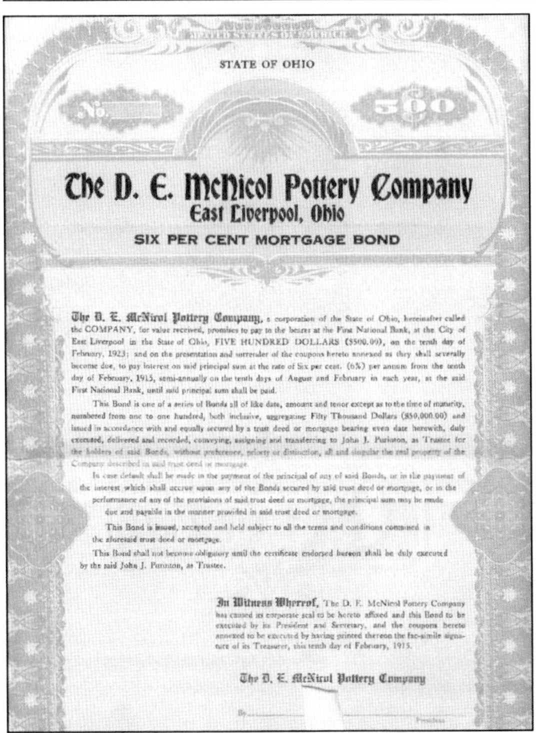

STATE OF OHIO

No. 500

The D. E. McNicol Pottery Company
East Liverpool, Ohio

SIX PER CENT MORTGAGE BOND

The D. E. McNicol Pottery Company, a corporation of the State of Ohio, hereinafter called the COMPANY, for value received, promises to pay to the bearer at the First National Bank, at the City of East Liverpool in the State of Ohio, FIVE HUNDRED DOLLARS ($500.00), on the tenth day of February, 1923; and on the presentation and surrender of the coupons hereto annexed as they shall severally become due, to pay interest on said principal sum at the rate of Six per cent. (6%) per annum from the tenth day of February, 1915, semi-annually on the tenth days of August and February in each year, at the said First National Bank, until said principal sum shall be paid.

This Bond is one of a series of Bonds all of like date, amount and tenor except as to the time of maturity, numbered from one to one hundred, both inclusive, aggregating Fifty Thousand Dollars ($50,000.00) and issued in accordance with and equally secured by a trust deed or mortgage bearing even date herewith, duly executed, delivered and recorded, conveying, assigning and transferring to John J. Purinton, as Trustee for the holders of said Bonds, without preference, priority or distinction, all and singular the real property of the Company described in said trust deed or mortgage.

In case default shall be made in the payment of the principal of any of said Bonds, or in the payment of the interest which shall accrue upon any of the Bonds secured by said trust deed or mortgage, or in the performance of any of the provisions of said trust deed or mortgage, the principal sum may be made due and payable in the manner provided in said trust deed or mortgage.

This Bond is issued, accepted and held subject to all the terms and conditions contained in the aforesaid trust deed or mortgage.

This Bond shall not become obligatory until the certificate endorsed hereon shall be duly executed by the said John J. Purinton, as Trustee.

In Witness Whereof, The D. E. McNicol Pottery Company has caused its corporate seal to be hereto affixed and this Bond to be executed by its President and Secretary, and the coupons hereto annexed to be executed by having printed thereon the fac-simile signature of its Treasurer, this tenth day of February, 1915.

The D. E. McNicol Pottery Company

By______________ President

The McNicol Pottery first opened in 1862 under John S. Goodwin, who soon sold it to the first of a succession of owners. In 1892, the company was taken over by Daniel McNicol and incorporated as D.E. McNicol Pottery Company. The company prospered and eventually included five plants, producing white and decorated dinnerware, decorated specialty pieces, and high-grade semiporcelain. Above, members of the McNicol clay department pose picturesquely in September 1896. At left, a seven-year McNicol's stock certificate promises to pay the bearer six percent semiannually on $500. Detachable coupons were included with the certificate and could be presented to the First National Bank of East Liverpool each February and August of the term. This certificate was issued February 10, 1915, and was redeemable in its entirety February 10, 1923. The full bond series amounted to $50,000. (Both Museum of Ceramics.)

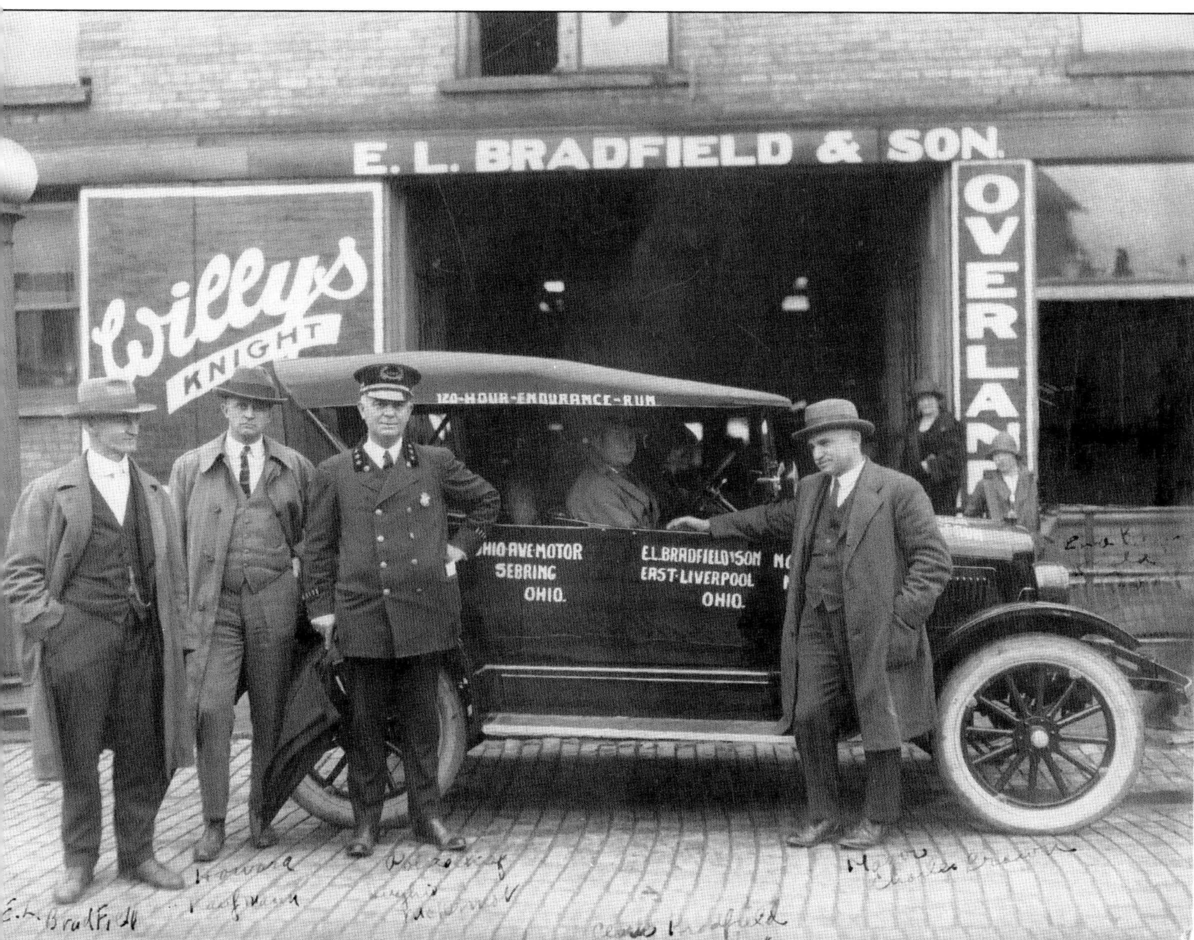

E.L. Bradfield & Son sold Ohio-built Willy's-Overland automobiles from a dealership on Broadway at the dawn of the 20th century. Pottery owners were, of course, among the first to buy automobiles and putter through the streets of East Liverpool, scaring horses and intriguing the populace. The first section of city streets was paved in 1889 on Fifth Street between Broadway and Market Street. Many major streets were paved with firebrick because of the easy availability of local clays, and some sections—bumpy but essentially complete—remain today. Celebrating the Bradfield company's participation in a 120-hour endurance run are, from left to right, E.L. Bradfield, Howard "Scoops" Kaufman, city police chief Hughie McDermott, Clark Bradfield (in the car), Ella Kannal Bradfield, and her sister Edna Kannal Wolford (in the doorway); the man behind the wheel is unidentified. E.L. and Ella Bradfield were maternal grandparents of Frank C. Dawson, a well-known city businessman. (Frank C. Dawson.)

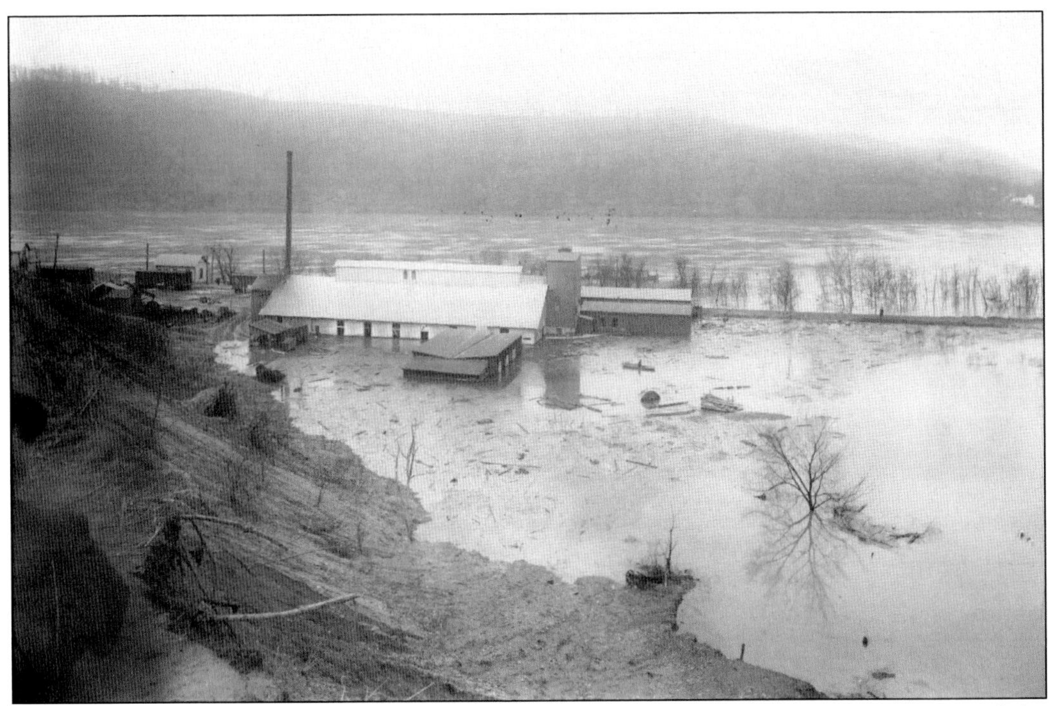

The Golding and Sons Company mill, built at the west end of town in 1876, was one of the ancillary industries that provided raw material—ground flint and feldspar for clay mixtures, in this case—to potteries all over the tristate area. The mill was one of several owned by Moses Golding of Trenton, New Jersey. The East Liverpool plant was considered both modern and efficient, able to produce 200 tons a month. Modern or not, it was flooded more than once. Local businesses that chose to locate on the riverfront for ease of transportation were used to periodic flooding. The photograph above was taken in 1900. The site of Golding's operation is now occupied by Westgate Middle School, but two of the mill's grinding stones, seen below, survive at the edge of the parking lot. (Above, East Liverpool Historical Society; below, author's collection.)

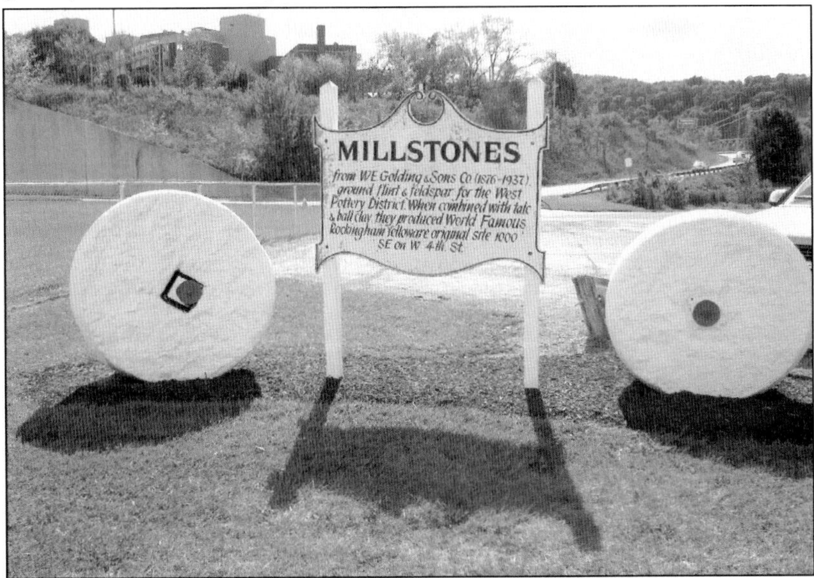

Four

Business, Pleasure, and Service

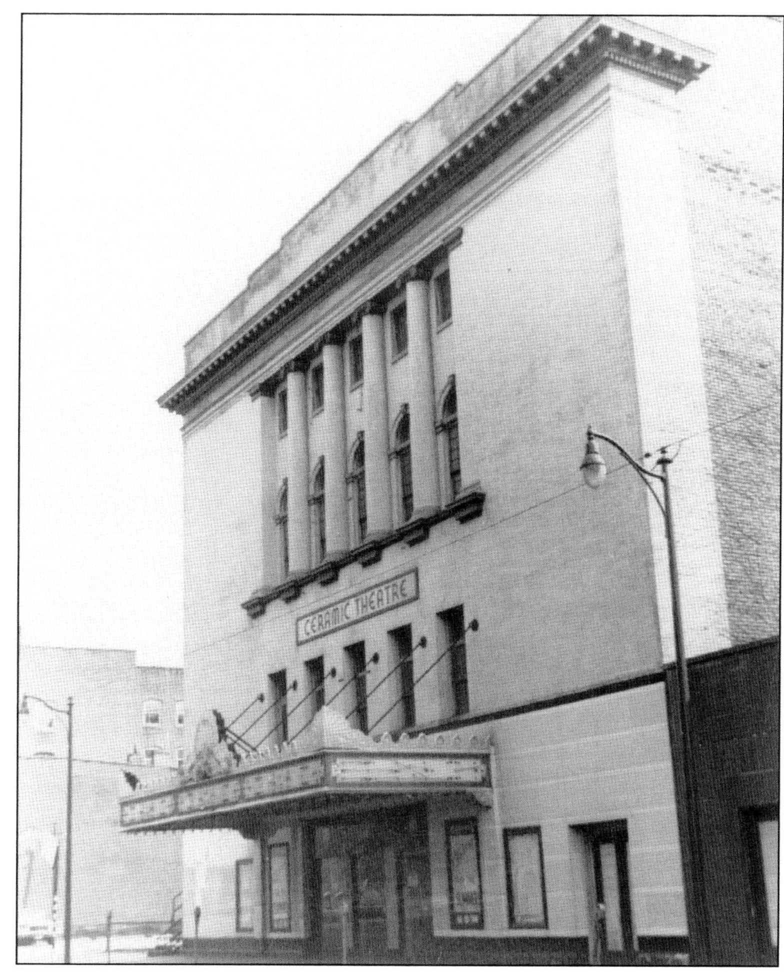

Built in 1904 at an astounding cost of $150,000, the Ceramic Theatre was for many years the premier theater in town, seating 2,000 people for first-run plays and later movies. It was the second-largest theater in Ohio and was rated one of the finest between New York and Chicago. (Frank C. Dawson.)

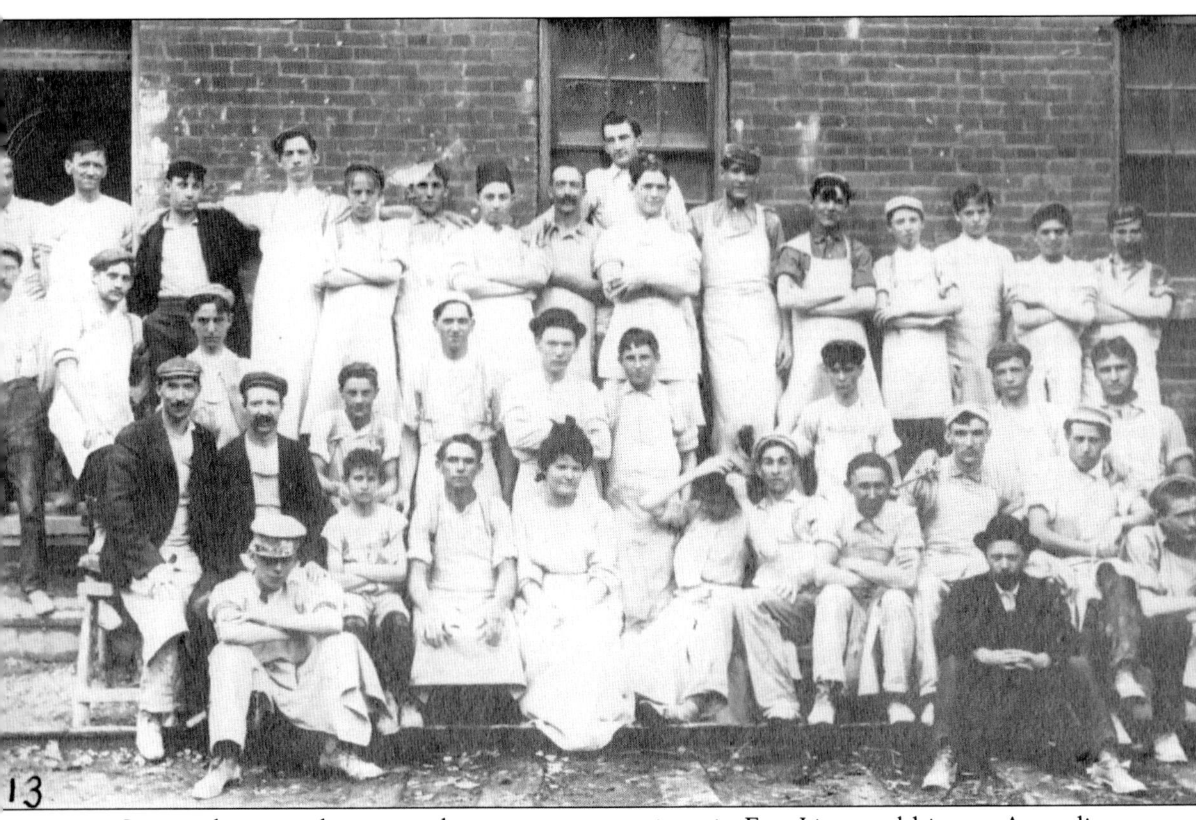

Cartwright is another name that appears many times in East Liverpool history. According to *The City of Hills and Kilns*, Thomas Cartwright was working at Harker Pottery by 1845 for "two or three dollars a week and to settle up once in two or three months, as may be convenient." Sometimes, in fact, Cartwright was not paid in cash but in produce and groceries. Brothers William and Joseph Cartwright were influential members of the family in the late 1800s and interested themselves in politics and real estate. The Croxall and Cartwright Pottery produced ware in 1888. A Cartwright Bros. Company was in business until May 1927, when the Potters Savings & Loan Company foreclosed. A few years later, the newspaper reported that several families that had lost their homes to the Depression were living illegally in an abandoned Cartwright pottery. This mostly male crew is posing outside their plant in 1902. (Museum of Ceramics.)

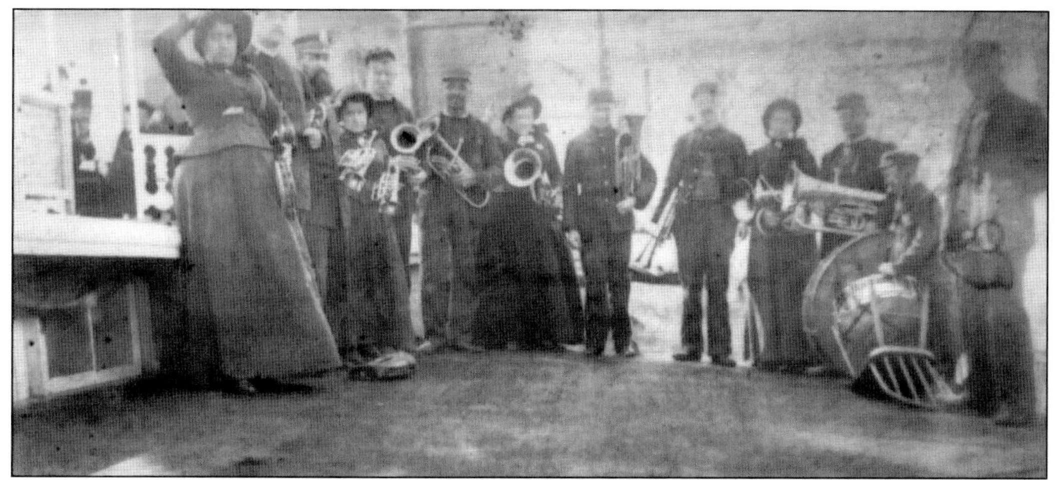

In 1894, the hardworking Salvation Army Band enjoyed a trip on the Hudson riverboat, headed to Cincinnati. Pictured are, from left to right, Mrs. Galley, cornet; P. Trumbell, cornet; Captain Galley, cornet; unidentified woman; H. Hughes, trombone; Tom Bridgett, alto; Maggie Carnabon, alto; Will Debee, tenor; Harry Webb, tenor; Ermma Childs, baritone; Dick Albright, bass; Harry Clunks, drummer; and Jim Kirkham, cornet. The original Salvation Army Citadel on Third Street was designed by founder William Booth and built in 1908–1909. It had seating for 600, plus an apartment for the commandant. At a dedication at the Ceramic Theater in 1914, Evangeline Booth, granddaughter of the Salvation Army's founder, was the speaker. Below are members of a Sunday school class at the original citadel, dressed in their best. (Both Museum of Ceramics.)

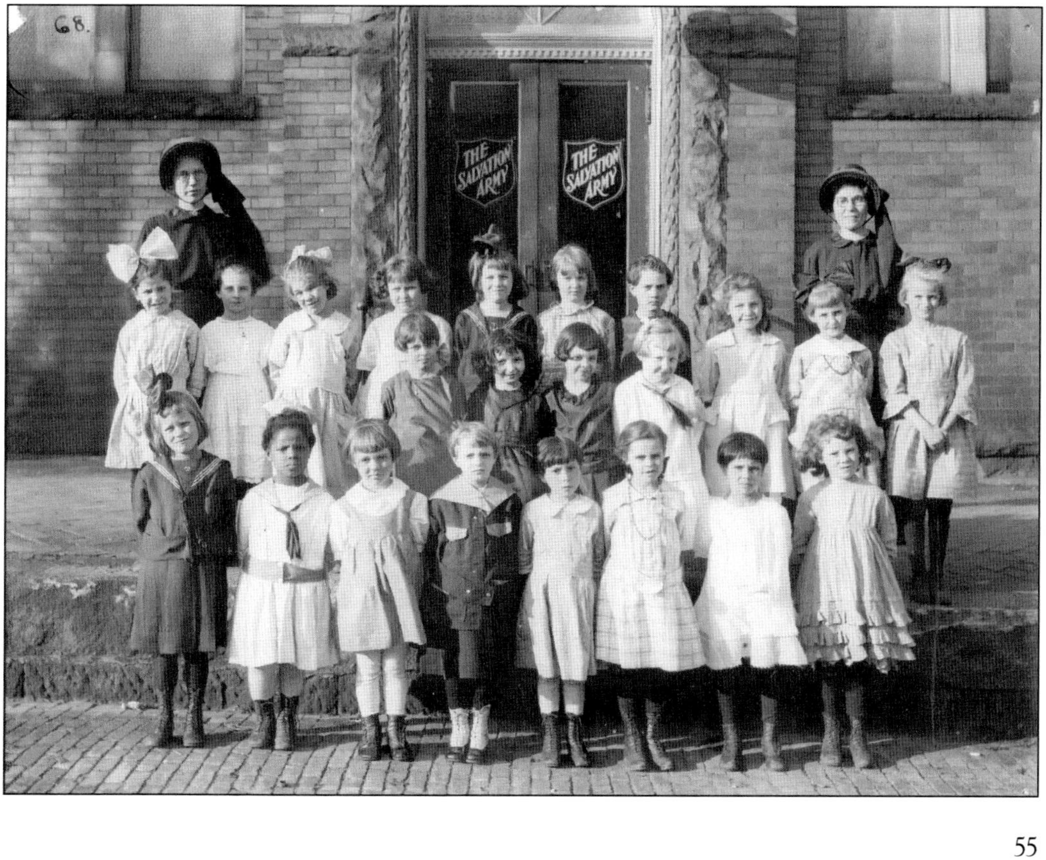

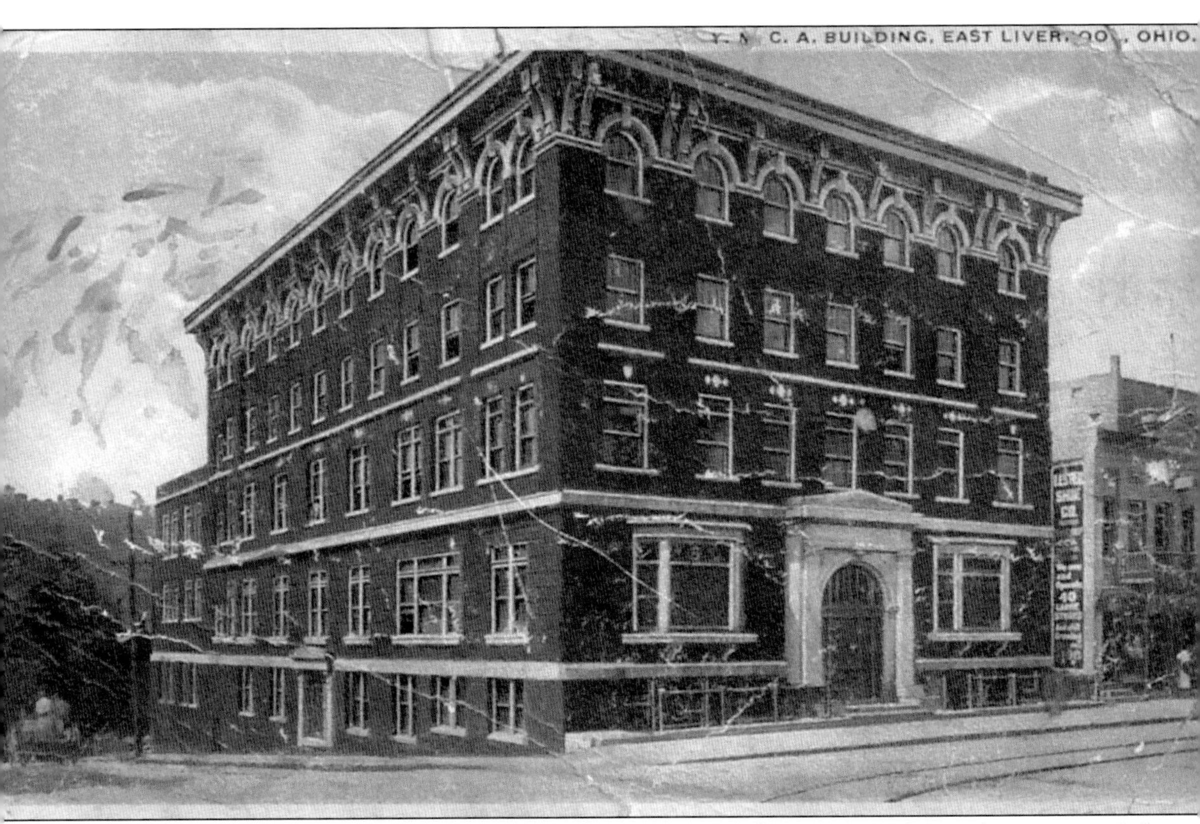

Built in 1913, the Classical Revival YMCA building on Fourth Street once boasted a spacious tiled lobby, three men's residential floors, a gymnasium with running track, two weight rooms, men's and women's health clubs, and a 20-foot-by-60-foot pool. The building still stands, though it is empty. The Y has opened new facilities in Memorial Auditorium, once part of East Liverpool High School. Many vintage postcards like this were never used, but this one was sent from the Klondyke Post Office in East End to Parkersburg, West Virginia, in 1918. On the back, the sender wrote in pencil, "Dear Clare will drop you a few lines. I got a letter from sis today she said you was talking about going to Fairmont don't you go far I am coming home real soon . . . write real soon." It was addressed to Mr. Clare Barnhart, Worthmore, Parkersburg, West Virginia. (Roxie Harsha.)

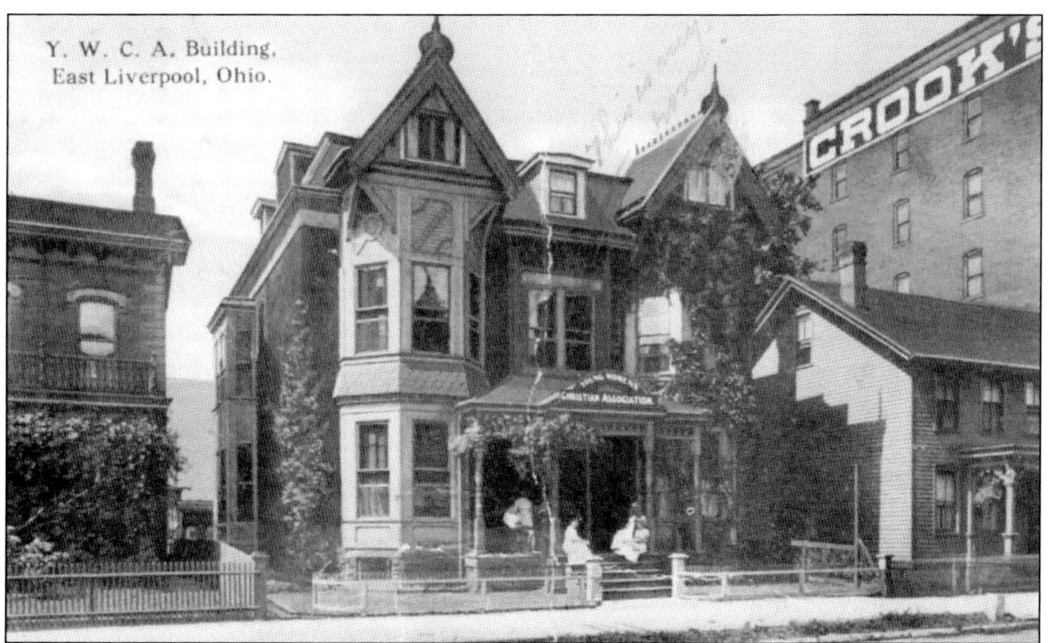

Although a YMCA has been a fixture in East Liverpool for more than 100 years, few people remember that a Young Women's Christian Association once existed here as well, in a pretty Victorian building on Fifth Street near Crook's Furniture. The YWCA operated from 1911 to 1920. (Museum of Ceramics.)

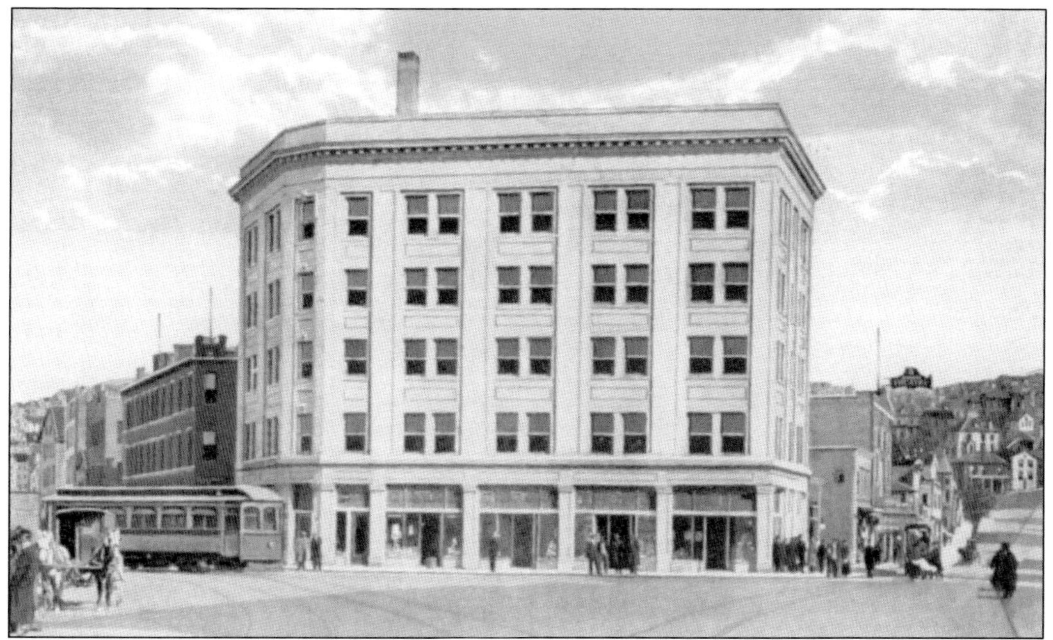

The five-story Little Building, housing retail shops and professional offices, was built on Sixth Street at the Diamond around 1912–1915, replacing the Surprise Clothing House. Through the first half of the 20th century, the Diamond was a bustling city center, full of pedestrians, vehicles, streetcars, restaurants, and businesses. The Little Building still stands, but it is mostly empty today. (Museum of Ceramics.)

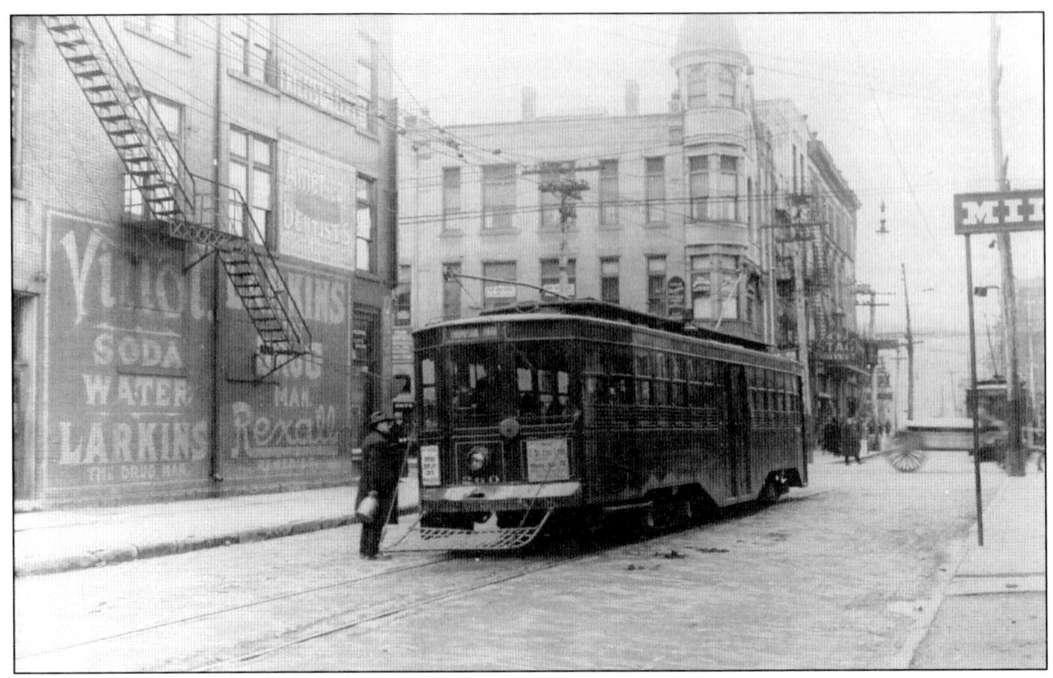

There was talk of a streetcar railway between East Liverpool and Wellsville in 1882, but the idea did not go any further. Talk surfaced again in 1888 and in 1890 with the same results, possibly caused by too much political maneuvering. On December 17, 1891, however, the first streetcar finally made the trip between the two cities. Despite more political controversy, it was not long before streetcars were traveling regularly throughout East Liverpool to its new suburbs, up and down the river, and into West Virginia and Pennsylvania. More than three million passengers were transported in 1902. Above, Car 260 heads up St. Clair Avenue from the Diamond to Thompson Park. The photograph below documents an unfortunate wintertime crash around 1912 that took out someone's front window at St. Clair Avenue and Grant Street. (Both East Liverpool Historical Society.)

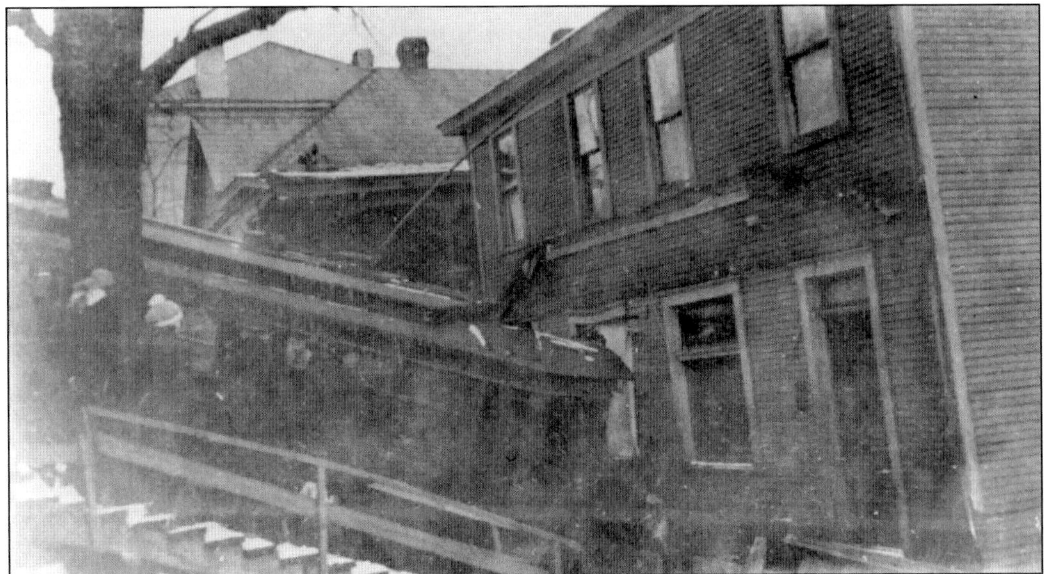

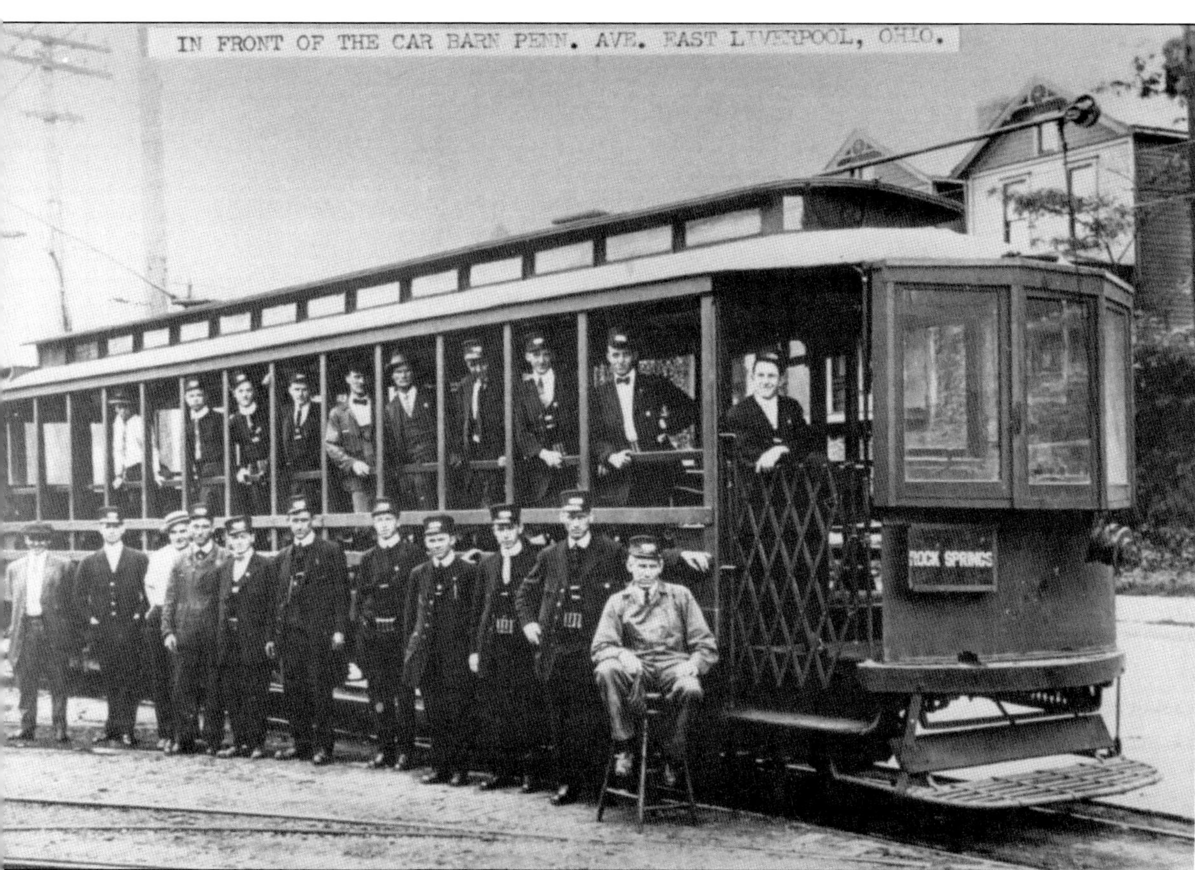

The East Liverpool Traction & Light Company built a carbarn and repair shop in the East End in 1909 next to Columbian Park on Pennsylvania Avenue to accommodate its growing fleet of streetcars. Conductors gathered there for this photograph with a car that traveled daily across the river to Chester's popular Rock Springs Park. Rail service expanded rapidly in these years. Companies such as the Youngstown & Southern Railroad Company; the Steubenville, East Liverpool & Beaver Valley Traction Co.; and the Ohio River Passenger Railway Company carried out plans for connections between cities. Soon, city residents could hop an interurban car, called the "Ceramic Flyer," which departed from the Diamond at the half hour. By connecting with other lines, passengers could travel in comfort to Steubenville, Pittsburgh, Wheeling, Cleveland, and beyond. The car barn continues to be used today by the city street department. (East Liverpool Historical Society.)

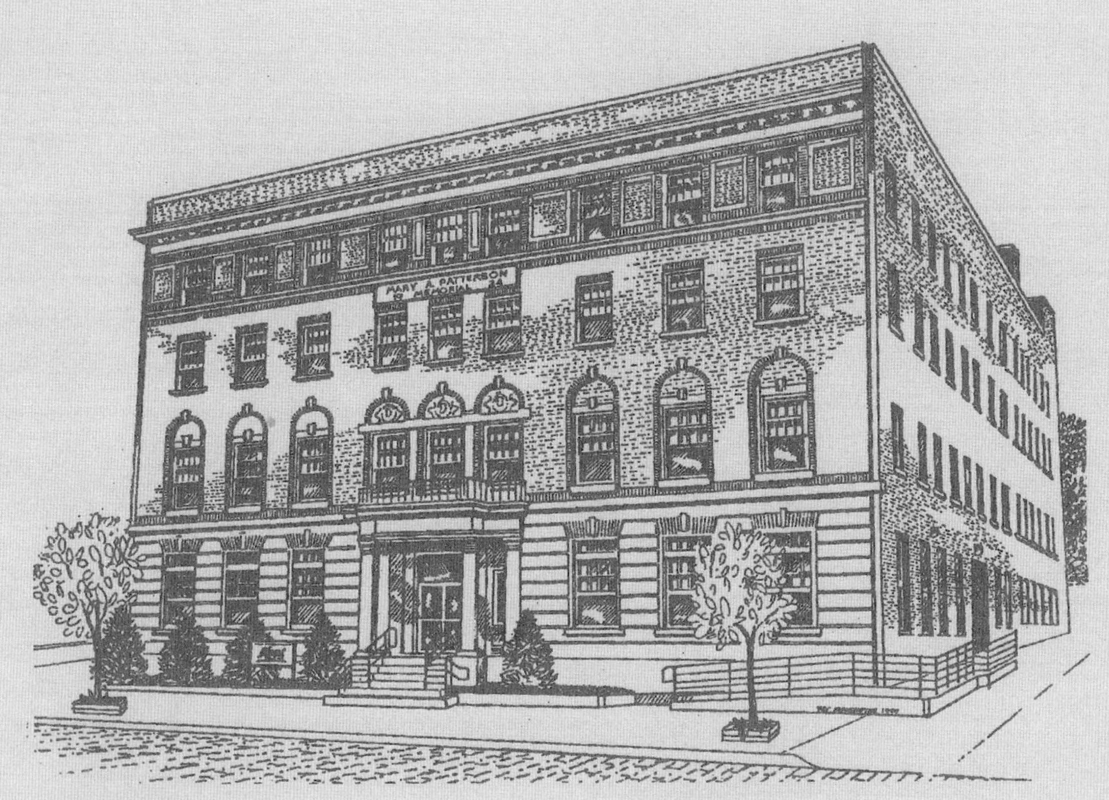

The Mary Patterson Memorial Home

The Mary A. Patterson Memorial Christian Home for Women has a tragic story with a good ending. Monroe Patterson of the Patterson Foundry and Machine Company (for whom the high school football field is also named) built it in 1925 as a gift to the city in honor of his late wife. Monroe died before the building was completed, and because of legal entanglements, the home was not opened to residents until 1932. The "Mary Pat," as it is called, had 116 furnished rooms meant for working women, along with a lounge, auditorium, and swimming pool. First-floor office space was used by both the Red Cross and the Columbiana County Motor Club. A combination of low residency and rising costs forced the Mary Pat to close in 1984. The Friends of Kent State University's East Liverpool campus bought the building in 1989 after it reverted to the Patterson heirs. Between private donors, the university, and the State of Ohio, enough money was raised for a $2 million renovation, and the building was reopened as part of Kent State in 2000. (Frank C. Dawson.)

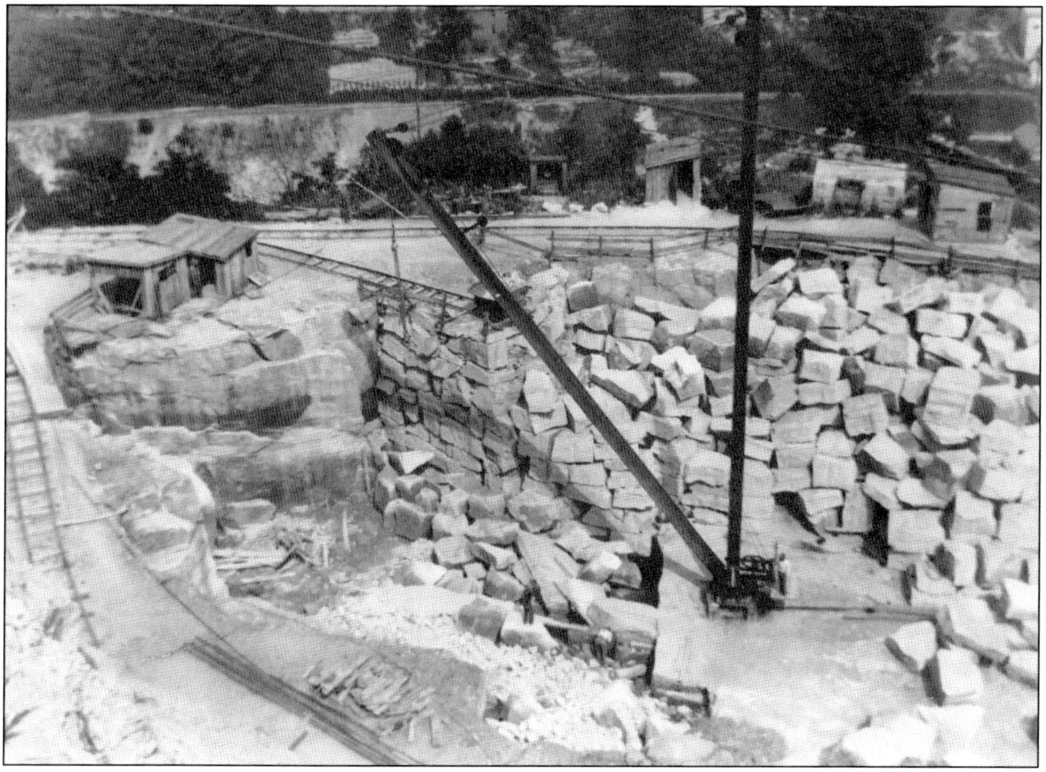

The Sunnyside Stone Quarry was operated by the International Pulp Stone Company from Empire, Ohio, early in the 20th century. Located in California Hollow on the hillside between Carpenter's Run and Pleasant Heights, it was in use for some 20 years, closing around 1920 when the "overbearing," or topsoil, became too deep. Austrian and Hungarian stonecutters, who lived nearby in company housing, began with a steam shovel to dig out the topsoil, then used dynamite to loosen the stone. Final quarrying was done with hand tools. Smaller stones that were to be used as building materials were dressed by hand with chipping hammers. Some of the building stones are still visible around town in retaining walls. (Both East Liverpool Historical Society.)

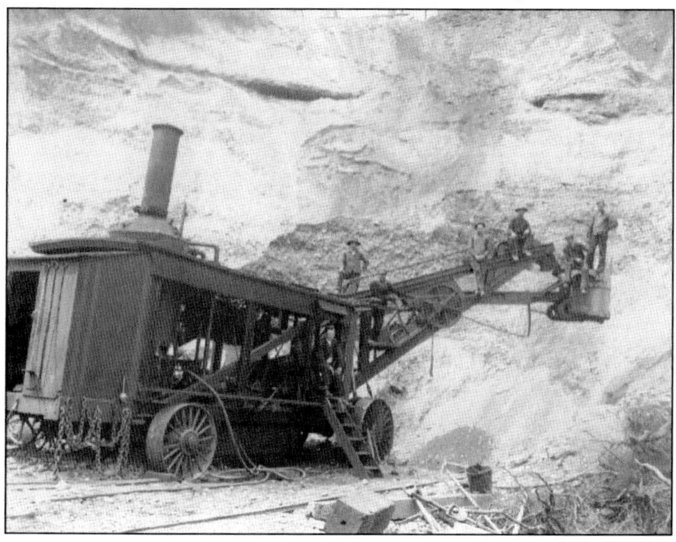

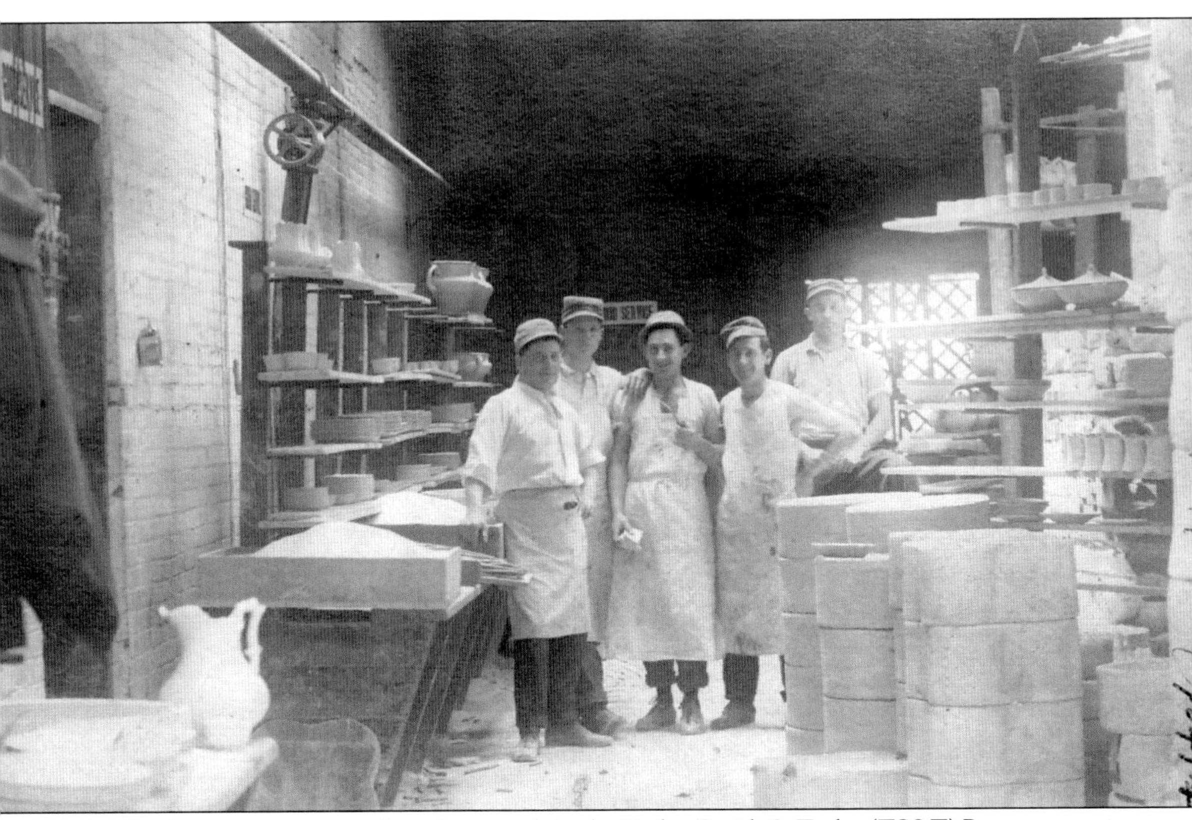

This five-man crew poses for a photograph in the Taylor, Smith & Taylor (TS&T) Pottery sometime in the 1910s or 1920s. Pottery work was reportedly dirty, damp, and exhausting and was known to cause lung ailments, but these workers look healthy, well rested, and relatively clean. The man in the center holding a pipe is probably the jiggerman. The man in the tilted cap, second from the right, is Jerry Hester. The proud crew is surrounded by the results of their labors: finished plates, cups, bowls, and tureens. Stacks of saggers and bins of what appears to be powdered clay are also visible. Note the tin cup hanging on the brick wall at the far left, probably used by all the crew members. TS&T expanded its operations in the late 1920s, converting to continuous kilns, and in the next few years was able to increase production by one-fourth. It operated until 1972. (Author's collection.)

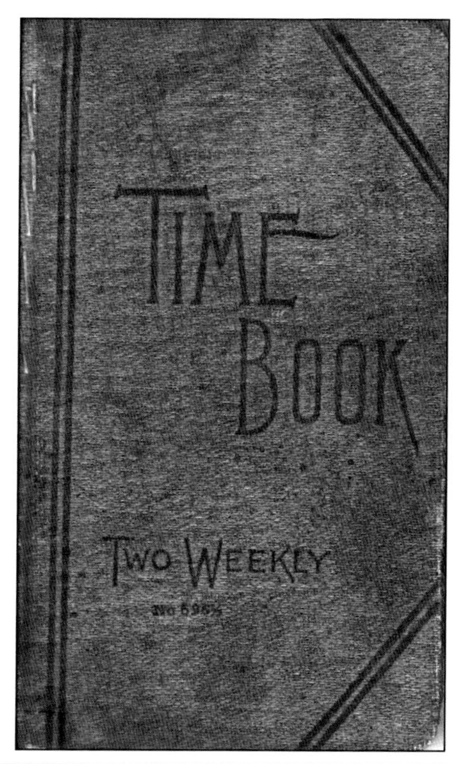

Between 1911 and 1913, a foreman or jiggerman at a local pottery used this book to keep track of his crew's hours. One page lists George B. Martin, George McGraw, F.B. Nash, R.E. Baxter, W.S. Baxter, and Albert Campbell, along with the notation, "Paid." Potters learned by experience, and different skills were needed. Some dug and dried the clay into crumbled bits; others mixed ingredients with water, using horses to turn the paddles. The liquid clay, or slip, was boiled to soft putty, pressed to remove extra water, then cast or pressed into molds. Jiggermen hired crews to handle the clay, transport it back and forth to the kiln, and finish the ware. Kiln firing and cooling could take 48 hours and might be repeated. Finally, packers placed the ware in straw-filled barrels for shipping. (Both author's collection.)

Time Book for Two Weeks, ending 1911

NAMES	S	M	T	W	T	F	S	S	M	T	W	T	F	S	Total Time	Rate	Amount	Remarks
Geo. B. Martin															4 ¼		13	
Geo McGraw															4 ¼		13	
F. B. Nash															4 ¼			
R. E. Baxter															4 ¼			
W. S. Baxter															4 ¼			
Albert Campbell															4 ½			
extra time															2			

Paid

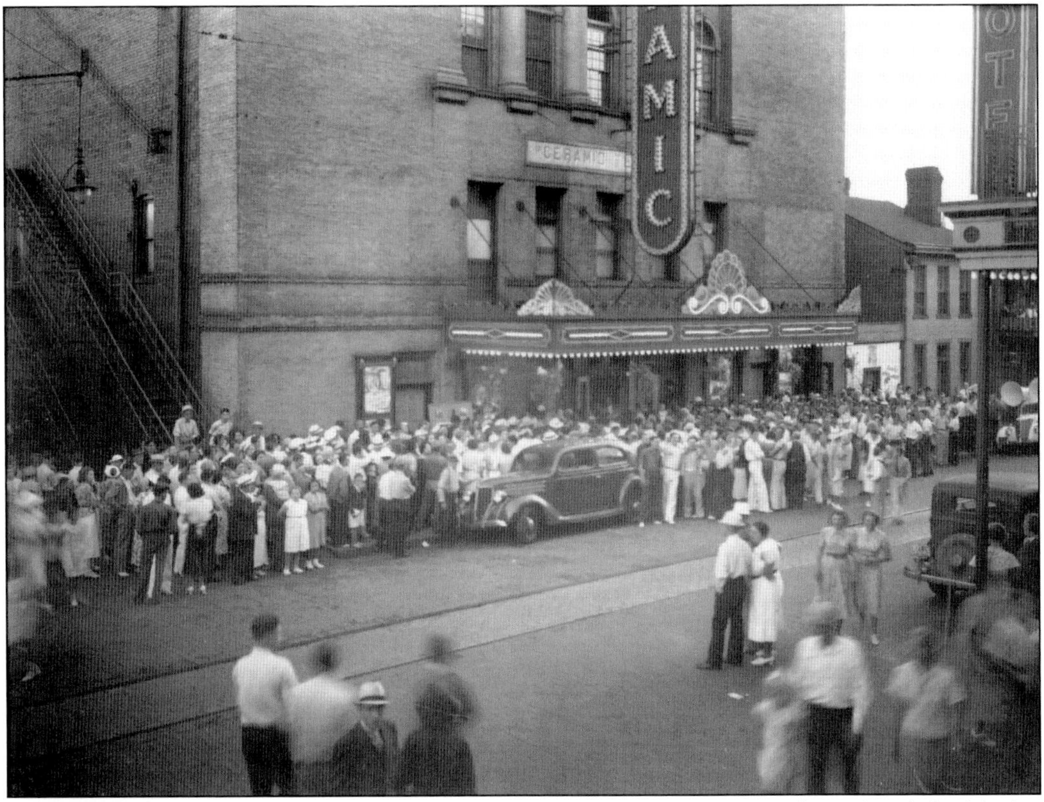

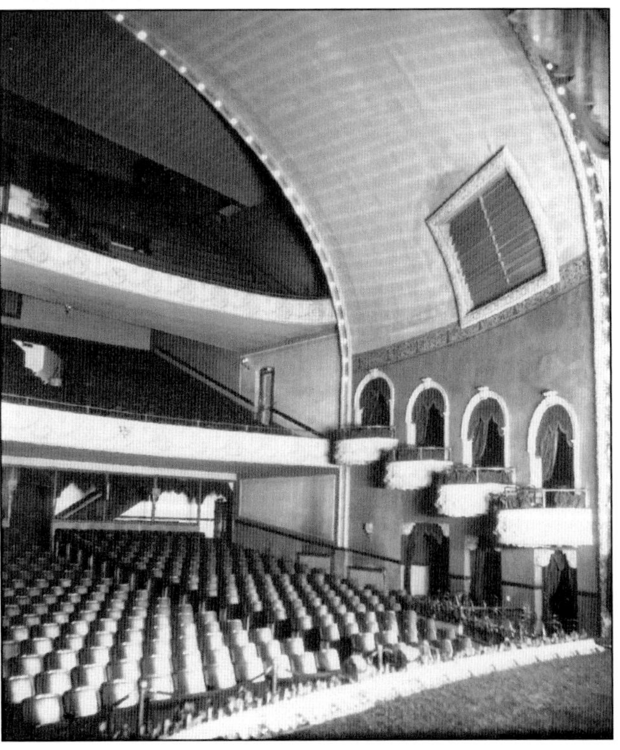

East Liverpudlians lined the block to see performances by leading stars like Will Rogers and Ethel Barrymore at the Ceramic Theater on Fourth Street. In 1912, a movie screen was installed, and movies alternated with live performances. Edison "talking pictures" were added in 1913, and in 1928 the Ceramic installed a Vitaphone, which synchronized voice and music with moving pictures, allowing talkies to be shown. In 1930, the Ceramic added radio performances, using the Vitaphone to present *Amos & Andy* every evening. Patriotic rallies, musical events, military groups, and speakers occupied the Ceramic. Presidential candidates Theodore Roosevelt and William Howard Taft campaigned there on the same day. The building was razed in the 1960s to make room for a parking lot. (Both Frank C. Dawson.)

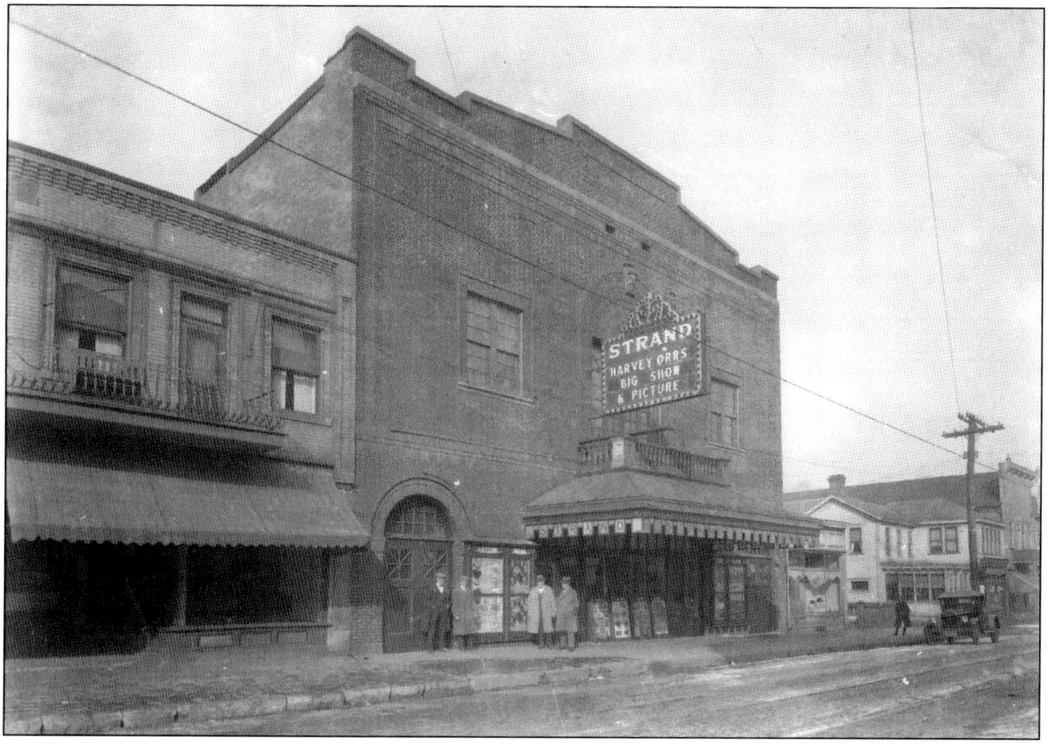

The building above opened for business on St. Clair Avenue in 1914 as the home of the McKinley Vaudeville Theatre. It was built by Col. John Walsh, who also owned the Walsh Hotel on East Sixth Street. Less than a year later, the theater's name was changed to the Strand, and it began to show silent movies such as *The Birth of a Nation*, *Way Down East*, and *The Ten Commandments*. By the late 1920s, the name had changed to the State Theater, which operated until the 1970s. Below, looking down West Sixth Street, the Columbia Theater is visible on the left, and the American Theater is on the right. The city bus terminal is at the far end. (Both Frank C. Dawson.)

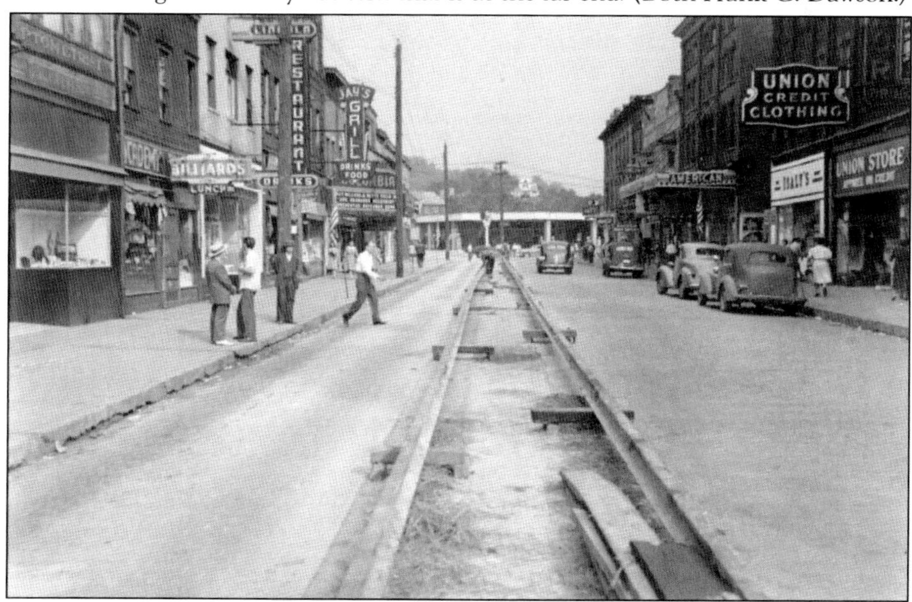

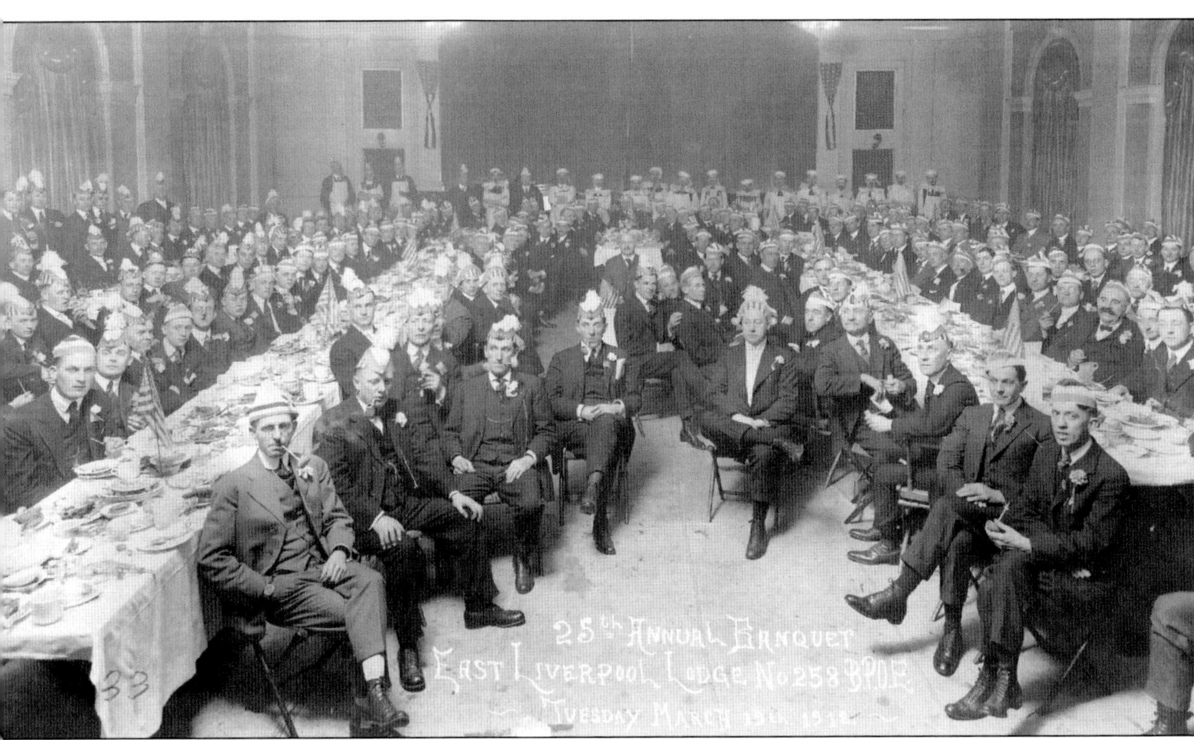

Dozens of lodge members gathered in their regalia for the 25th anniversary of the Benevolent Protective Order of Elks East Liverpool Lodge 258 on March 19, 1918. Many of them seem to be smoking the same type of corncob pipe. Their imposing Fifth Street lodge, built in 1916, is part of the National Register of Historic Places. The Elks members have since moved to smaller quarters, but the original building still stands. Besides fraternal, cultural, and service organizations, social clubs in the city provided entertainment and purpose and fostered networking opportunities. For industry leaders, social organizations included the Cosmopolitan Club, the Phoenix Club, and the Belmont Club. The New Century Club, the Baedeker Club, the Colonial Club, and the Monday Literary Club for women were also active in the 1900s, and some still meet today. (Museum of Ceramics.)

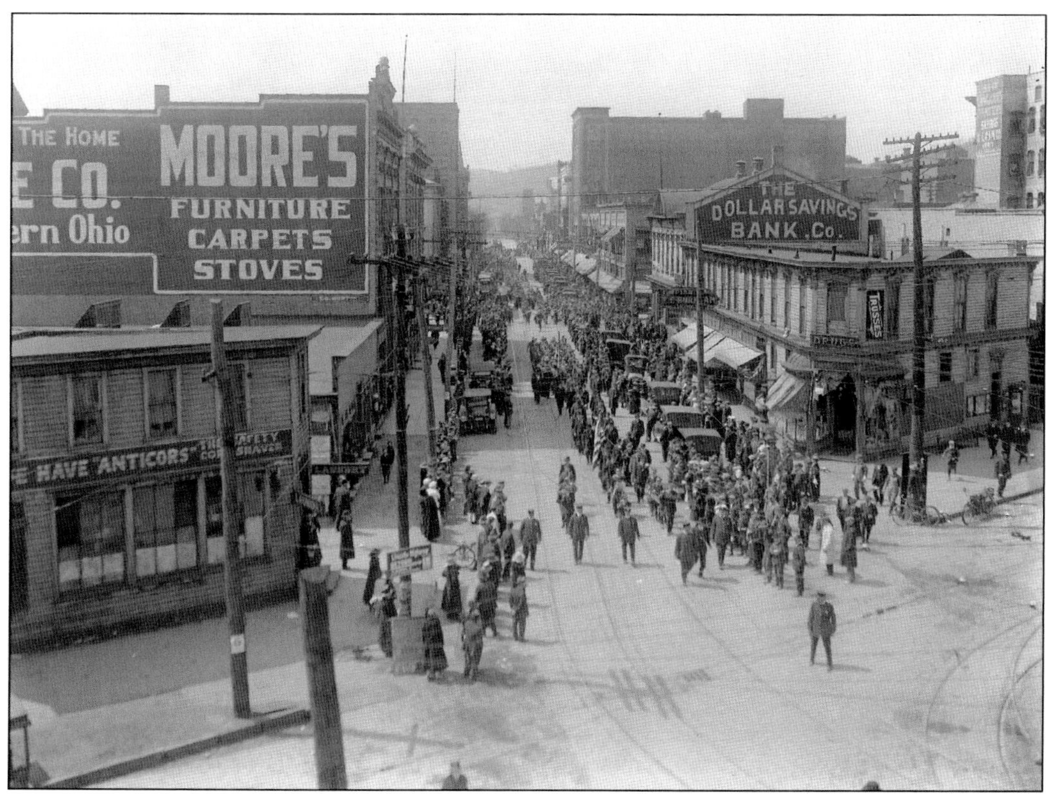

East Liverpool welcomed its veterans home after World War I ended in 1918. Even before war had been declared, Ohio National Guard recruits drilled on Sixth Street, and a local company was organized in March 1917. More than 300 East Liverpool men had joined the fight by April 1918. Some 150 local men made up Company E, a machine gun unit in the 37th Buckeye Division of the 135th Regiment that served in France. Potteries prospered during the war, between large orders from the War Department and the disruption of pottery production in Europe. Residents gave to Liberty Loan drives and participated in meatless Tuesdays and lightless Mondays. In all, 1,185 East Liverpool men served, along with at least five female Red Cross nurses; 38 citizens died. (Both Museum of Ceramics.)

Home-Coming Banquet For Our World War Heroes

B. P. O. ELKS HOME, No. 258

Thursday, November 20, 1919

7 O'clock P. M.

ABLE SPEAKERS, INCLUDING

Major General E. F. Glenn

Assessment to all except Soldiers, $4.00 per plate.
Reservations should be made in advance with the Steward

JOIN NOW!

★

ANNUAL
MEMBERSHIP WEEK

MAY 24th TO 29th

★

HEADQUARTERS

TRAVELERS HOTEL
PHONE 356

SEASON 1937-38
Adults $5.00 **Students $2.50**

★

Admission to Concerts by Membership Card Only
No single tickets sold at any time

Membership Closes Saturday, May 29th at 10 P. M.

★

RRANGED IN COOPERATION WITH
IVIC · CONCERT · SERVICE · INC ·
NATIONAL BROADCASTING COMPANY SUBSIDIARY

EVERYONE IS INVITED TO JOIN

★

THE CIVIC MUSIC ASSOCIATION PLAN LEADS THE MUSICAL WORLD IN THE BUILDING OF AUDIENCES, ENABLING YOUR CITY TO PRESENT CONCERTS ON A FINANCIALLY SOUND, PERMANENT AND ORGANIZED BASIS

★

OFFICERS

MRS. ROBERT T. HALL....... Chairman of Board
W. H. EMERSON....... President
ALBERT FROSCH....... Vice-President
MRS. E. J. GASTON....... Vice-President
H. B. BARTH....... Secretary
MISS MARY IRWIN....... Treasurer

EAST LIVERPOOL

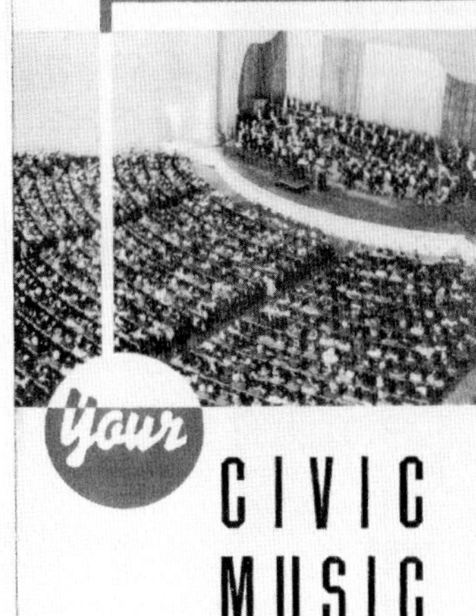

your

CIVIC MUSIC ASSOCIATION

...and why you should join

The town's movie theaters brought outside entertainment to the area on a regular basis, but Liverpudlians also provided their own. Both local and nationally known musicians appeared in revues sponsored by clubs, fraternal organizations, and the chamber of commerce. The East Liverpool Civic Music Association, seen above, presented regular concerts with "admission . . . by membership card only." This flyer urged citizens to join up for the 1937–1938 concert season. The names of the association's officers were a roster of the social elite. Mrs. Hall was the wife of the founder of Hall China. Frosch was a city official. Mrs. Gaston was also a pottery owner's wife, and H.B. Barth was the author of *History of Columbiana County, Ohio.* Below is the Jefferson Dramatic Club (plus one small boy), which might have put on plays and orations for Liverpudlians. (Both Museum of Ceramics.)

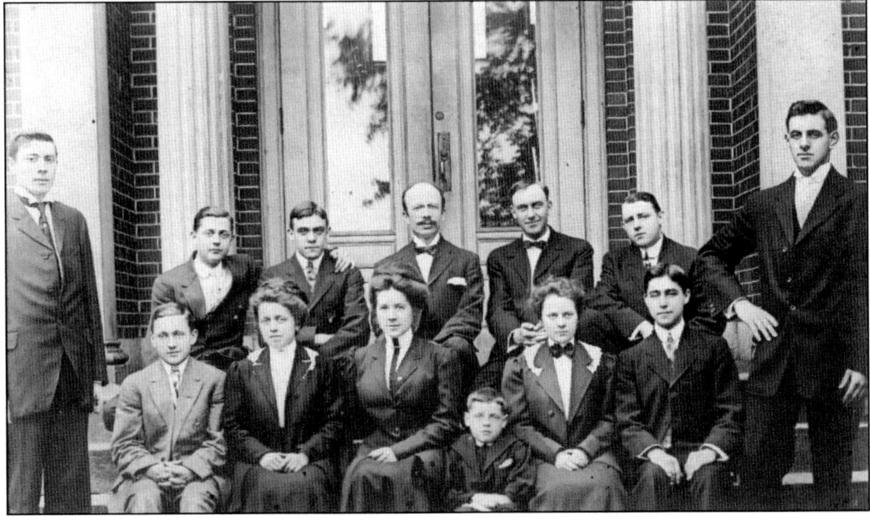

The first city hall (right) was built in 1878 at the southeast corner of Market and Third Streets and housed offices for both the city and the township. Citizens felt the imposing structure was fitting for the prosperous community. The three-story hall was spacious enough that civic groups were sometimes accommodated. The Silver Cornet Band, for instance, had its own band room there. By 1911, though, city residents were tired of the shabby building, calling it "a relic of the dead past." Over the next 25 years, there were repeated calls for a new building, which the city could not afford. (At right, Frank C. Dawson; below, Museum of Ceramics.)

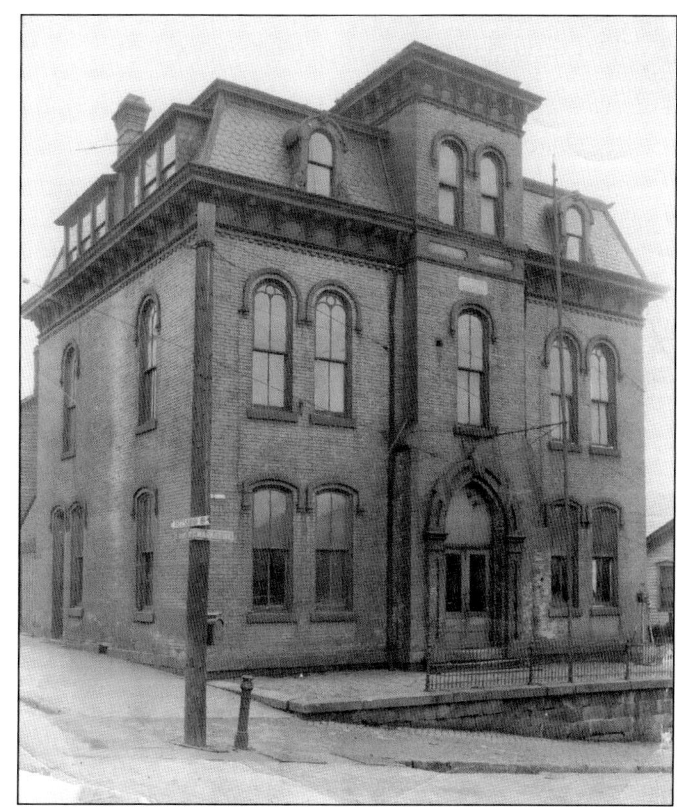

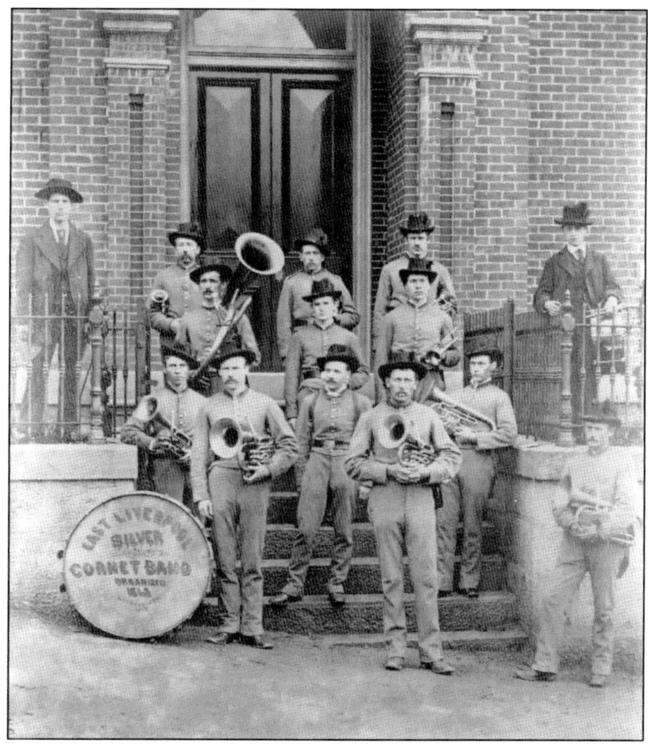

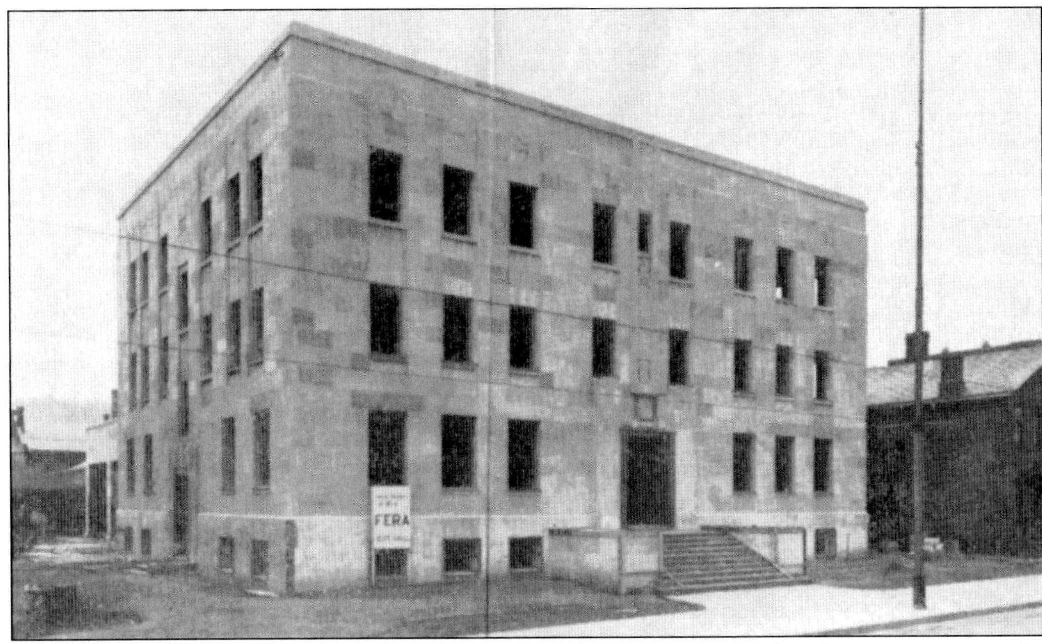

In the middle of the Depression, city officials found the means to order the construction of a new sandstone city hall and jail on East Sixth Street in the popular Art Deco style of the time. Through the Civil Works Administration and the Federal Emergency Relief Administration, the federal government contributed $95,000 for labor and $28,000 for material, leaving city residents to furnish the balance of $75,000. The new building was dedicated with much fanfare in 1935. It was added to the National Register of Historic Places in 1985. When the original city hall was torn down in 1934, its bell was given a second life at the Third Street Park, pictured below in 1951; balancing on top is Harold Walderhaug. (Above, Museum of Ceramics; below, Inger Lloyd.)

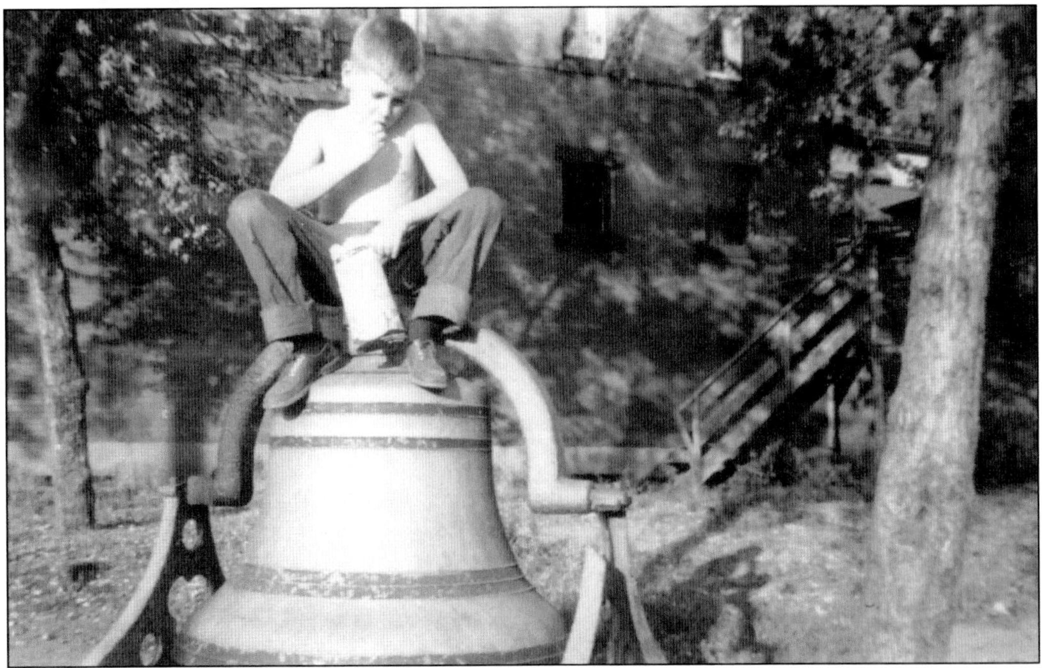

Five

ONWARD AND UPWARD

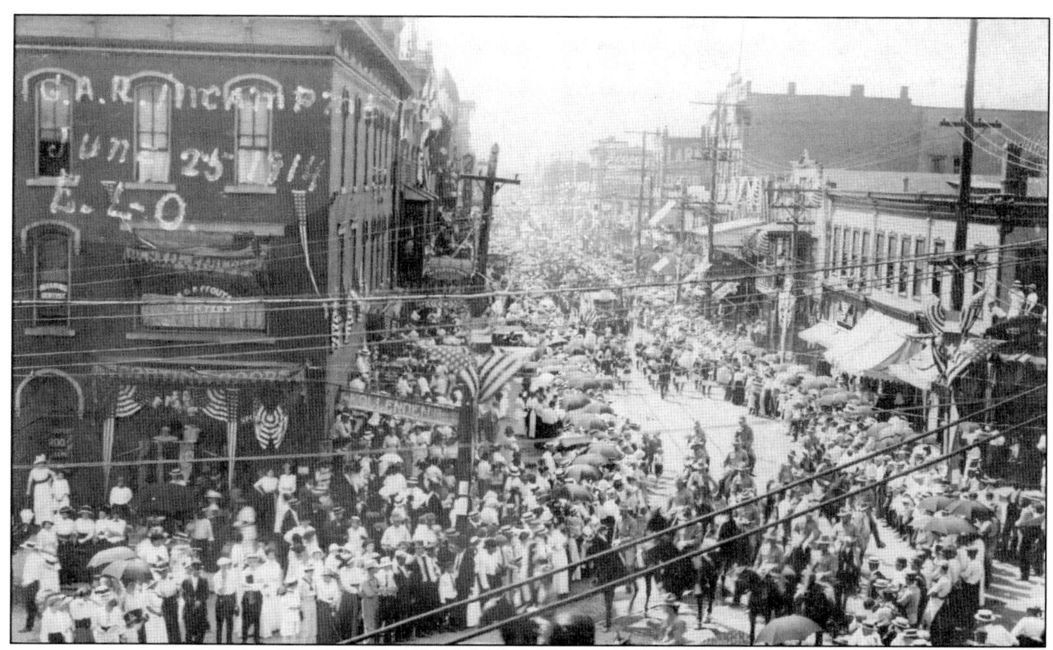

Marching east on Fifth Street on June 25, 1914, on the rainy final day of the 1914 Ohio Encampment, are members of the Grand Army of the Republic (GAR). The GAR, a fraternal organization of Civil War veterans, was active from its formation in 1856 until its dissolution in 1956, when the last member died. (Frank C. Dawson.)

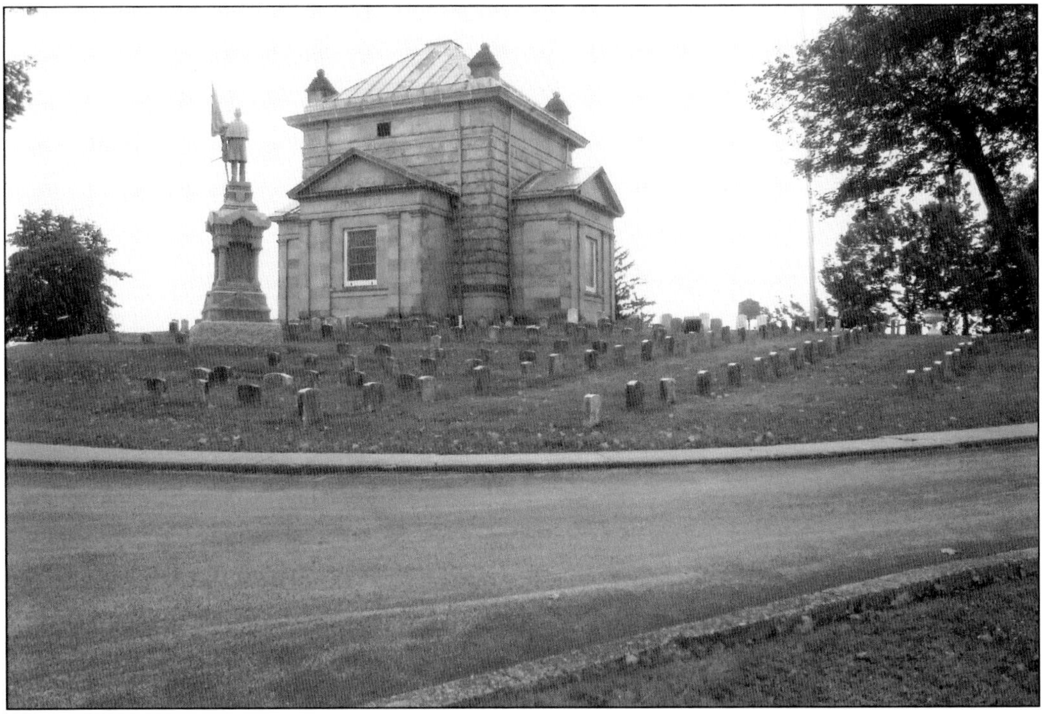

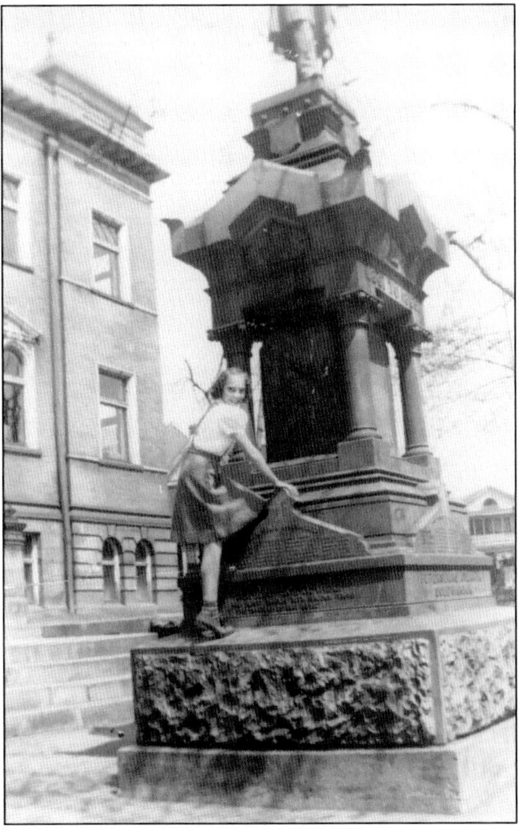

One of East Liverpool's most recognizable—and well-traveled—landmarks is the Civil War Soldier. The statue was donated to the city by the GAR in 1890 and stood on the Diamond for 19 years. It was then moved to City Park for seven years. The soldier was moved again, guarding Carnegie Library for 26 years. Since 1942, the statue has stood with Riverview Cemetery's Memorial Chapel, overlooking a circular arrangement of inward-facing veterans' tombstones. On the statue's 100th anniversary in 1990, the city historical society held a rededication ceremony. The Memorial Chapel, for which local GAR members raised more than $17,000, contains plaques listing 702 Civil War veterans from Ohio, Pennsylvania, and West Virginia. Some 311 of those are buried at the cemetery. Plaques also list veterans of World Wars I and II, Korea, and Vietnam. The photograph at left, of Phyllis Hutchison Conley, was taken in 1938 during the Civil War Soldier's tour of duty at Carnegie Library. (Above, author's collection; at left, Phyllis Conley.)

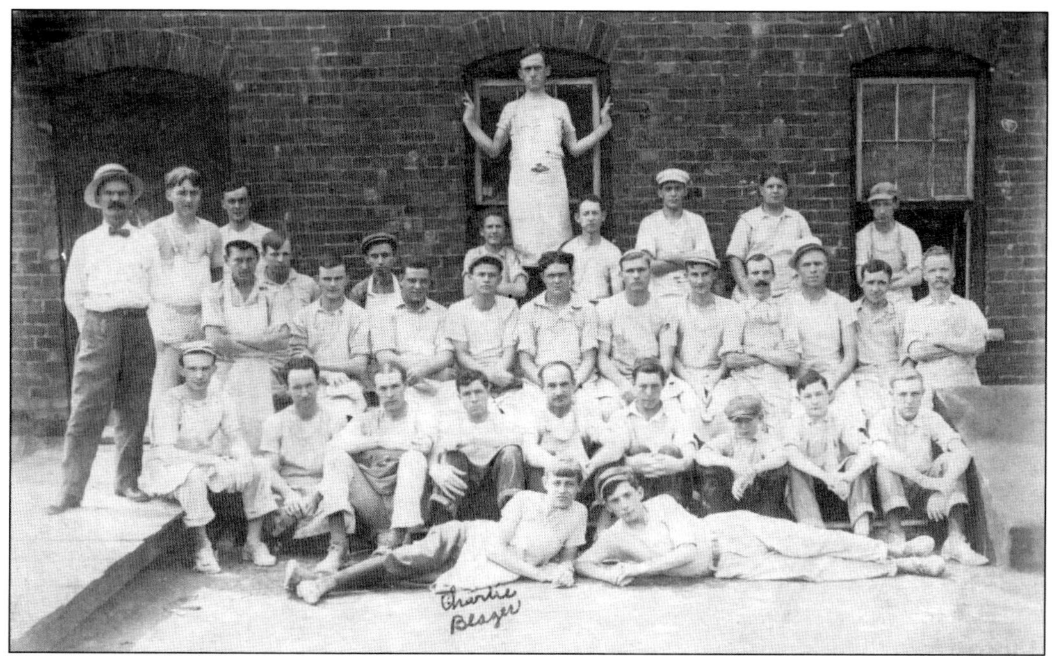

Above, Charlie Blazer (first row, left) was 13 and just out of eighth grade when he joined this Harker pottery crew, probably around 1912. It was not uncommon to hire children, sometimes against their wishes. In 1849, a 10-year-old girl started a fire in the Ball & Morris Pottery with the hope of getting out of work. When R.M. Hull, a state inspector, visited East Liverpool in 1896, a "great number" of child workers were let go until the inspector left town. By the early 1900s, potters were making enough money to keep their children in school longer. Below, American Porcelain Company employees, including at least two children, gather in front of the plant. American Porcelain was in business from 1914 to about 1922 on Second Street. (Above, Donna Blazer McComas; below, East Liverpool Historical Society.)

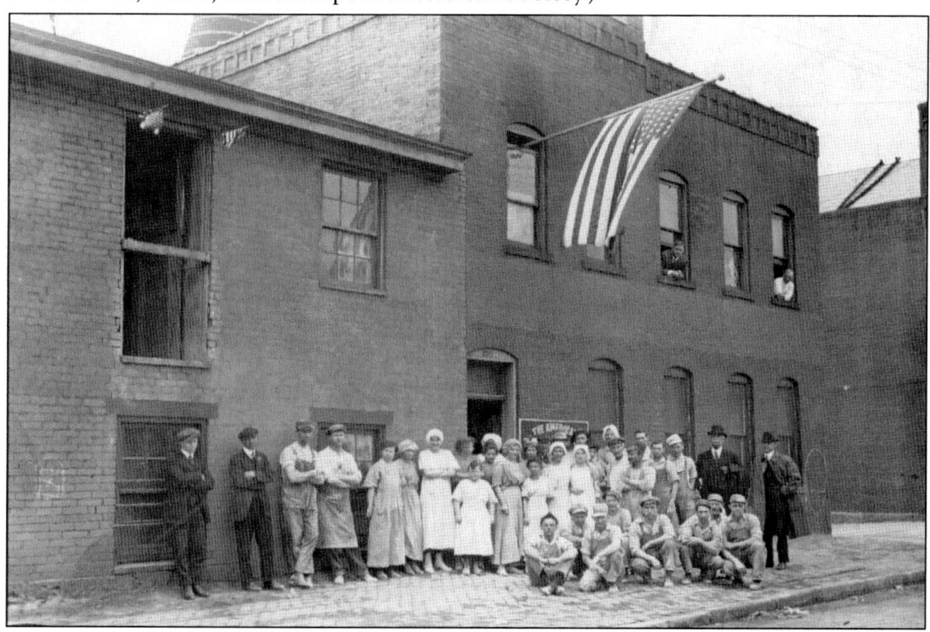

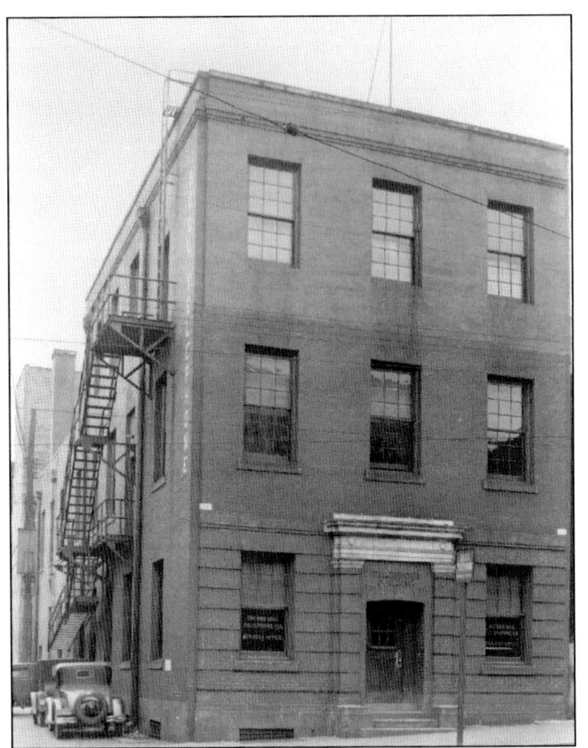

Telephone service first came to East Liverpool in 1880, with offices in the First National Bank building at Broadway and Railroad Street, courtesy of the Central District Telephone and Printing Company. Urcilla Kinsey was the first operator at a time when most telephone operators were male. This modern building was erected on Market Street in 1923 by the Ohio Bell Telephone Company. By 1938, an entire crew of operators was at work. One might wonder how comfortable the operators pictured below could be in summertime, with the electric fans several feet above their heads and pointing sideways. (Both East Liverpool Historical Society.)

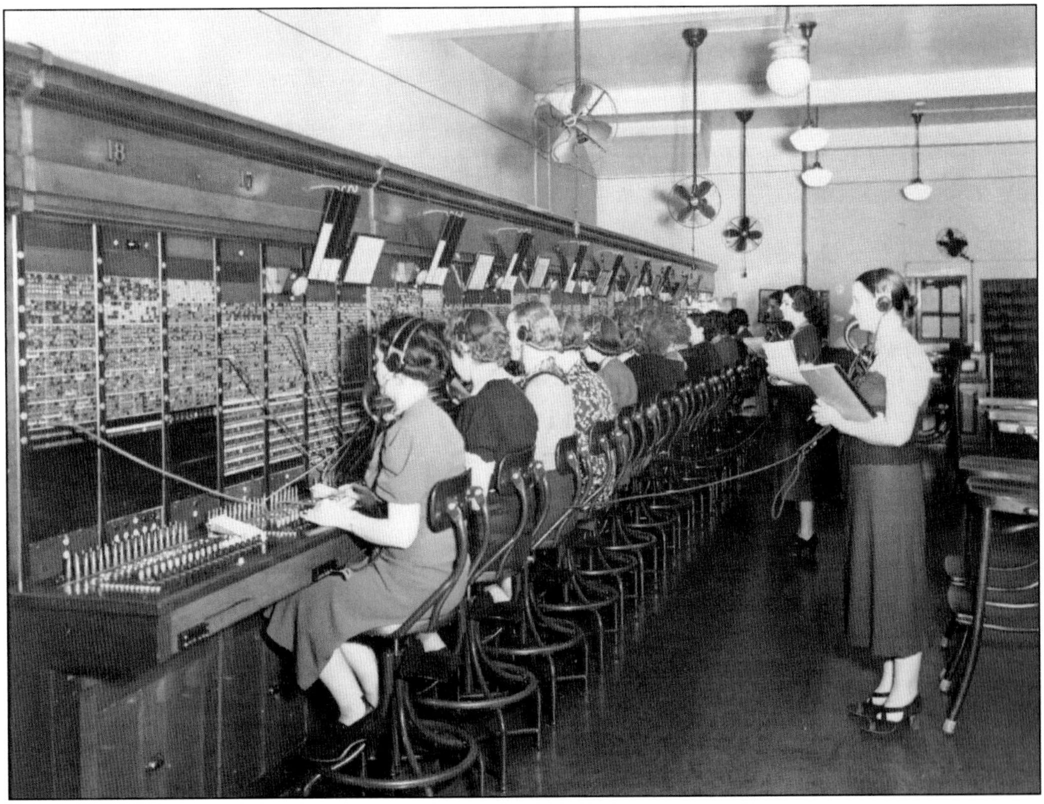

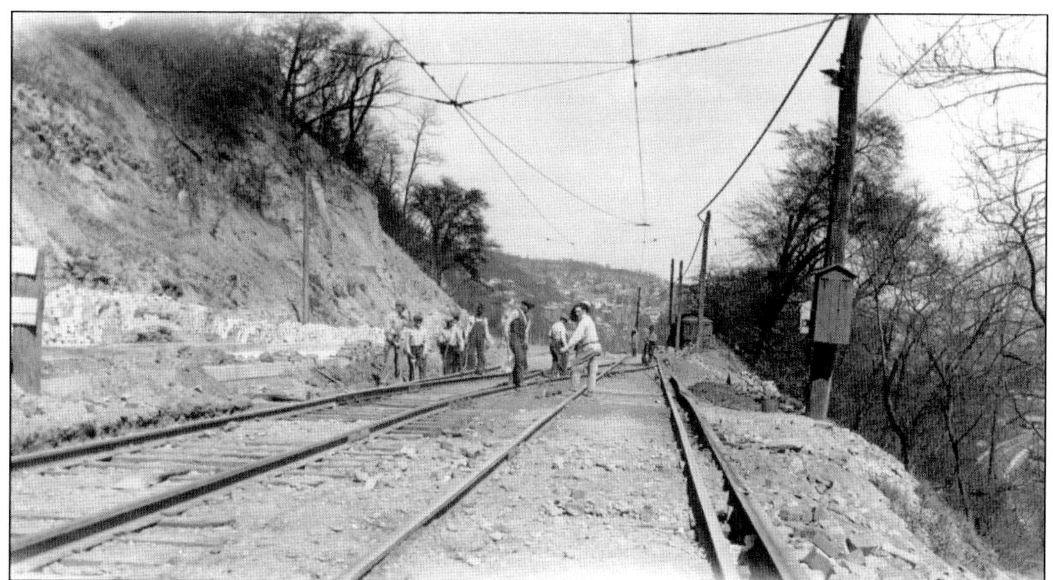

In the summer of 1926, the crew above assembled crossover tracks between East Liverpool and Wellsville in a neighborhood known as Jethro Hollow. Below, on the East Liverpool end of Jethro Hollow, a train passes under the Newell toll bridge. Rail service had been available since the 1850s and greatly benefitted local businesses, allowing freight to move in and out of town almost unimpeded by weather. City residents were not always so happy about train service. Under pressure from voters, the city council passed an ordinance in 1861 that trains be restricted to five miles per hour within the city limits. (Above, Museum of Ceramics; below, Inger Lloyd.)

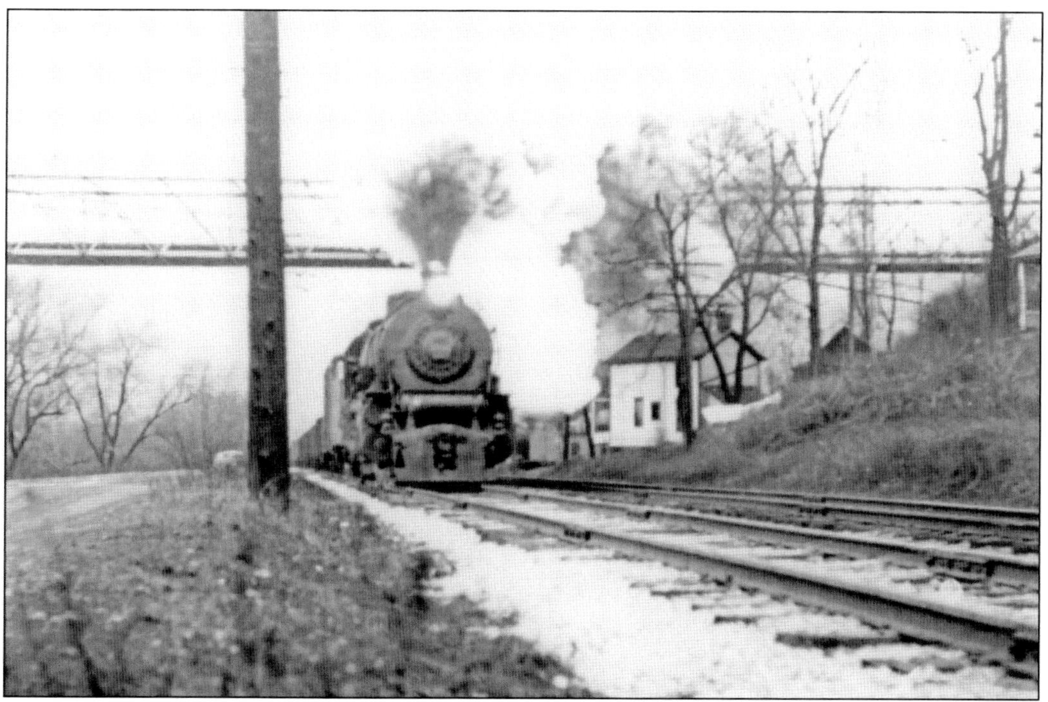

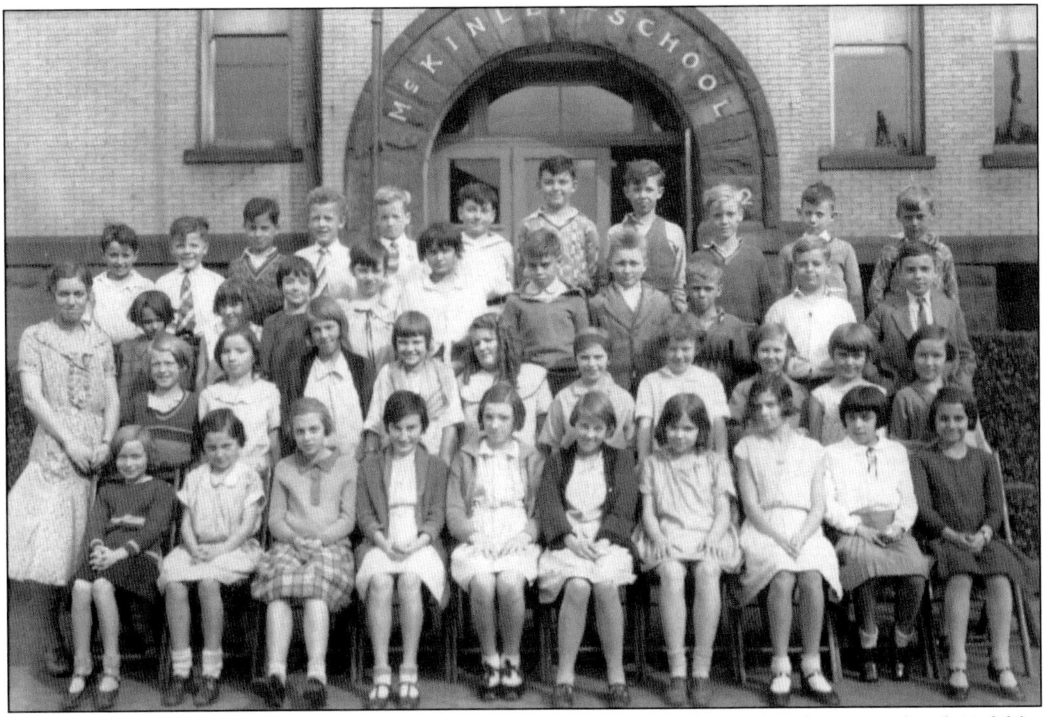

The rapid growth of the town in the early 1900s is evident in this 1930 photograph of 41 fifth-graders, and one teacher, at McKinley Elementary. The suburban school had been erected in 1902, one of half a dozen built around that time to alleviate overcrowding. It was named for Pres. William McKinley of nearby Canton, who had good friends and supporters in town. (Museum of Ceramics.)

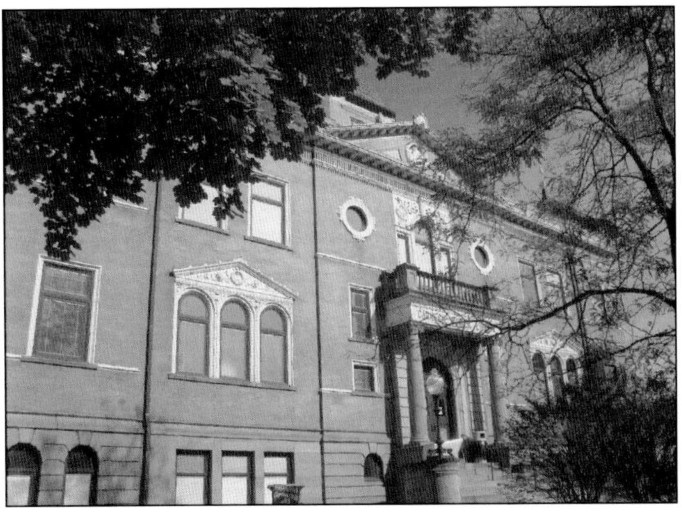

City businessmen T.Y. Travis and M.E. Miskall approached Pittsburgh philanthropist Andrew Carnegie in 1899 for funds to build a public library. He agreed, and 20 local men purchased the Bradshaw property on Fourth Street. Construction on the Beaux Arts building began in 1899, and city businesses including Milligan Hardware and the Lewis Brothers Furniture Store provided infrastructure and furnishings. The library opened in 1902. (Author's collection.)

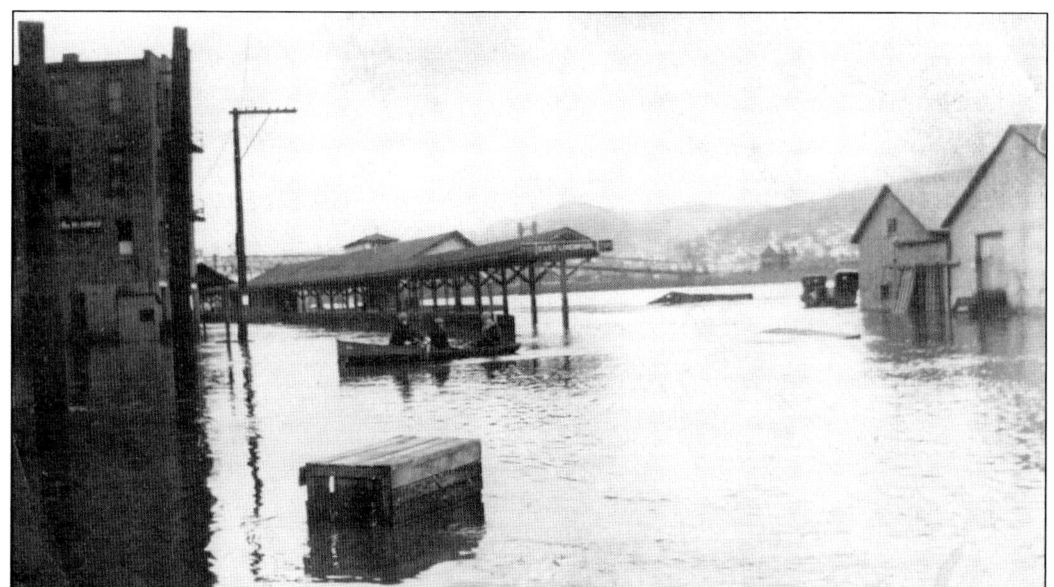

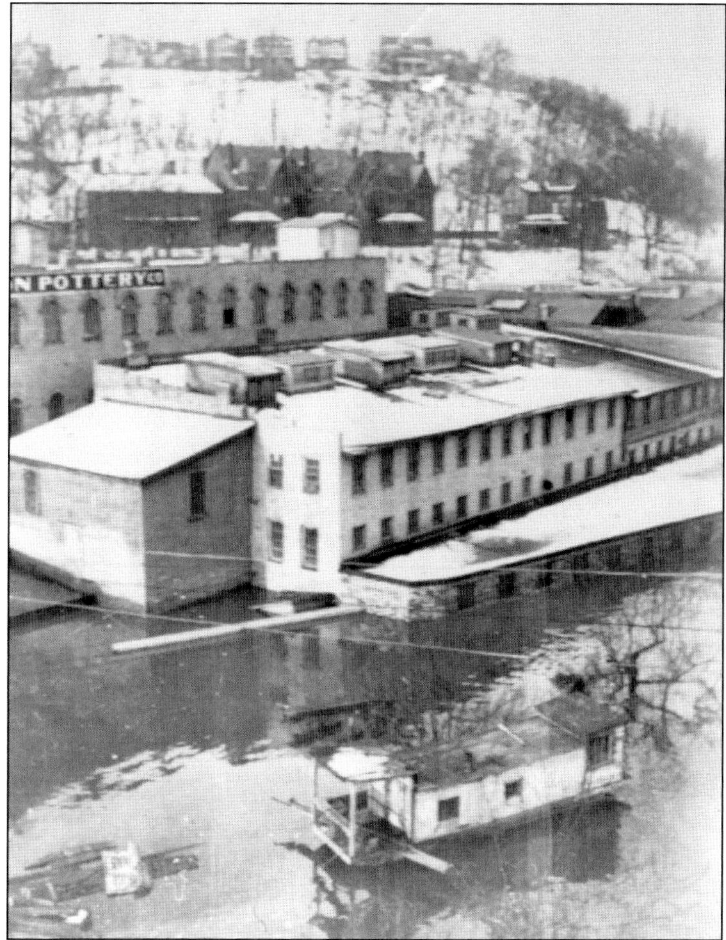

Though East Liverpool barreled into the 20th century with modernity, there was still not adequate flood control on the Ohio River, where businesses and homes crowded the shoreline. In 1832, 1852, 1898, 1900, and 1907, serious flooding disrupted production at local plants. In 1936, it happened again, and a trolley stop in the lower part of town (above) and the C.C. Thompson Pottery (at right) were affected. A local story tells of Rebecca Williams, nine months pregnant, who was forced to evacuate her Second Street home with her five-year-old daughter, Jenny, and three-year-old grandson, Ray. She walked about a half mile to Ravine Street, a steep climb, and delivered a healthy boy, David, on her oldest son John's living-room couch. (Both Museum of Ceramics.)

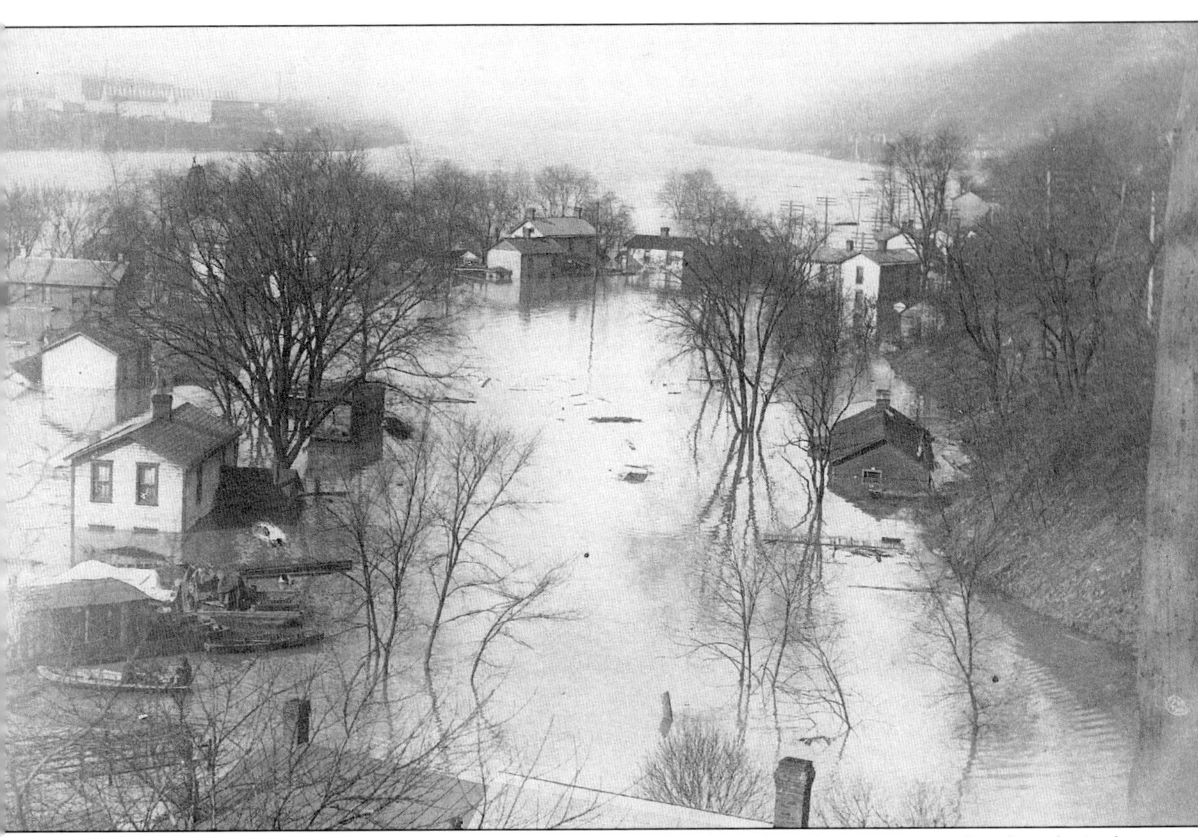

Some homeowners had a more difficult time with flooding than businesses and railroads. Jethro Hollow, a low-lying neighborhood at the west end of town, suffered greatly in 1937. Homeowners can be seen at the lower left, either evacuating or salvaging with small boats. After the devastating 1937 flood, which caused millions of dollars in damages from Pittsburgh to Cairo, Illinois, President Roosevelt sent WPA workers to assist with rescue and recovery and to provide food and temporary housing. Both business and civic leaders along the river pressured the federal government for a more effective system of flood control. The recently formed US Army Corps of Engineers spent the next several years on the project, designing and building more than 70 storage reservoirs to keep floodwaters out of the towns. The new system greatly reduced flood damage. (Museum of Ceramics.)

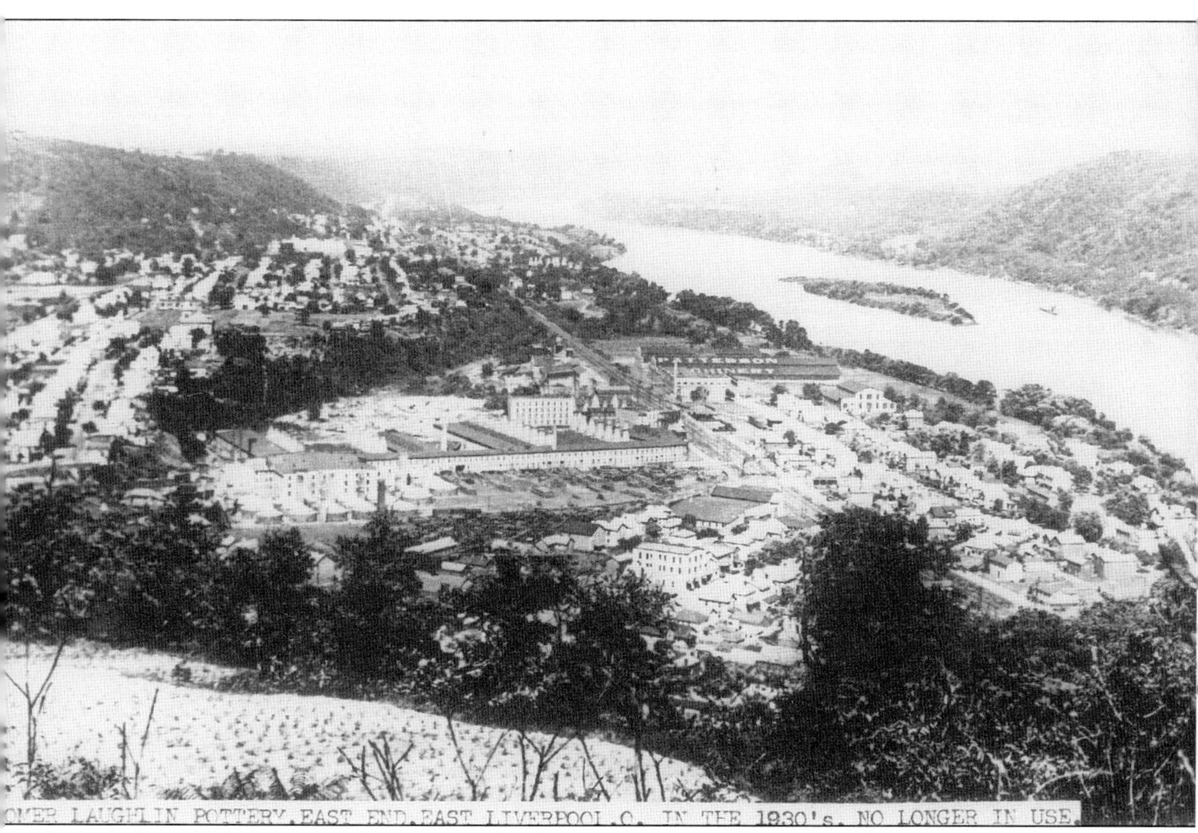

Founded in 1896 along the Ohio River, the Homer Laughlin China (HLC) Company built its second and third plants in East End in 1899 and 1901. By 1906, it was the largest pottery in the United States, with 28 kilns and 1,030 operatives. In 1907, a fourth plant with 30 kilns was constructed in the new town of Newell, West Virginia, and the total workforce expanded to 1,800. This photograph of an East End plant was taken in 1930. During the Depression, HLC maintained its reputation for development of new technology, modern equipment, and innovative product design. It was responsible for one quarter of the tableware sold in the United States. The East Liverpool plants were closed by the end of the Depression, but the Newell plant is still in operation. The company's Fiesta line, first introduced during the Depression in 1936, continues to be popular and collectible today. (East Liverpool Historical Society.)

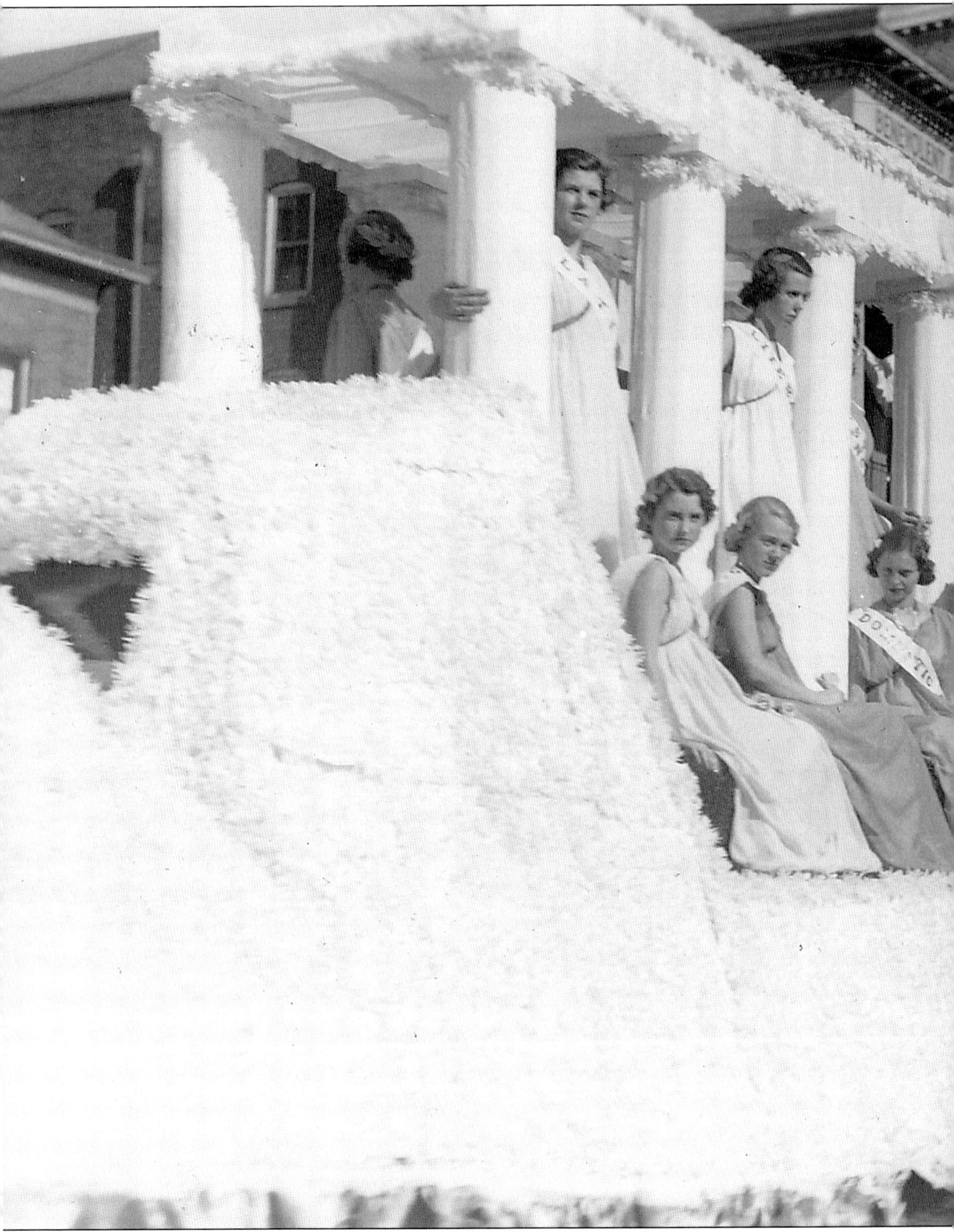

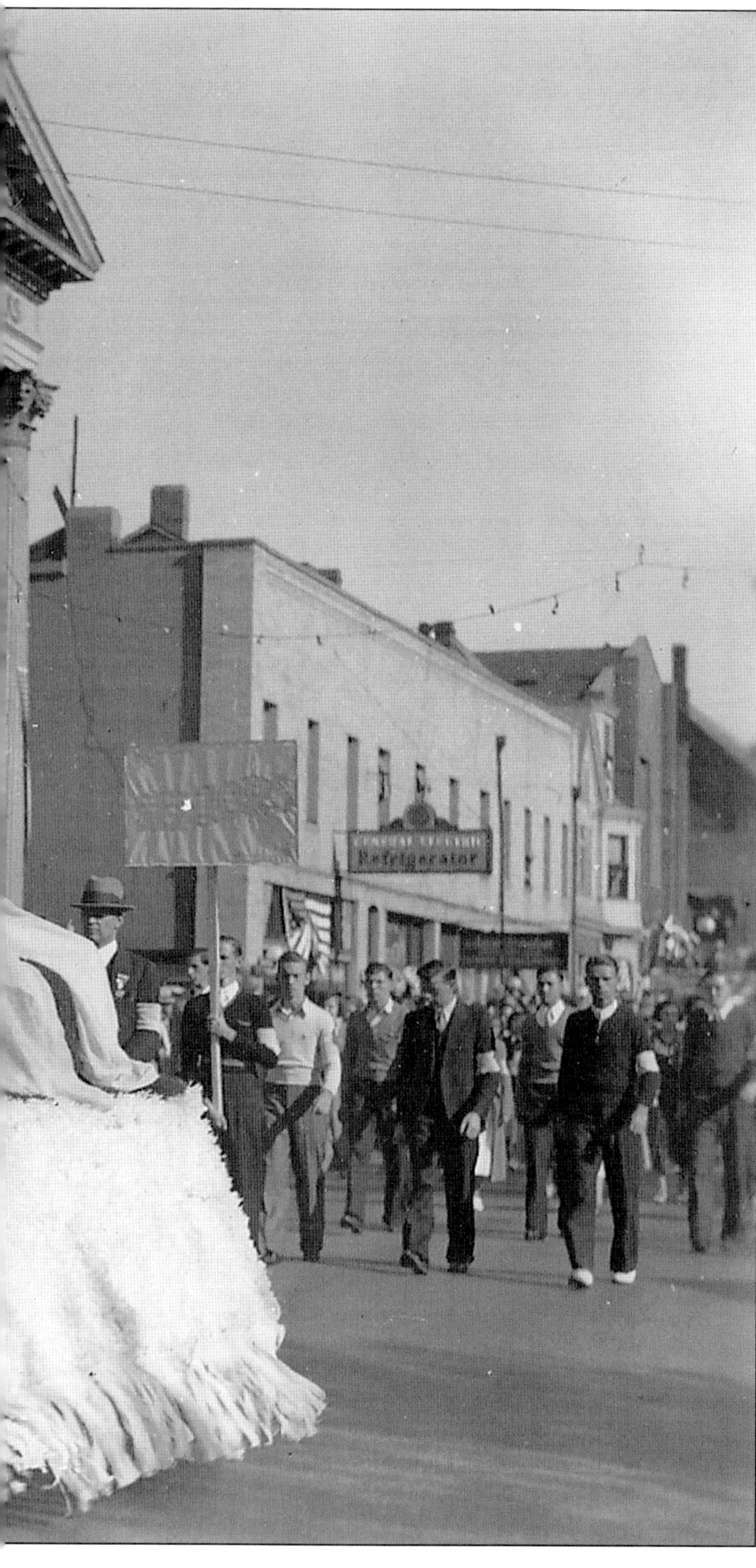

East Liverpool businesses participated eagerly in city centennial activities in 1934, including this October 12 educational and pet parade. Elks Lodge 258 is visible behind the Crockery City floats, draped in bunting. The Crockery City Ice & Products Company had begun business in 1900 as the Crockery City Brewing Company, but it became an "ice and products" company with the advent of Prohibition. During the Depression, the company earned the city's goodwill when it donated a daily supply of milk to the Salvation Army for families hit hard by unemployment. In its heyday, the company averaged 60 to 75 employees with an average annual payroll of $200,000. Renamed the Webber Brewery after the end of Prohibition, the company continued until the early 1950s. The original building still stands on Webber Way. (Museum of Ceramics.)

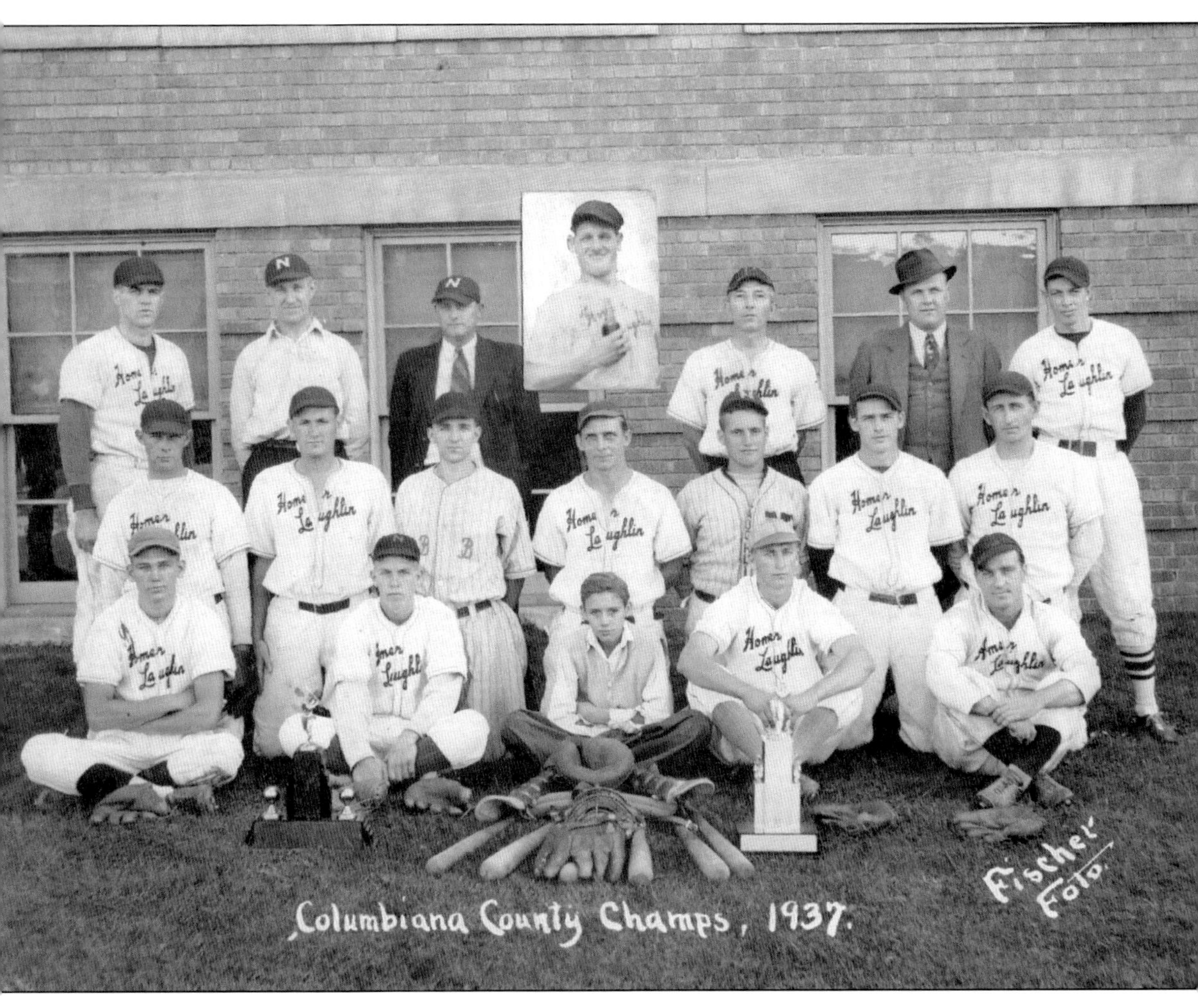

Baseball had been a popular sport in East Liverpool since 1867, when the Etruria Base-Ball Club was organized. The team lost its first game to the Crescent Club of New Lisbon, 108-15. Cy Young played here for a year or two in the 1890s at the beginning of his career. The YMCA Industrial League, organized in 1921, included teams from half a dozen potteries. Thousands of fans attended the games, where competition was fierce. The YMCA bowed out in 1925 because potteries had begun hiring workers just for their sports abilities, but the City Industrial League was formed to carry on the games. The 1937 city baseball championship was won by this team from Homer Laughlin China Company. From left to right, the members are (first row) E. Mosser, ? Meeks, ? Simmons, R. Mosser, and ? Christy; (second row) ? Watson, S. Aronson, T. Mosser, ? Rairden, ? Pittenger, ? Simmons, and ? Ashe; (third row) ? Thorne, F. Bailey, S. Bailey, W. Booth, ? Dickey, ? Manson, and ? Kimball. (East Liverpool Historical Society.)

Six

Notoriety, Danger, and Everyday Life

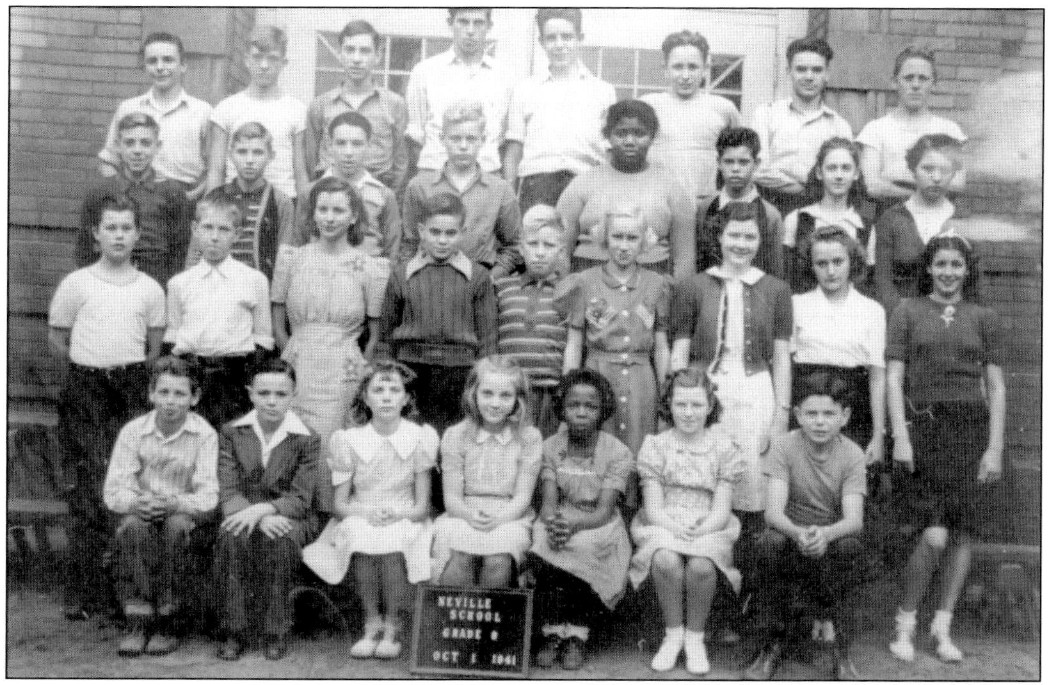

Eighth-graders at Neville School pose with grins and frowns in 1941. The school was located in Klondyke, a neighborhood in East End near Hall China. Some of these boys may have gone to war a few years later. A previous school known as the Neville Institute had been founded in the 1830s as a private secondary school. (East Liverpool Historical Society.)

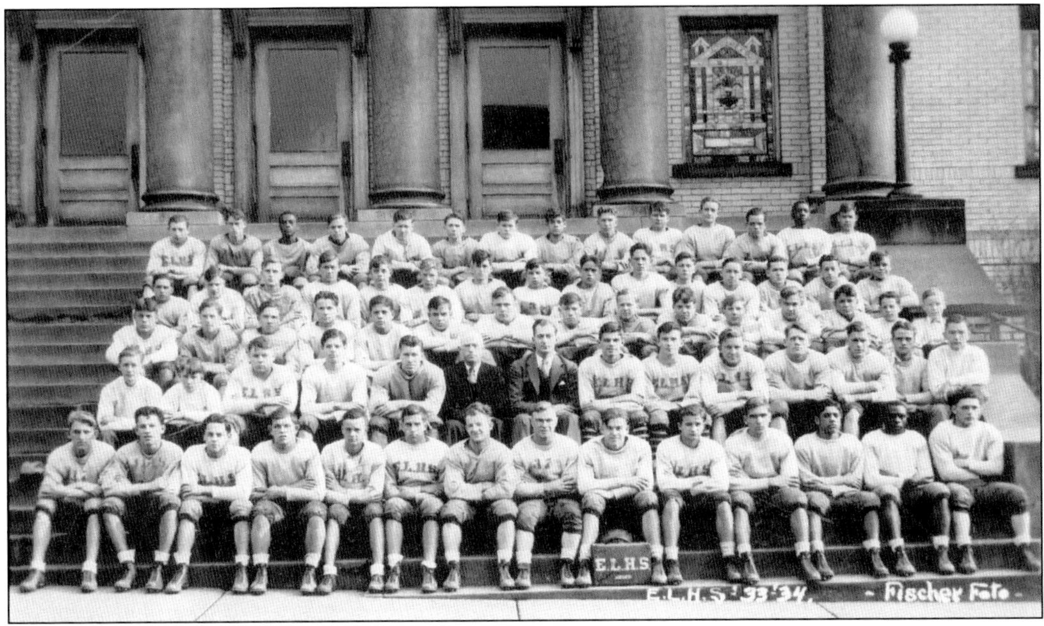

The 1933 East Liverpool High School Potters football team, seen above on the steps of the First Church of Christ (Disciples) across from the high school, included one of the city's most beloved players. Bill Booth is in the second row, fourth from the right. Booth, born in 1916 in Newell, West Virginia, started out at Wells High but transferred to East Liverpool and graduated in 1934. He had also played baseball for the Homer Laughlin team. During his college career, he was a halfback for Illinois State University, later transferring to Ohio State University. In the summer of 1937, he was killed in a car accident. That year the Bill Booth Memorial Award was established and is given each year to a Potter senior who best meets the criteria of "ability, sportsmanship, scholastic standing, character, and leadership." Bill Booth's brother Dick, also an ELHS football star, became a punter with the Detroit Lions. Below is the 1931–1932 ELHS women's basketball team. (Both Frank C. Dawson.)

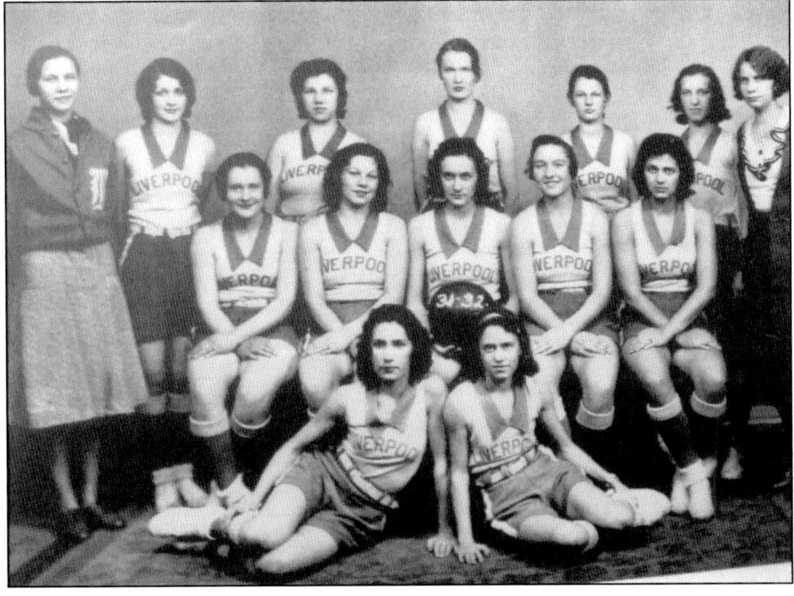

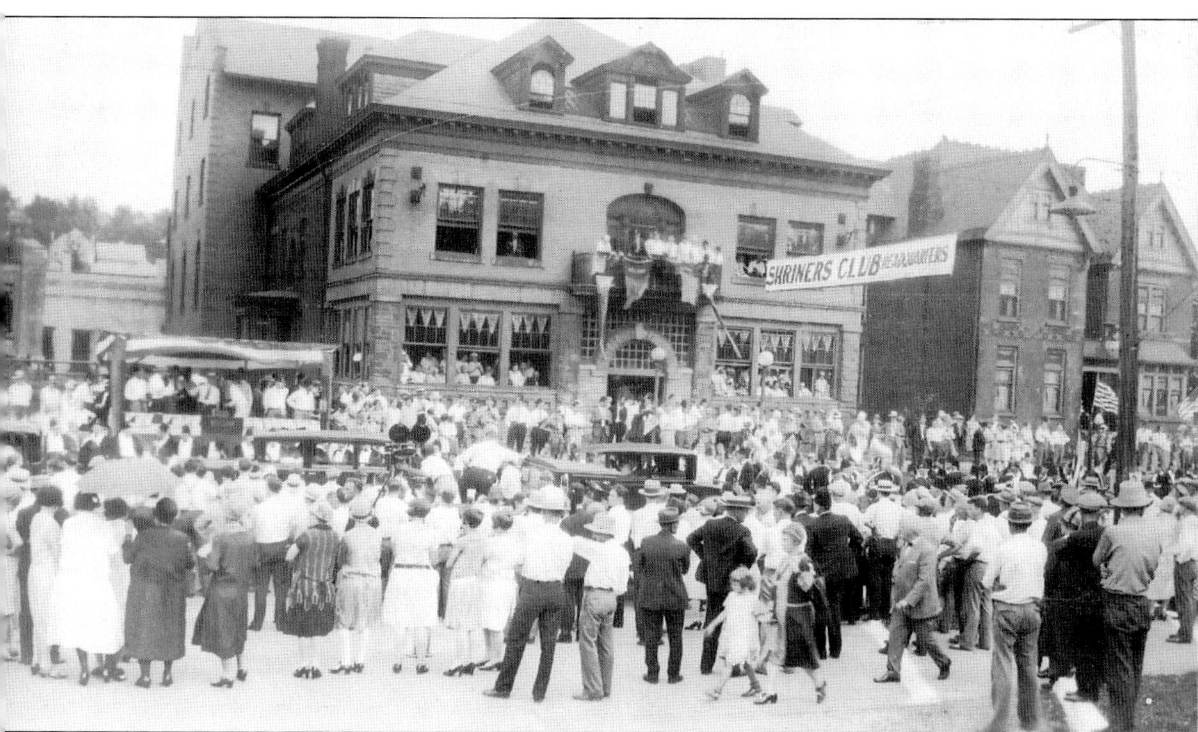

A Depression-era event at the East Liverpool Masonic Temple filled Broadway to capacity. The Colonial Revival building was constructed in 1890 as the Goodwin House, home of early pottery leader John Goodwin and his family and later occupied by his nephew Homer Knowles, also a pottery owner. It was sold to the city Masonic lodge in 1910. The front porch was enclosed at that time, and the building was expanded. Items such as the roof and new dormers were built to blend with original features. The Goodwin-Knowles house was added to the National Register of Historic Places in 1985. Today, it is one of the best-known pottery mansions in the city and sees regular use. At the right side of the photograph, the Homer Laughlin house is visible. It had been in the National Register of Historic Places until it was torn down in 2013. (Museum of Ceramics.)

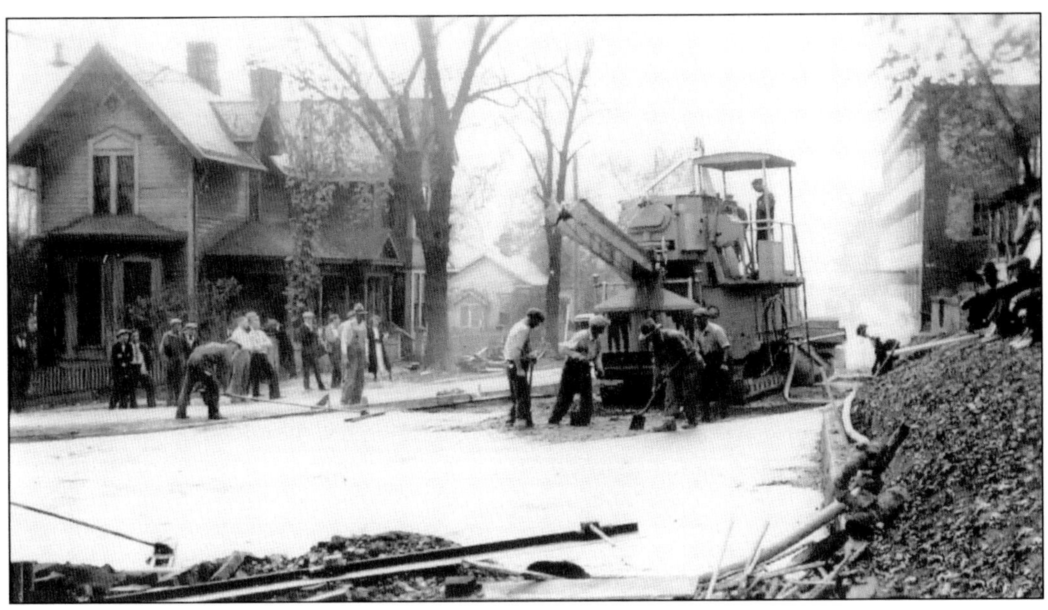

A street-paving project drew the usual contingent of sightseers in the 1930s at East Third and Walnut Streets. The idea had been controversial, but by 1895 five and a half miles of city streets had been paved. Mulberry Street in East End, the hub of the commercial district there, was not paved until 1906. In 1911, the city spent $100,000, but even in the center of town, many alleys remained unpaved. A survey in 1912 showed that in 106.5 miles of alleys and streets in the city limits, only 2.5 miles of alleys and 22 miles of streets were paved. Below, Norman Hamilton is second from the right in a photograph taken outside Hamilton's Barber Shop. (Above, Inger Lloyd; below, Frank C. Dawson.)

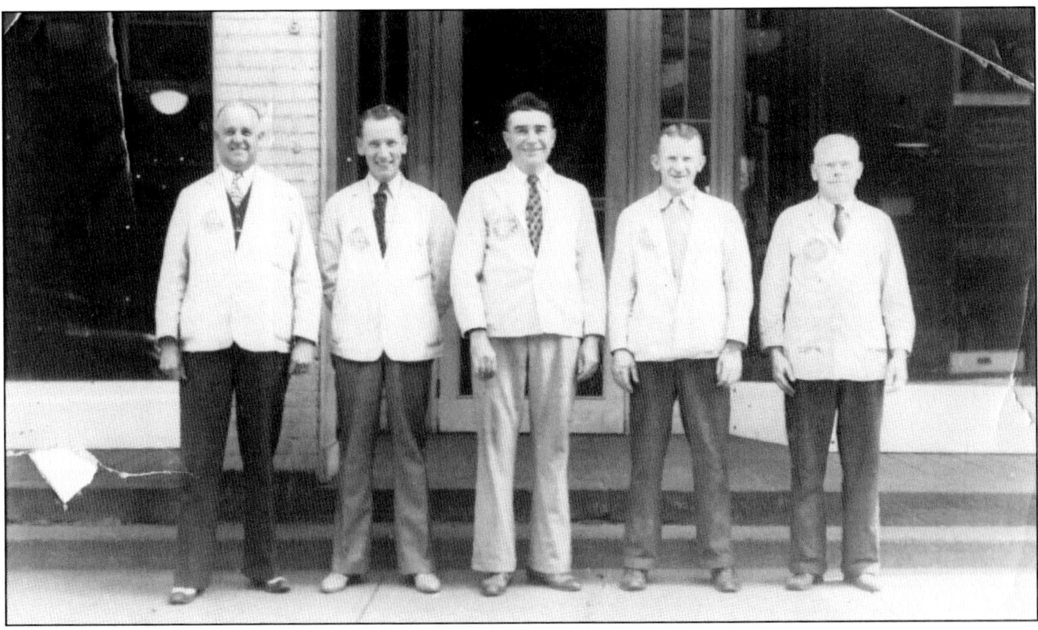

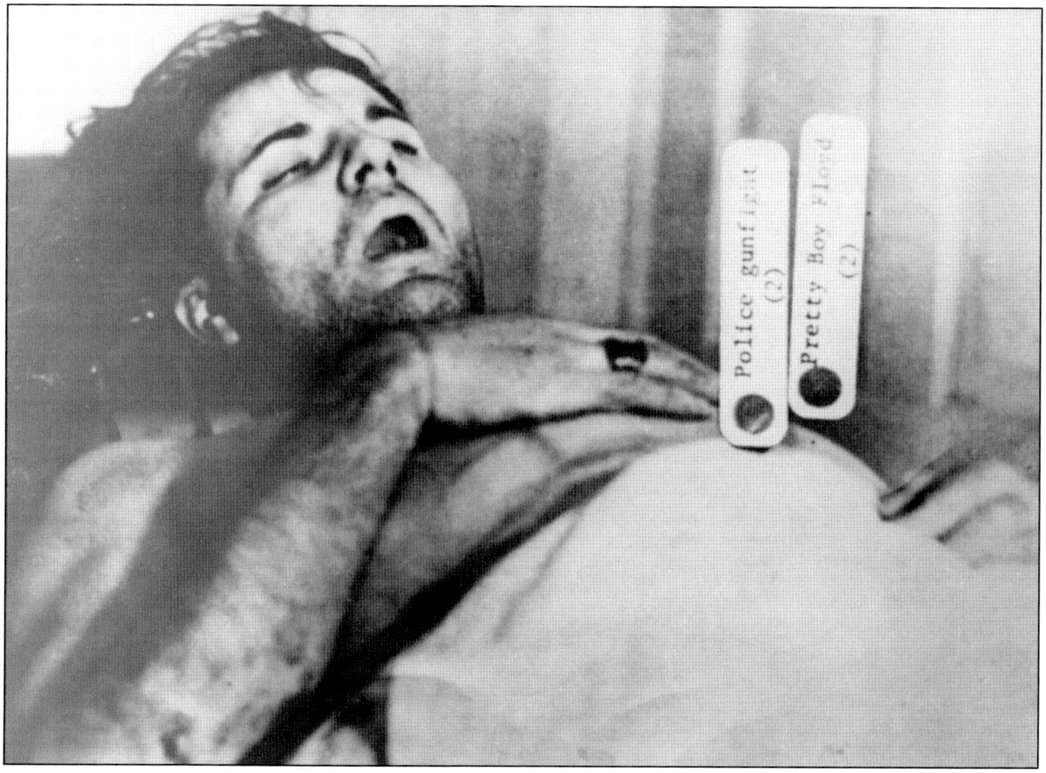

Prohibition and the crime wave that followed it kept the local police busy in the early 1930s. Hell's Half Acre at the state line was a notorious hangout. John Dillinger and Baby Face Nelson were reportedly seen there. Charles "Pretty Boy" Floyd, who was Public Enemy No. 1 after Dillinger's death, famously made his last stand in the area in October 1934. After a chase of several days, FBI agent Melvin Purvis and an East Liverpool police posse caught up to Floyd on the Conkle farm on Sprucevale Road outside town. Accounts of the final showdown differ, but all agree that he was shot once, got up, ran, was shot again, and stayed down. City police officer Chester Smith may have fired the first and second shots, though Purvis claimed otherwise. The body was taken to the Sturgis Funeral Home in town, embalmed by Frank A. Dawson and fingerprinted by, from left to right, Elwyn Shenkle, Curley Montgomery, Chester Smith, and Ernie Sturgis. (Both Frank C. Dawson.)

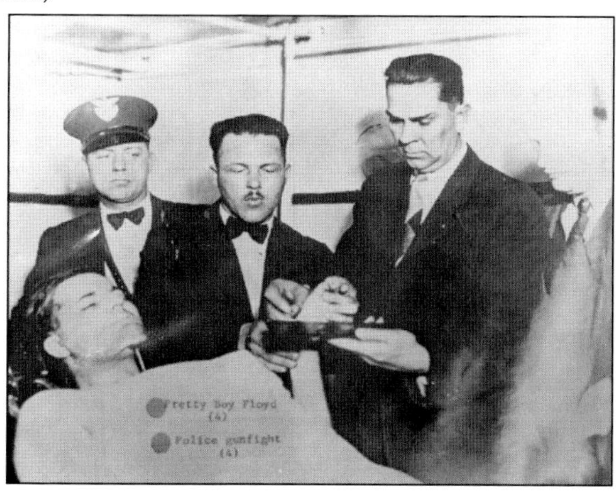

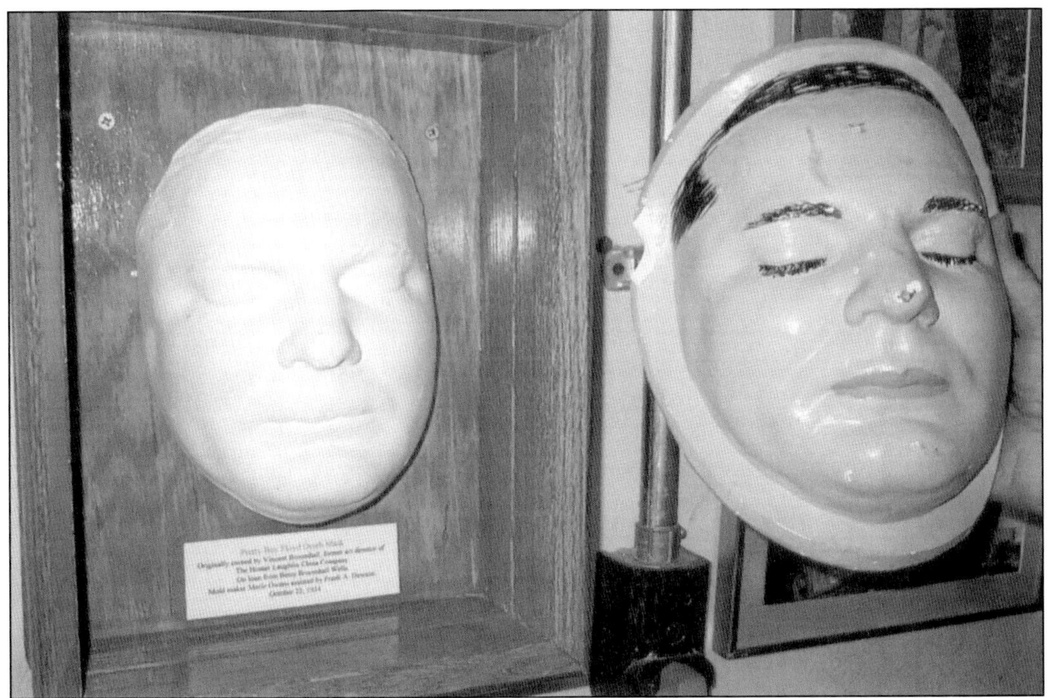

A pottery worker was called in to make a cast of Pretty Boy Floyd's face for a death mask, and copies were given to participating police officers. Though Floyd's mother asked that the body not be shown to the public, her request came too late. Floyd's body had already been displayed on a daybed in the middle parlor of Sturgis Funeral Home. Crowds of locals paraded through the viewing parlor that evening and the next day to see the famous outlaw. The funeral home was later purchased by Frank A. Dawson and moved to a different location on Fifth Street. The original building is now the Sturgis House Bed and Breakfast, still owned by the Dawson family. A small museum in the basement displays artifacts of the capture, including several Floyd death masks. (Both Frank C. Dawson.)

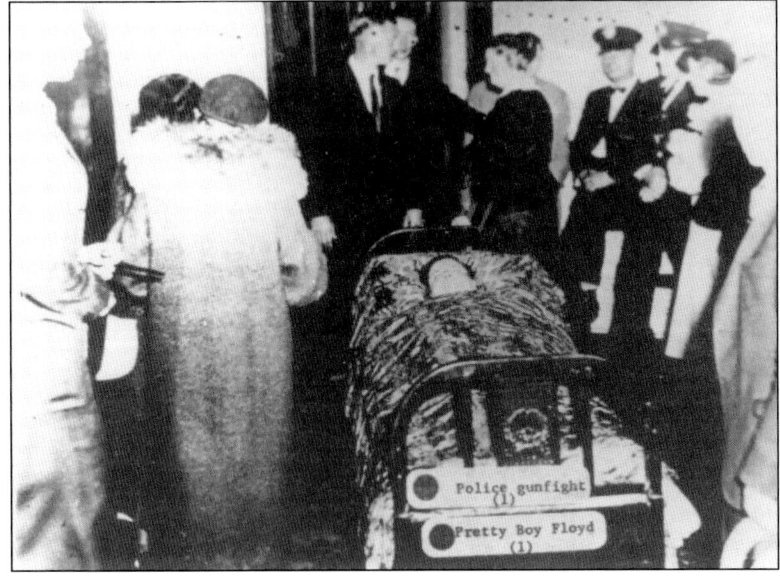

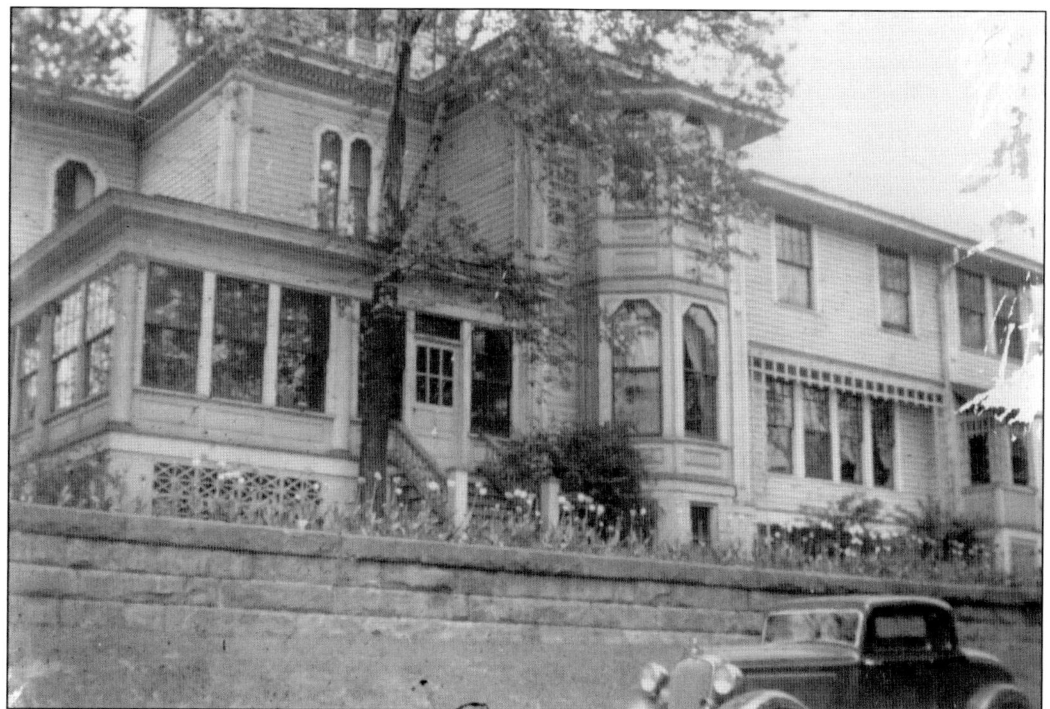

The photograph above of the Harker home was taken in 1940. Benjamin Harker, patriarch of the East Liverpool Harkers, had established East Liverpool's second pottery 100 years earlier. He built a plant, dug clay and coal from his own land, and hired professional potter John Goodwin to operate the business. Goodwin taught Harker and his sons everything they knew about making pottery. Harker potteries became famous for ovenproof Bakerite ware, Cameo ware and Cameo shell ware, White Rose oven ware in blue and pink, and Royal Gadroon with rope accents on the edges. The firm sometimes called itself "the oldest pottery in America" because it outlasted the Bennett pottery by more than 100 years, closing in 1972. The abandoned works, below, decayed on River Road for years before being torn down. (Both East Liverpool Historical Society.)

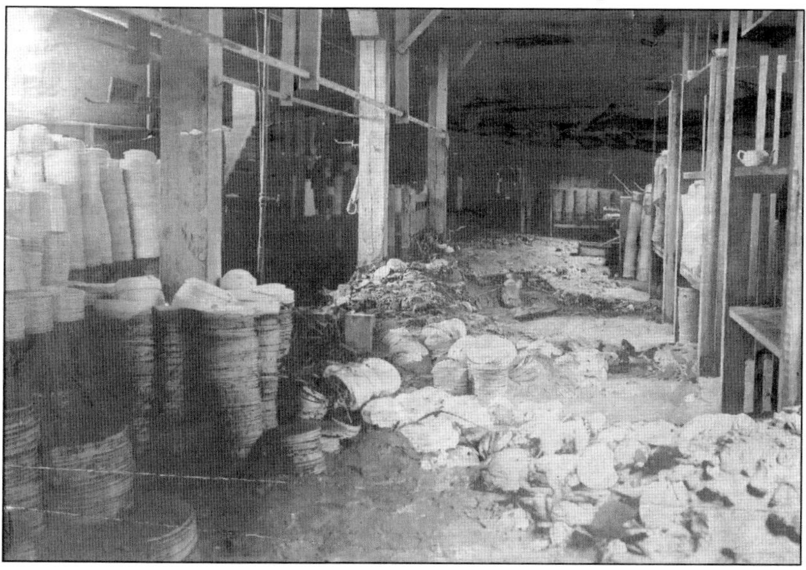

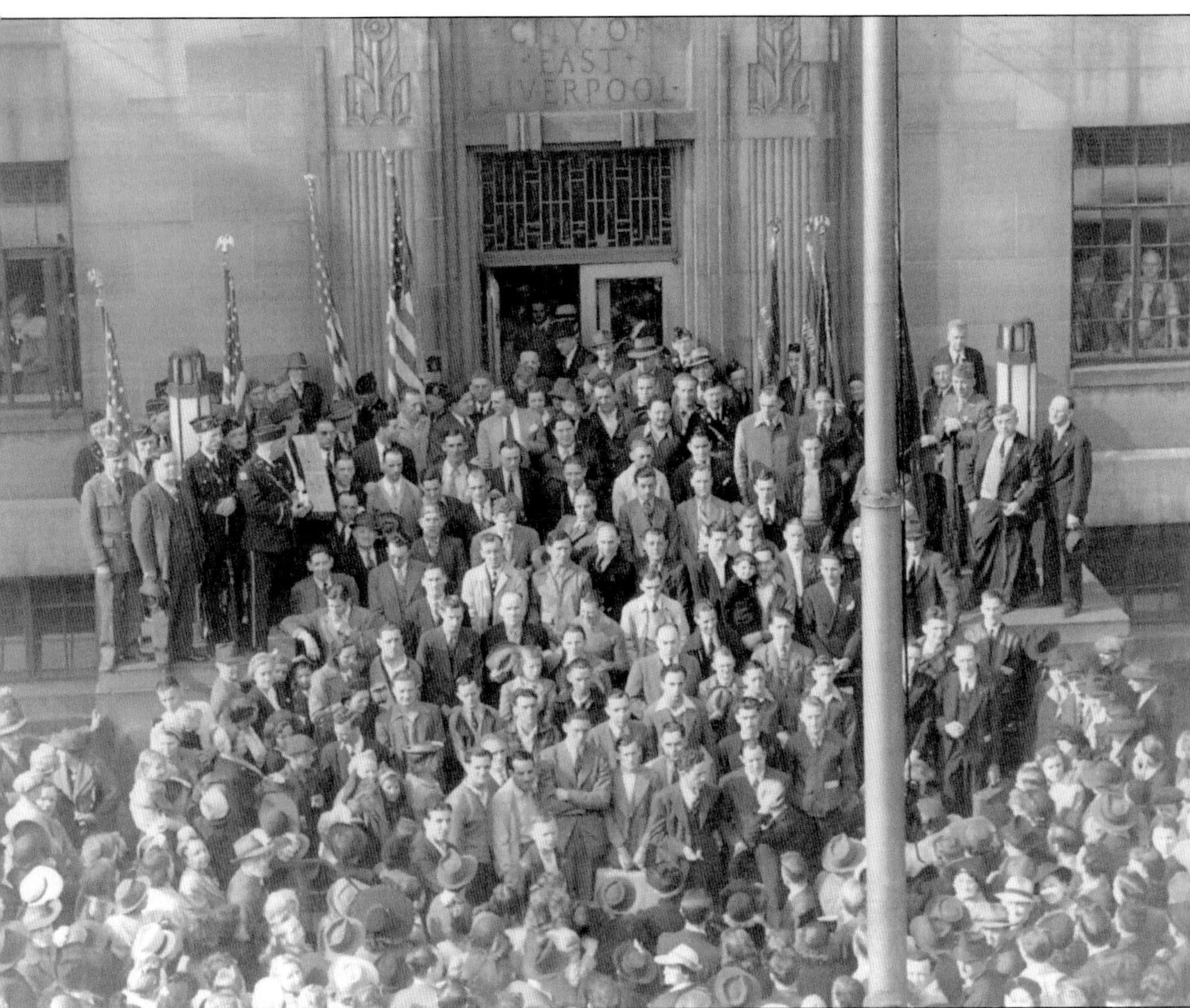

April 25, 1942, was a big day for East Liverpool, when more than 50 draftees gathered with friends, family, and city officials before leaving for training. The Selective Training and Service Act went into effect well before the war, in 1940, and required men between the ages of 21 and 45 to register. A memorial plaque at the front of city hall remembers 101 East Liverpudlians, mostly enlisted men, who were killed in action. Many of those who stayed at home worked at Crucible Steel in nearby Midland, Pennsylvania, making bullet casings. Manpower shortages were so severe, in fact, that high school students were released to work in manufacturing, business, transportation, and public utilities. In the photograph, Naomi Green and her brother Ira are at the lower left, both looking over their right shoulders toward the camera. They were on hand to see off their brother Arry Green. (Liane Elliott-Gorby.)

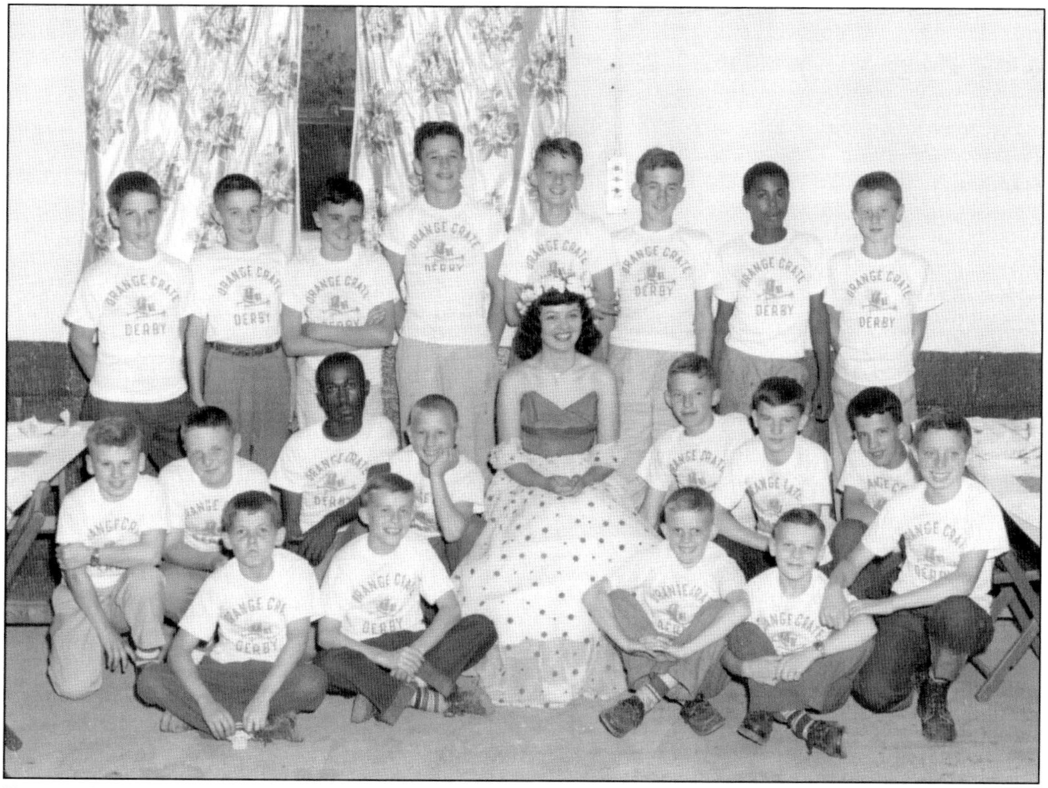

During East Liverpool High School's Homecoming Week in 1950, one of the activities was the Orange Crate Derby. The boys seen above were treated to commemorative T-shirts and a banquet after the race, which started halfway up Bradshaw Avenue and finished on Walnut Street. They were congratulated by that year's homecoming queen, Connie Buck. The boy behind the queen, whose name was Kaufman, was the winner. Below, in another local contest, the winner of the Golden Star Dairy baby contest at Rock Springs Park in July 1956 was 22-month-old Joey Clark, shown at left with his mother, Marilyn Clark. (Above, Caryle Buck; below, Richard W. Bangor.)

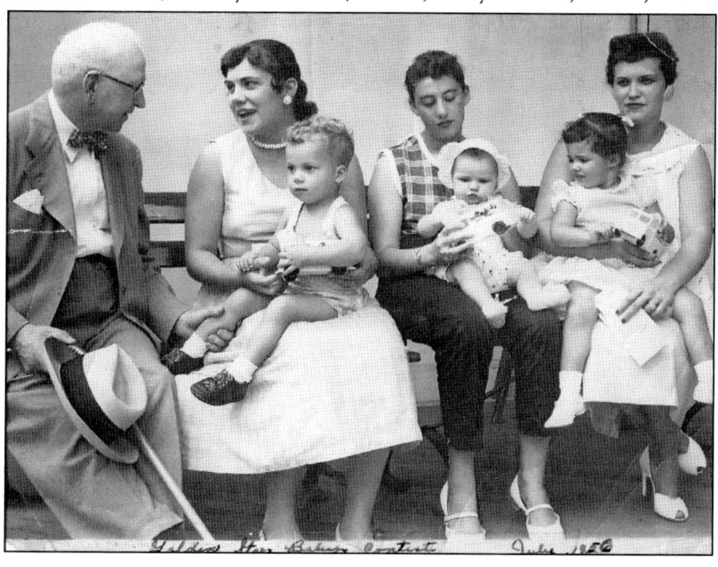

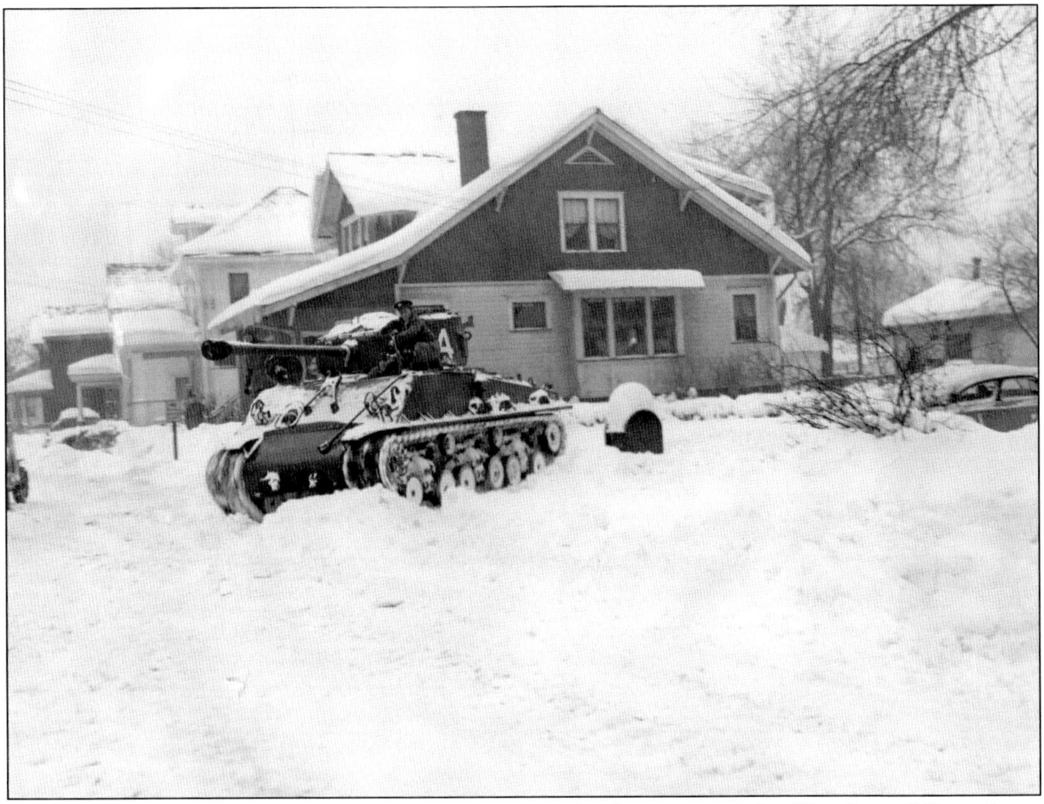

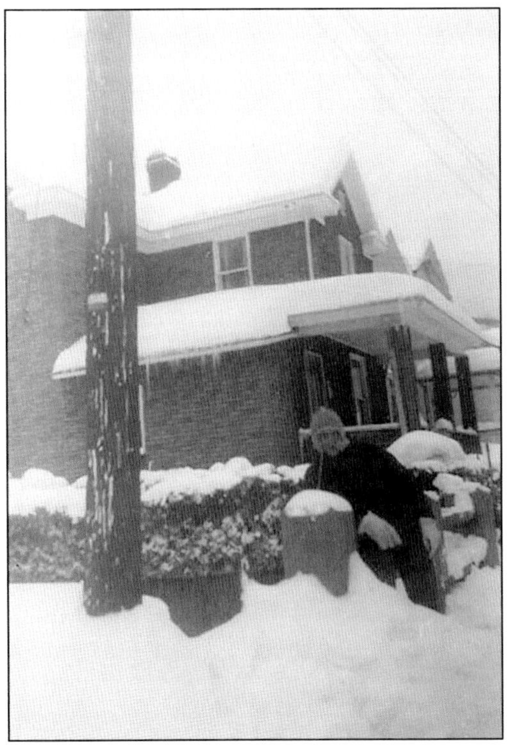

In the first stage of the "Big Snow," Saturday, November 24, 1950, twenty-four inches fell, with more expected. There was no mail, no newspaper, and no grocery delivery. The National Guard sent a Sherman tank (above) to beat a path across town to East End. Santa was to have come to town to pass out candy at the Diamond, but children were informed that he had not been able to land at nearby Swaney Airport. At the corner of Mapletree Street and Virginia Avenue, snow was three feet deep. Vince Maola Jr. (at left) remembers that his father, an auxiliary police officer, called the police department to send a Jeep to pick up a neighbor who was about to have a baby and transport her to the hospital. "It worked out fine," Maola reports. (Above, Museum of Ceramics; at left, Vincent Maola Jr.)

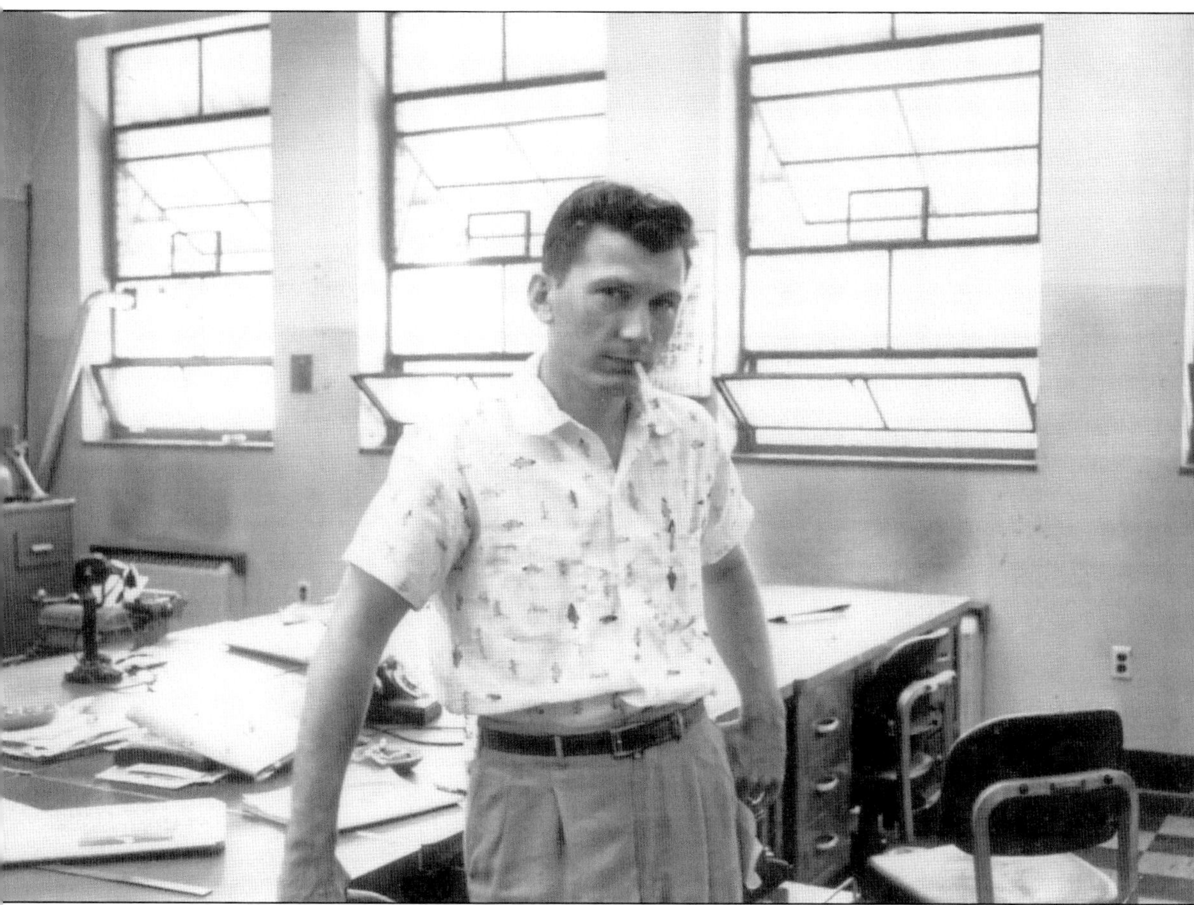

Harry L. Stewart was a familiar name in the pages of the East Liverpool *Review* in the 1950s and 1960s. He started his career in the circulation department in October 1951 while he was still in business school. He later worked as an apprentice printer and proofreader before being promoted to the newsroom as a general-assignment reporter and feature writer. He also worked the wire desk before moving to the *Midland News* and later the *Salem News*. For many years, he wrote a Saturday outdoors column for the *Review*. The *Review*, in one form or another, has been around since the *Saturday Review* was founded in 1878 by William McCord. It was in daily publication as the *Review* by 1885. With a change of owner in 1892, it became the *News Review*. Again as the *Review*, the paper moved to its present building on East Fourth Street in 1949, changed its name to the *Evening Review*, reverted to the *Review*, and is now a morning publication seven days a week. (Pam Stewart Banfield.)

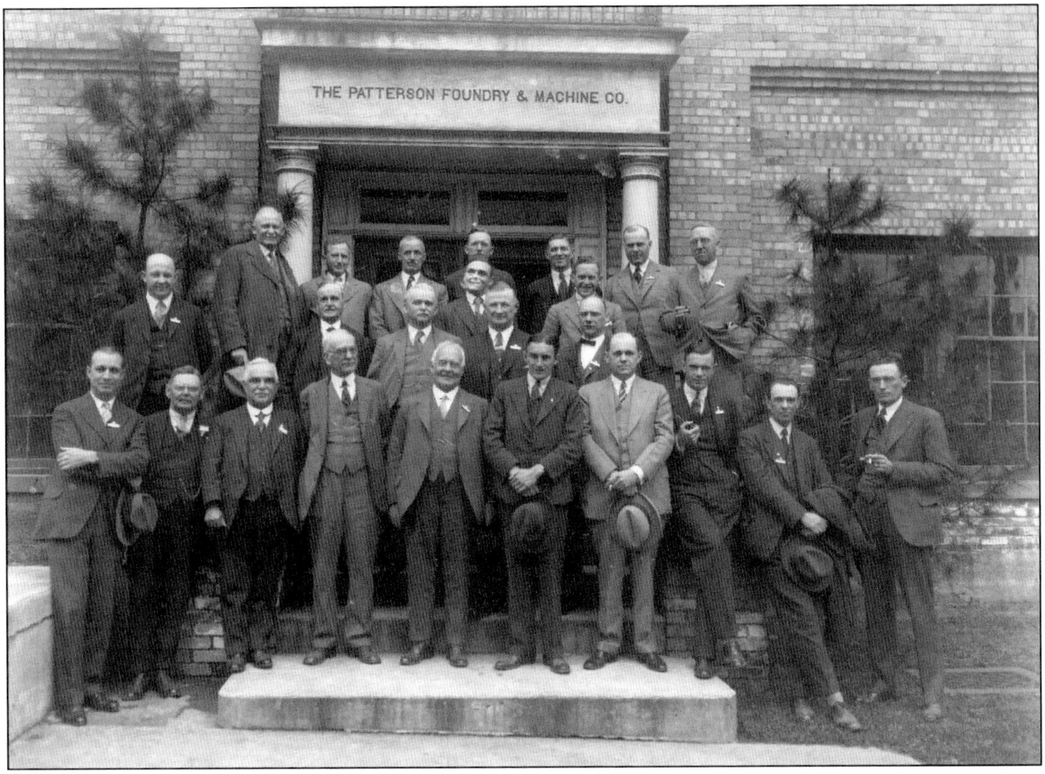

What later became the Patterson Foundry and Machine Company began in 1865 as a machine shop owned by Andrew J. Boyce on East Sixth Street. It was reportedly the first American foundry to specialize in clay-working machinery. After his death, Boyce's shop was acquired by the Patterson Machine Company, begun in 1878 by brothers Dixon, Monroe, and John W. Patterson. At the East End plant, above, this group is probably made up of owners and executives. Director Richard A. Caywood is at right, holding a cigar. Under Caywood's leadership, the company constructed a steel mill next to its East End plant. The new Patterson Steel Products Company provided almost 100 more jobs for the community and built steel castings for use in the foundry. The Patterson upper works lab at Fifth and Walnut Streets is pictured below. (Both East Liverpool Historical Society.)

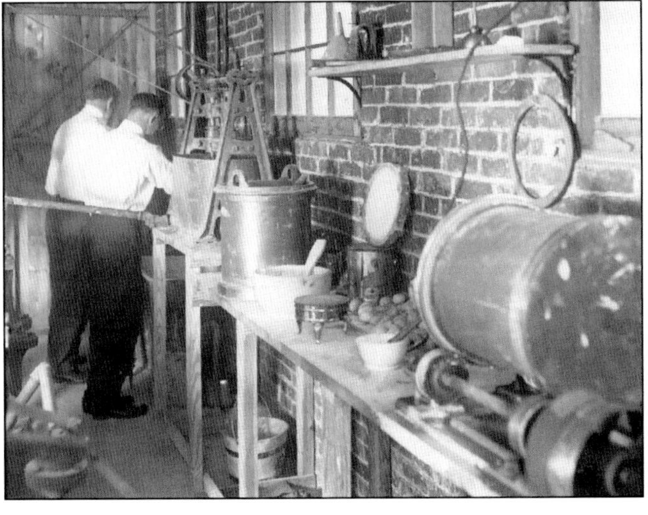

Seven

The Boom Years

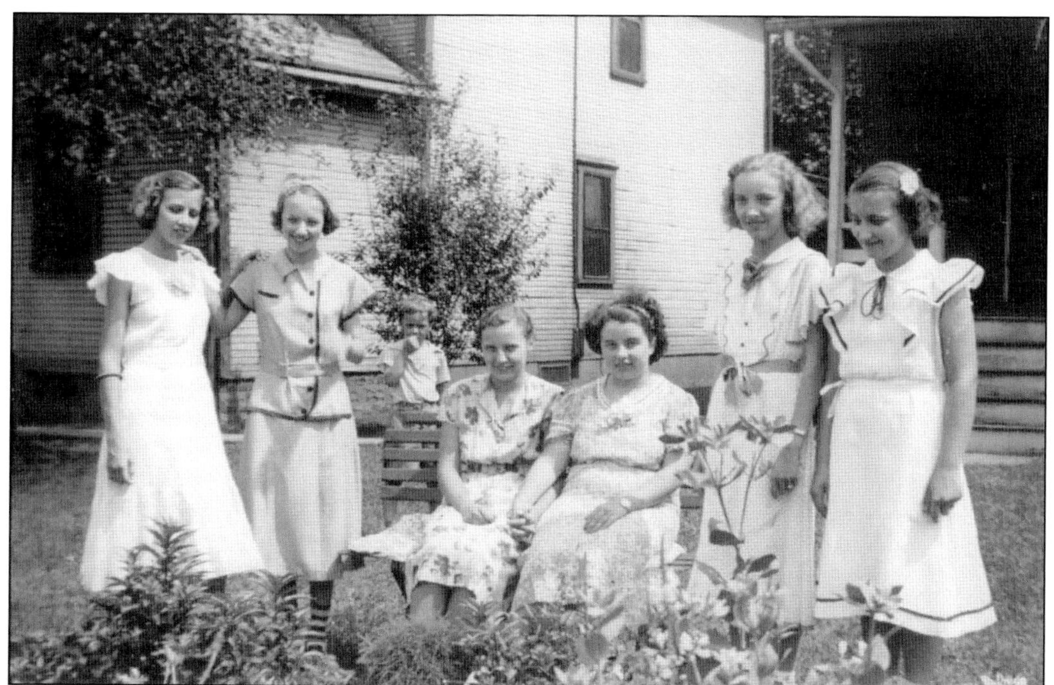

Members of the Jolly Six Swing Club (plus one curious little brother) pose prettily on a lawn in their best dresses and suits, complete with hair bows and striped socks. From left to right, they are Fae Mansfield, Elizabeth Metsch, Sara Mountford, Josephine Rigby, Rachel Ketchum, and Evelyn Cooper. (Frank C. Dawson.)

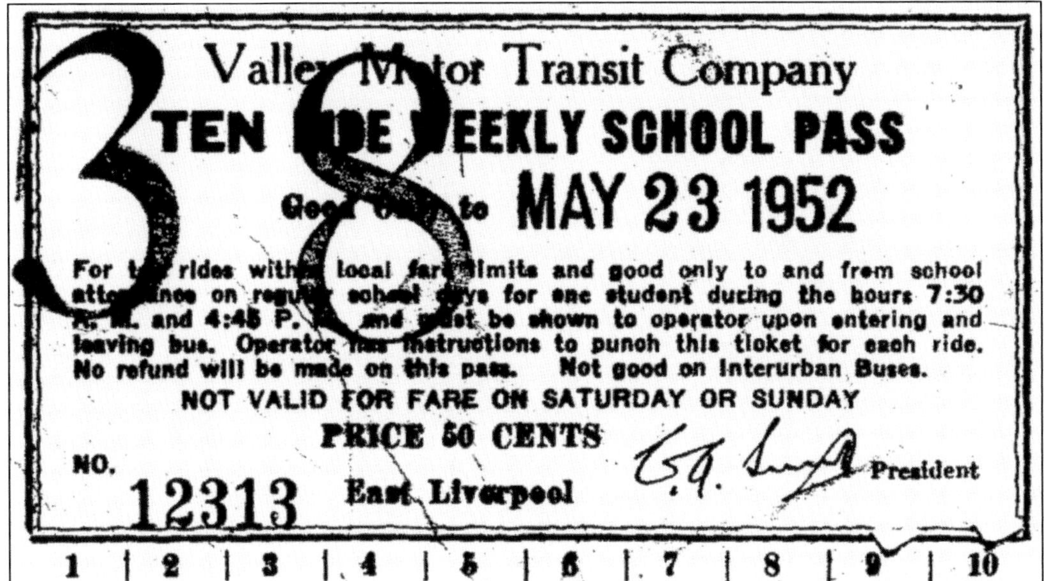

38

Vall[illegible] M[illegible]tor Transit Company

TEN [illegible] [illegible]EEKLY SCHOOL PASS

Goo[illegible] to MAY 23 1952

For t[illegible] rides with[illegible] local far[illegible]imits and good only to and from school atte[illegible]nce on regu[illegible] school [illegible]s for one student during the hours 7:30 [illegible] and 4:45 P.[illegible] and [illegible]st be shown to operator upon entering and leaving bus. Operator [illegible] instructions to punch this ticket for each ride. No refund will be made on this pass. Not good on Interurban Buses.

NOT VALID FOR FARE ON SATURDAY OR SUNDAY

PRICE 50 CENTS

NO. 12313 East Liverpool

President

1 | 2 | 3 | 4 | 5 | 6 | 7 | 8 | 9 | 10

In the 1940s, the city school board hired the Valley Motor Transit Company to transport students who lived more than a mile from their school. The school board owned three of its own buses by 1947, but Valley was still providing school passes for 50¢ that were good for 10 rides in a week. (Frank C. Dawson.)

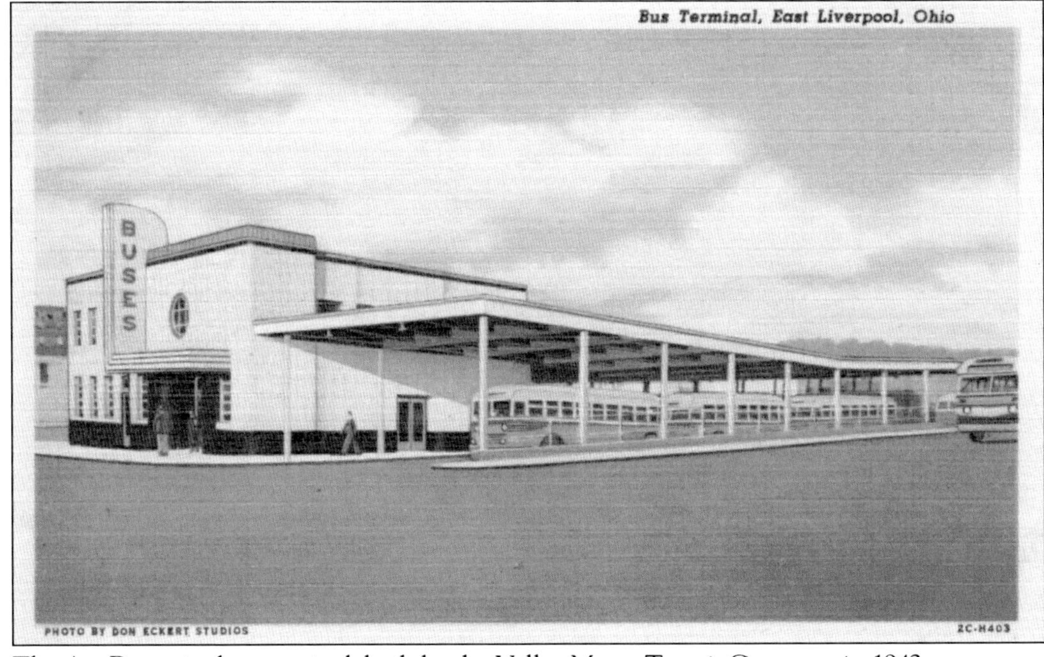

The Art Deco city bus terminal, built by the Valley Motor Transit Company in 1942, was a very modern travel center that included a restaurant, newsstand, and lockers for travelers. In later years, it was the home of Gus's Party Center. The building has since been torn down, suffering the same fate of other landmarks that outlived their usefulness. (Museum of Ceramics.)

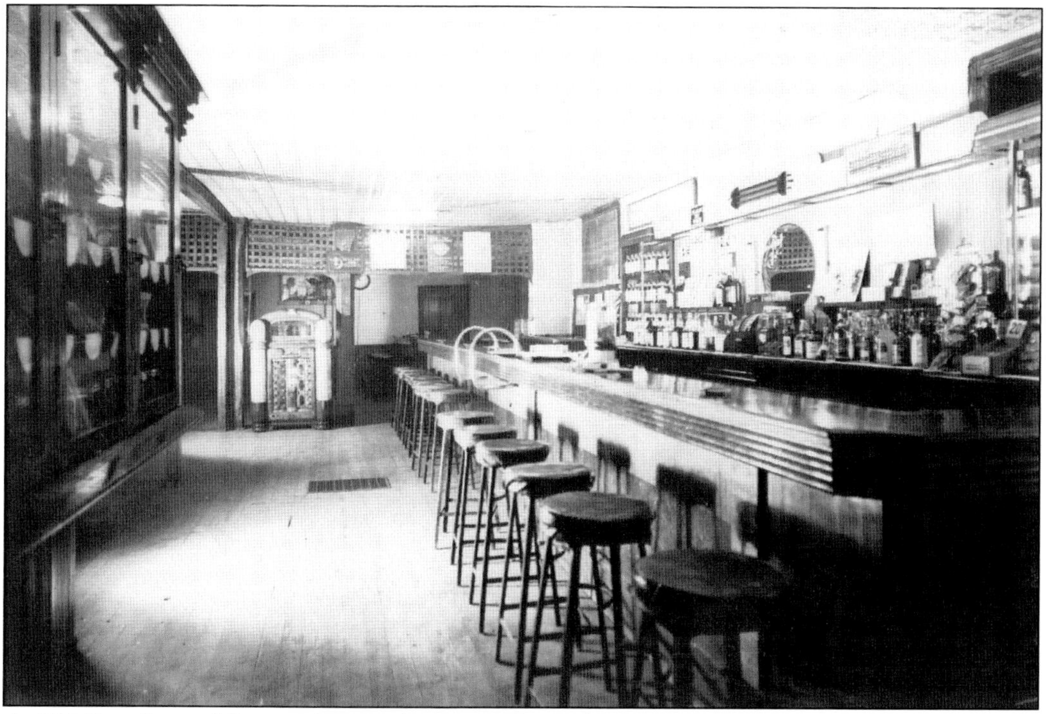

At 300 East Second Street, the Manhattan Café was known as the "Bucket of Blood" on Friday and Saturday nights, when town dignitaries mixed with potters, steelworkers, and employees of Milliron's Concrete Company across the railroad tracks. Owner Robert J. Freed always employed an off-duty police officer to stand at the door. Above, notice the Model 800 Wurlitzer Jukebox. Freed also owned Veterans Vending, Veterans Cab Company, Freed's Bar and Grill on Sixth Street, Freed's Welding, and the Buckeye Club. His daughter and son-in-law, Jackie and Kelsey Hedrick, and their son Eddie lived next door to the Manhattan in an attached house and worked in the various businesses. In the 1945 photograph below are, from left to right behind the bar, owners Velma and Robert J. Freed and bartenders Robert Sutherin and William Brewer; in front is waitress Gracie Martin. (Both Eddie Hedrick.)

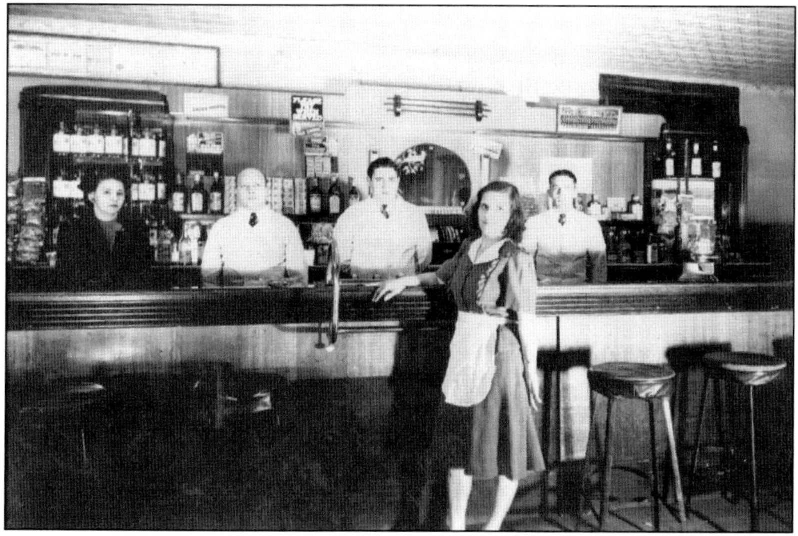

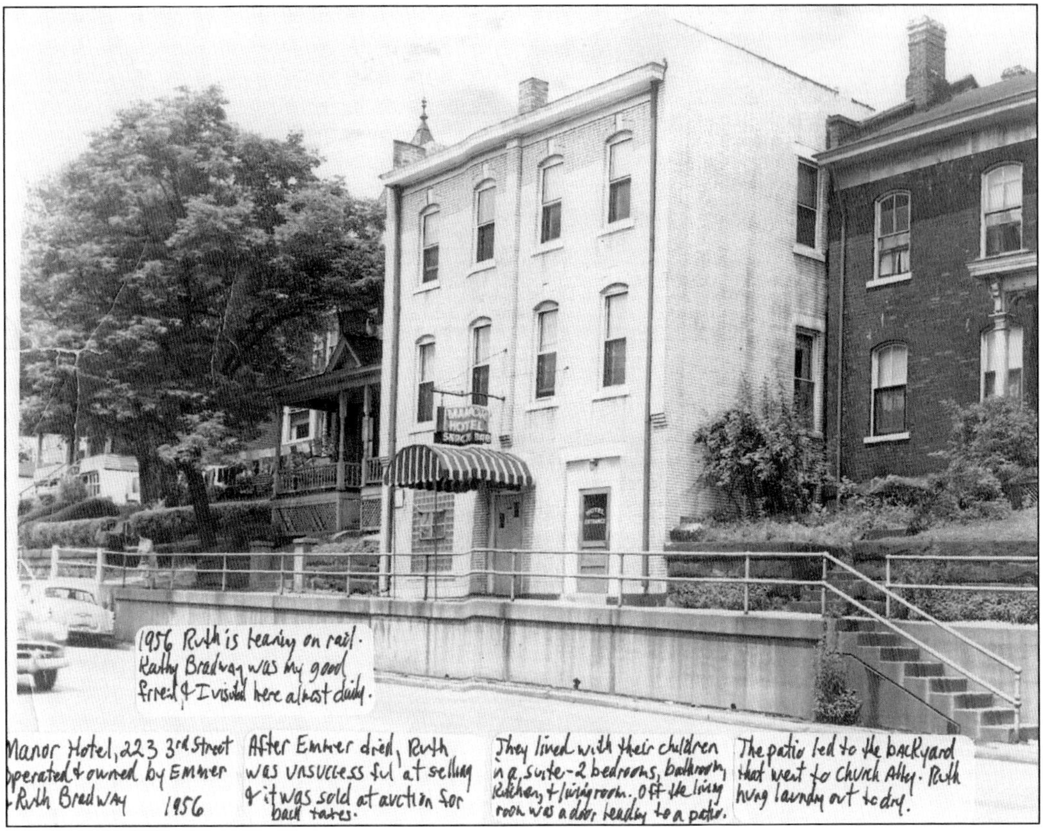

1956 Ruth is leaning on rail. Kathy Bradway was my good friend & I visited here almost daily.

Manor Hotel, 223 3rd Street operated & owned by Emmer & Ruth Bradway 1956

After Emmer died, Ruth was unsuccessful at selling & it was sold at auction for back taxes.

They lived with their children in a suite-2 bedrooms, bathroom, kitchen, & living room. Off the living room was a door leading to a patio.

The patio led to the backyard that went to Church Alley. Ruth hung laundry out to dry.

At 223 Third Street, the Manor Hotel was owned and operated by Emmer and Ruth Bradway. The couple lived at the hotel with their children in a suite that included a living room, kitchen, bathroom, and two bedrooms. In the 1956 photograph above, Ruth is leaning on the rail at the front left. Off the living room of the owners' private suite was a back door that led to a patio and backyard facing Church Alley and flanked by a garage and the rear of ELHS Central School. On fine days, the proprietress hung her laundry, including guests' linens, in the backyard. After Emmer died, Ruth tried without success to sell the hotel, and it was later sold at auction for back taxes. (Both Inger Lloyd.)

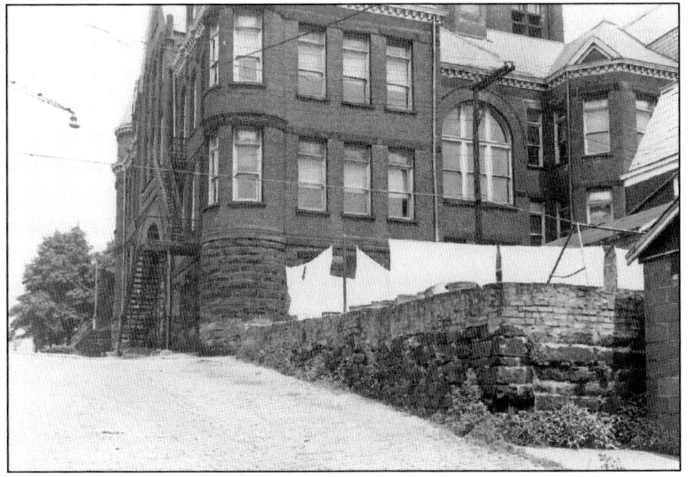

The East Liverpool pottery industry supported many ancillary industries. Louthan Manufacturing Company, formed in 1901, produced pins and stilts for kilns. Louthan's also made porcelain heater plates, insulators, and radiants and back walls for gas heaters. Shown at a Louthan's pressing machine in 1957 is Bill Barrett, whom Mr. Louthan called "Willie Westinghouse" for his ability—like the cartoon character—to fix most anything. (Dawn Chapman.)

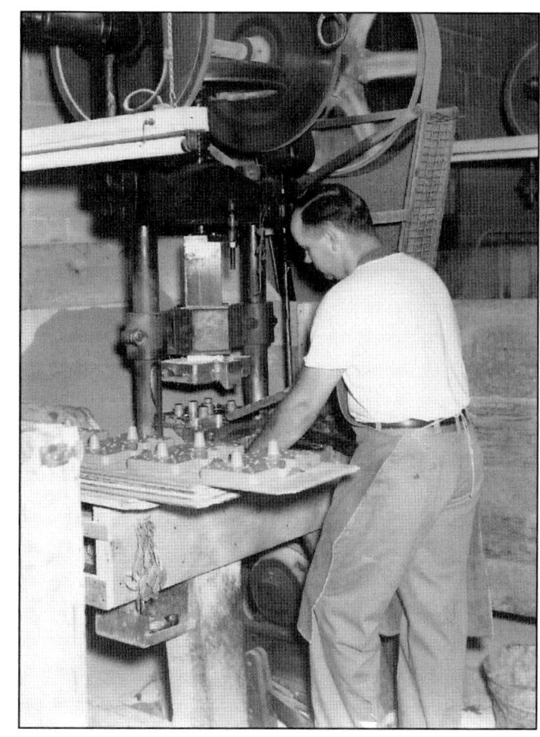

The Amoco station at East Third and Washington Streets was a longtime downtown fixture. Children in the backseats of cars, waiting for station attendants to fill the tank, check the oil, and wash the windshield, could amuse themselves by inspecting the map of the Lincoln Highway, visible here just above the right-side garage door. (Inger Lloyd.)

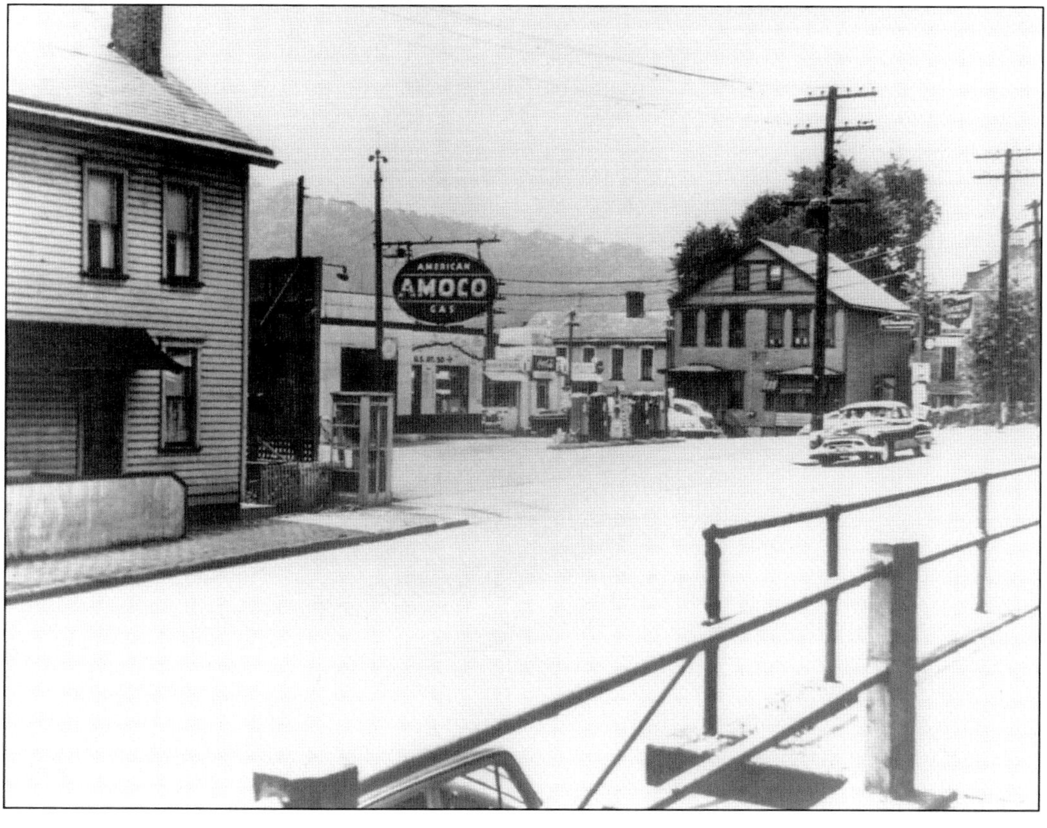

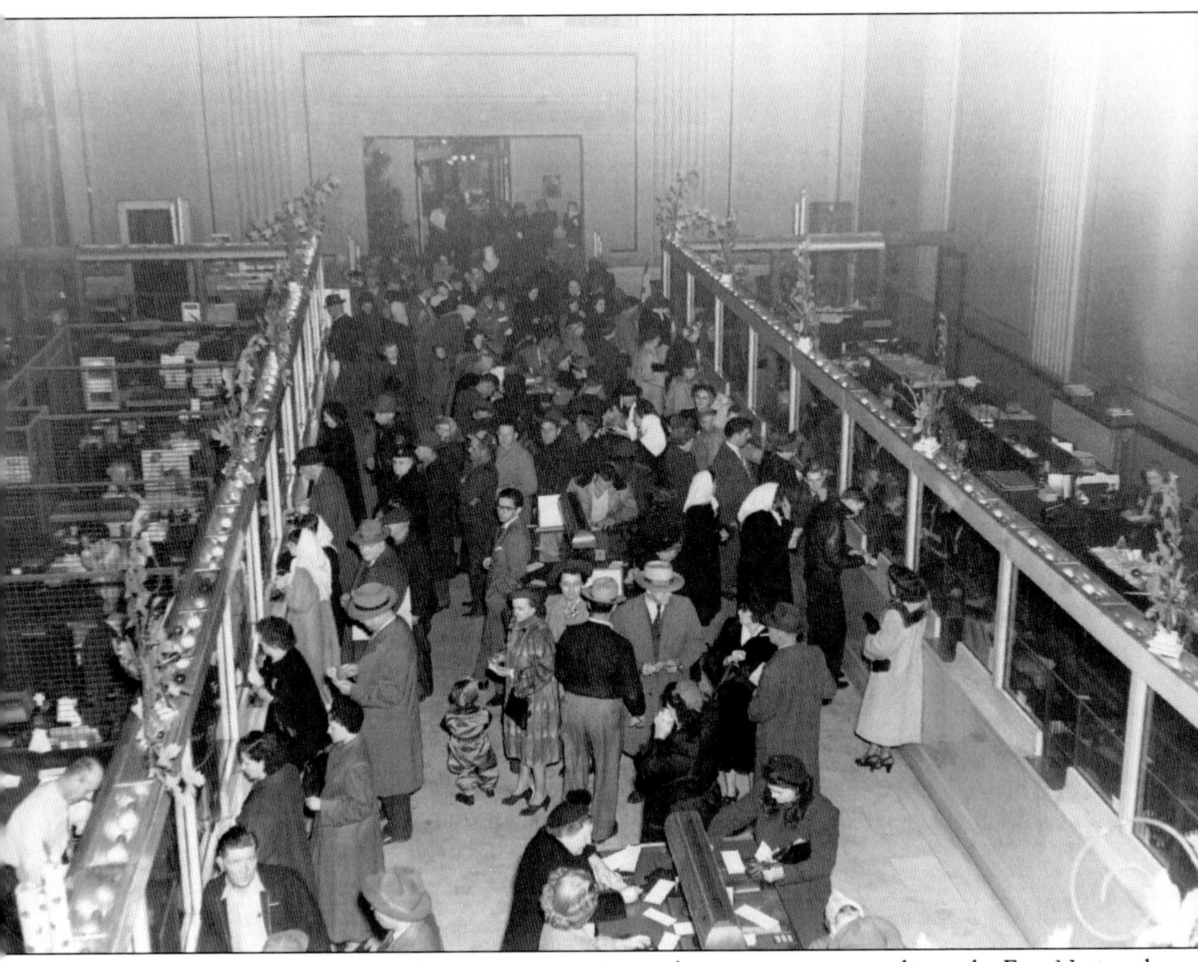

In the postwar years, it was a big event every winter when customers poured into the First National Bank on Fifth Street to cash their Christmas Club accounts and start shopping. Downtown businesses were open late on Thursday nights, and people thronged the streets to shop, eat, and visit with friends and neighbors. The First National Bank, for many years a downtown fixture, first opened its doors in 1874 on Broadway and Second Street, then moved to Washington Street in 1889. The original bank officers included David Boyce, Josiah Thompson, I.M. Kelly, William H. Vodrey, N.B. Hickman, N.A. Frederick, and George Morley. This building, at the center of the Fifth Street shopping district, was built in 1922–1923 at a cost of $260,000. Today, the building is occupied by the Lou Holtz/Upper Ohio Valley Hall of Fame. (Frank C. Dawson.)

Someone was just clowning around when they shot this promotional picture of the ELHS Marching Band Color Guard in the 1960s. The clowns are David Maola (left) and Rusty Glasure (right). The guards are, from left to right, Bob Carroll, Tom Snow, Tom Thornton, and John Capraruolo. The photograph was taken up the street from the high school's Memorial Auditorium at the First Church of Christ (Disciples). (Vince Maola Jr.)

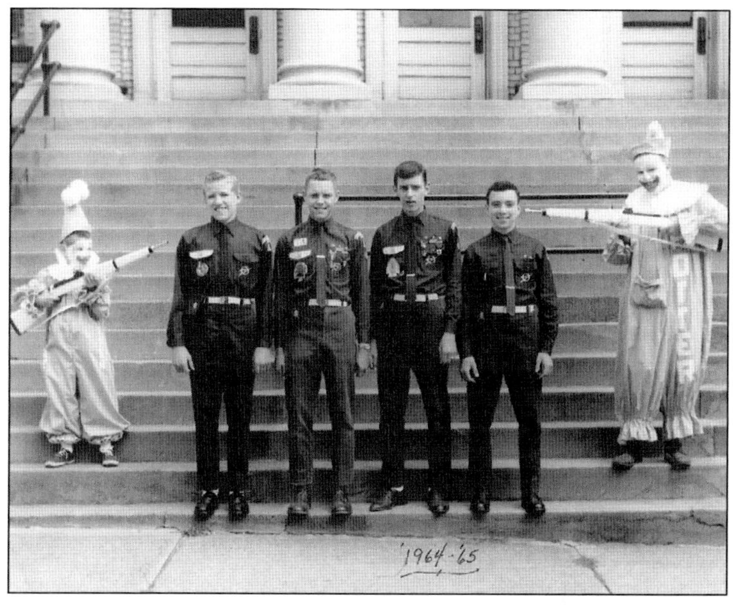

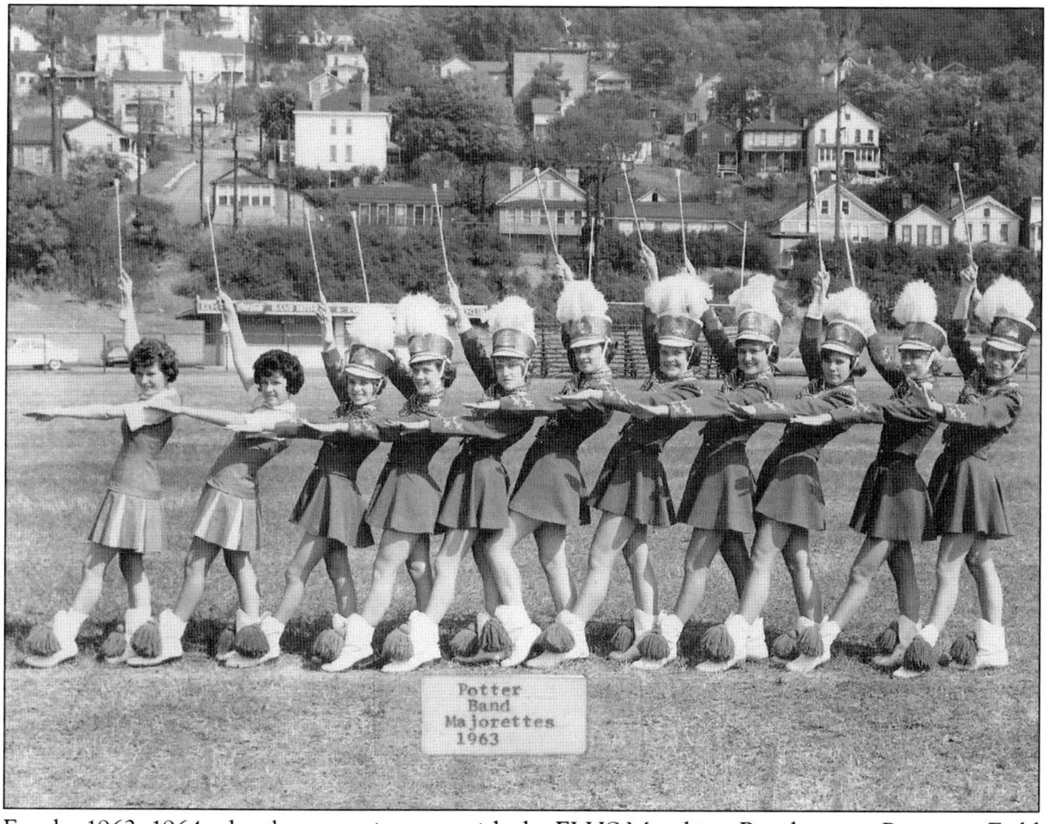

For the 1963–1964 school year, majorettes with the ELHS Marching Band pose at Patterson Field in a promotional shot for the band program. They are, from left to right, Cindy Kidder, Mary Beth Fone, Amy Siebert, Susan Jones, Kay Simpson, Nancy Watson, Vicki Myers, Terry Looman, Cheryl Standley, Mary Lou McGaffic, and Patti Campbell. (Vince Maola Jr.)

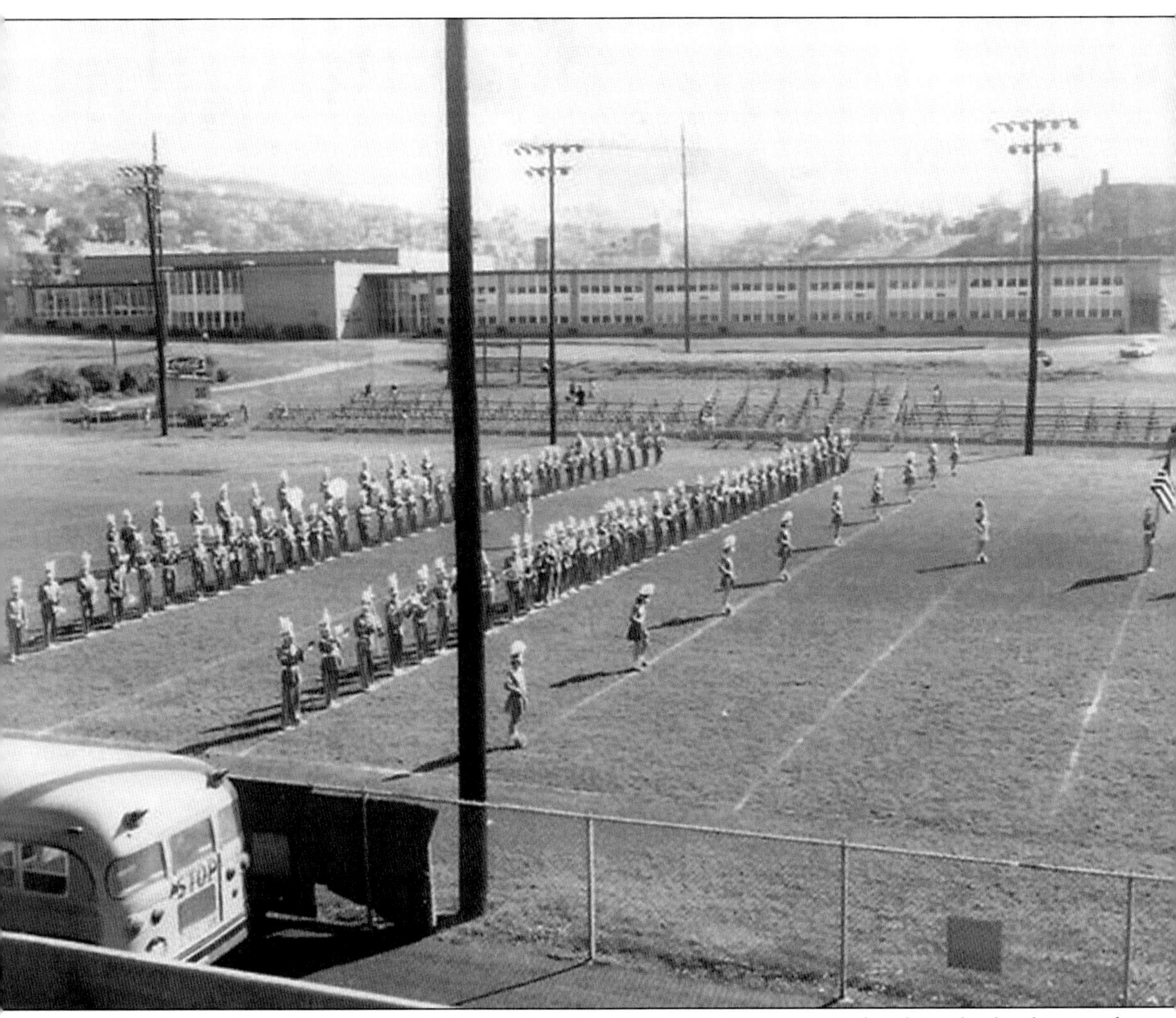

Band practice at Patterson Field, seen here in 1964 with Westgate School in the background, was serious business. That year, there were 166 playing members of the band, divided into two equal sections of 75 each, with a 16-piece percussion section at midfield. The section on the left worked from the 45-yard line to the 15-yard line, and the opposite one did the same thing. The drum section in the middle held it all together, with band director Vince Maola conducting the percussionists and a drum major conducting each side. One of their presentations was the Wrigley's "Double Your Pleasure" jingle. The bands presented seven different shows at home and away games, at Ohio Wesleyan University, Geneva College, and Pittsburgh Steelers' games, for hometown parades, and in Philadelphia at the Gimbel's Thanksgiving Day Parade. At practices, each band member carried a transistor radio and used earphones to listen to directions over a student-built three-watt transmitter. (Vince Maola Jr.)

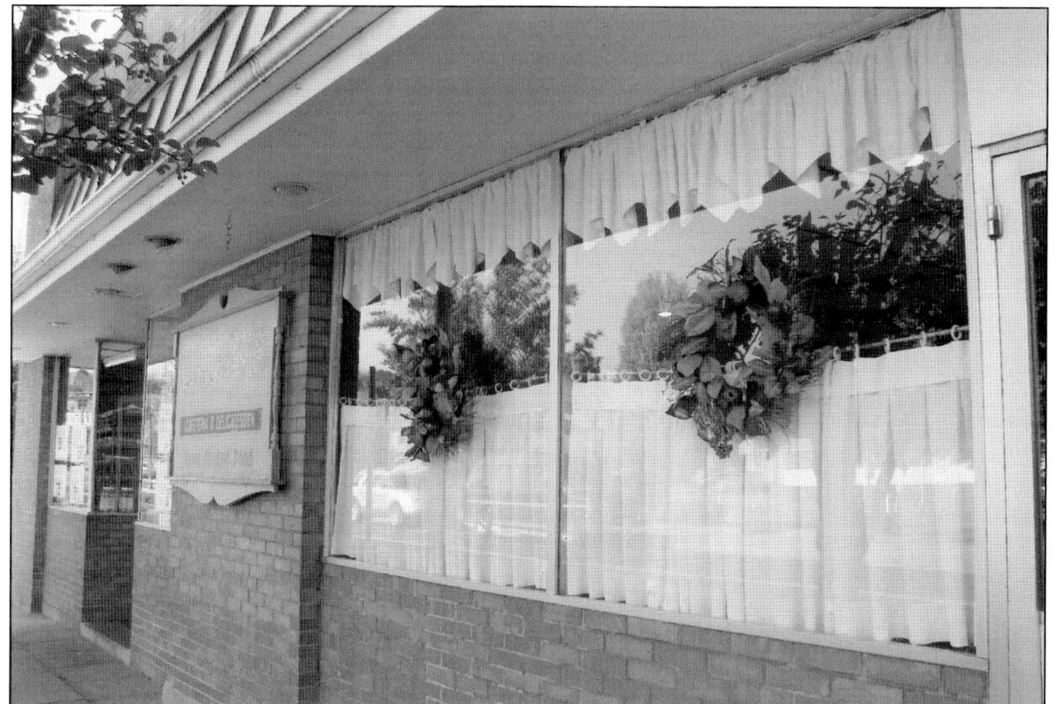

Lee Bricker opened a cafeteria and delicatessen on East Sixth Street in 1930. His son Harold later took over the business, which he remodeled just before the Diamond Fire in March 1968. The top two floors were removed, and Bricker's reopened in May. Skyscraper ice cream cones were big attractions in the 1960s. Dan Dietz, Harold's son-in-law, is now the owner, assisted by his sister-in-law Sarah Bricker. (Author's collection.)

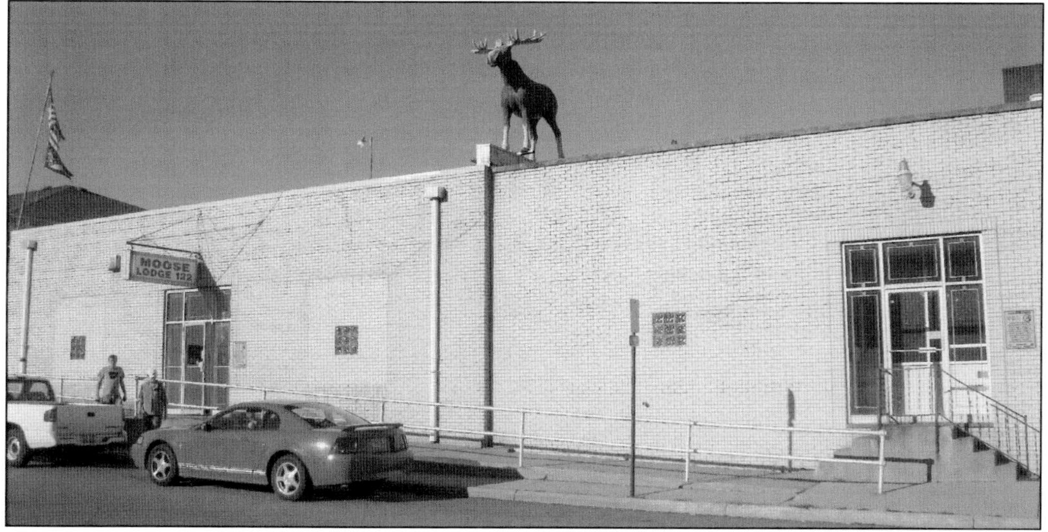

The Loyal Order of Moose dedicated East Liverpool Lodge 122 in 1912. The fraternal organization's first building was on Fourth Street at the present location of the *Review*. This building on Third Street was erected in 1957. Lodge members today describe themselves as a "family organization," with 457 men and 412 Women of the Moose. Parties, picnic, dances, and charitable events are popular activities. (Author's collection.)

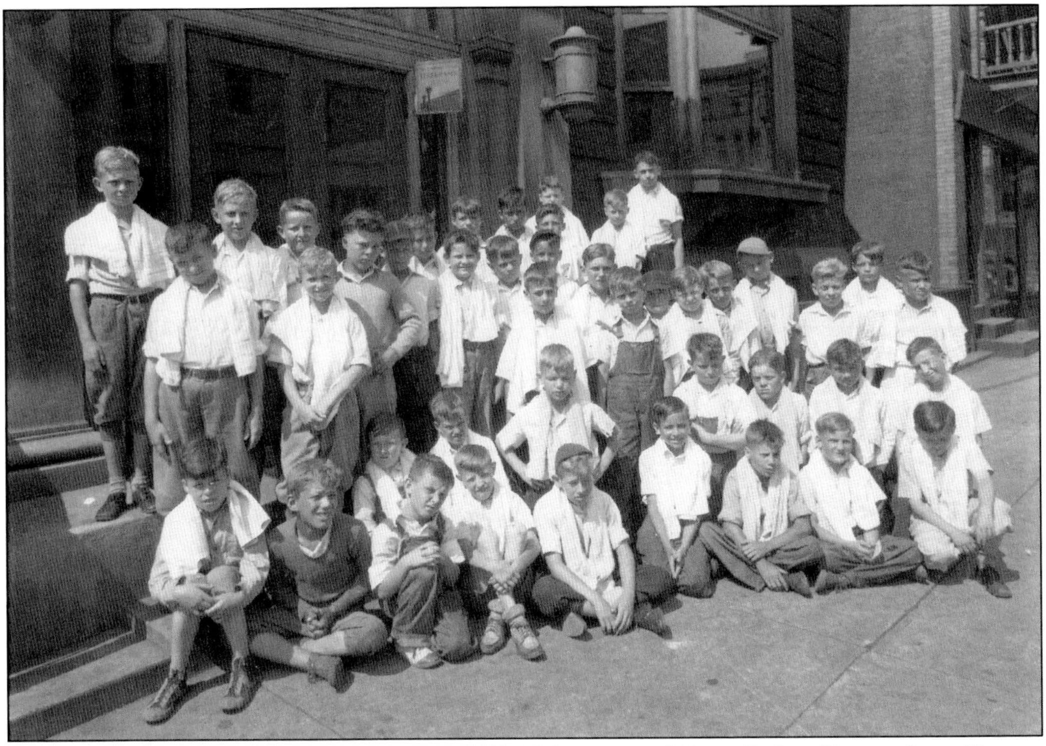

From 1923 until 1974, the East Liverpool YMCA operated Pine Ridge Camp along Beaver Creek near Lisbon. Carl "Pop" Werner, longtime director at the Y, devoted his summers to camp sessions. Campers remember taking baths in the creek with a bar of soap and tumbling out of the cabins at the sound of the morning whistle. The last cabin out had to clean "Zero," the pit toilets at the end of the cabin row. The boys' photograph is from 1950 and the girls' photograph is from 1967. From left to right, the girls are (first row) Barbie Stover, Yvonne Crowder, Maria Musuraca, Cathy Coleman, Amy Todd, Vicki Woomer, Gretchen Kennedy, Cindy ? , Christy Williams, and Barbara Hester; (second row) Barbie Ferguson, Sherri Thorne, Sue Standley, Patty Webber, Gerry Young, Valene Burheister, Arden ? , Carole Hile, and Cathy Hester; (third row) Joann Stepanovich, an unidentified cook, Penny Thorne, Peggy Porter, Sue Green, Mary Wilkinson, Debbie Price, Jenny ? , Suzann Cunningham, an unidentified cook, and Jane Swogger; (fourth row) Barbara Yeager, Pam Price, Sue Vohar, Randy Young, and Sandy Young. (Above, East Liverpool Historical Society; below, author's collection.)

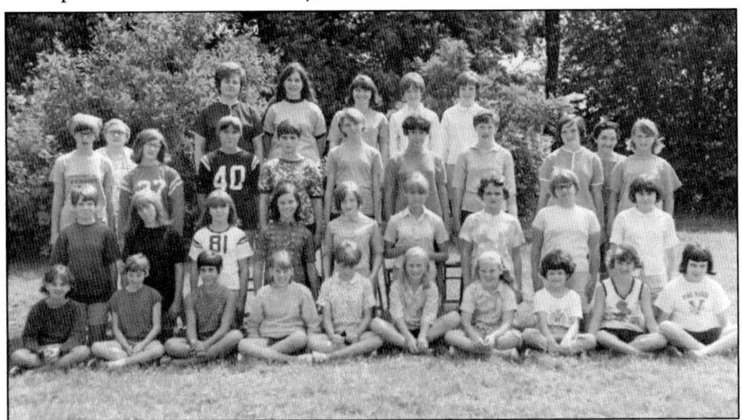

Eight

The Realignment Years

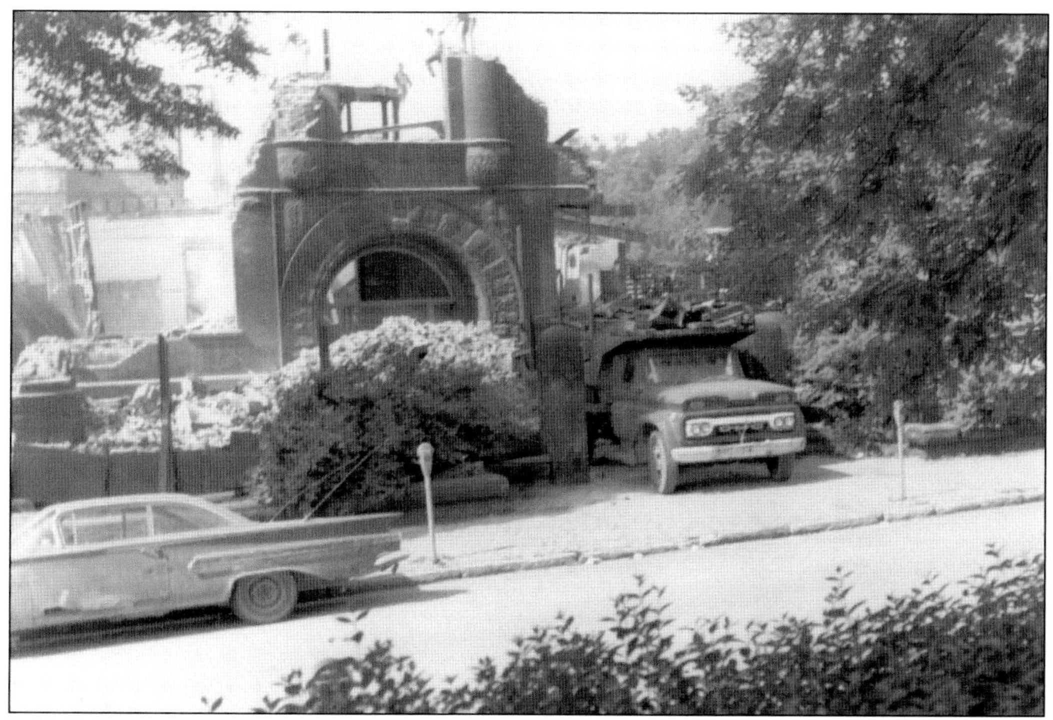

When Central School, built in 1894–1895, was demolished in 1969 or 1970, it marked the end of an era in East Liverpool. The site on East Fourth and Union Streets had held a school building since 1825, but the newest high school would be constructed on Maine Boulevard above town. (East Liverpool Historical Society.)

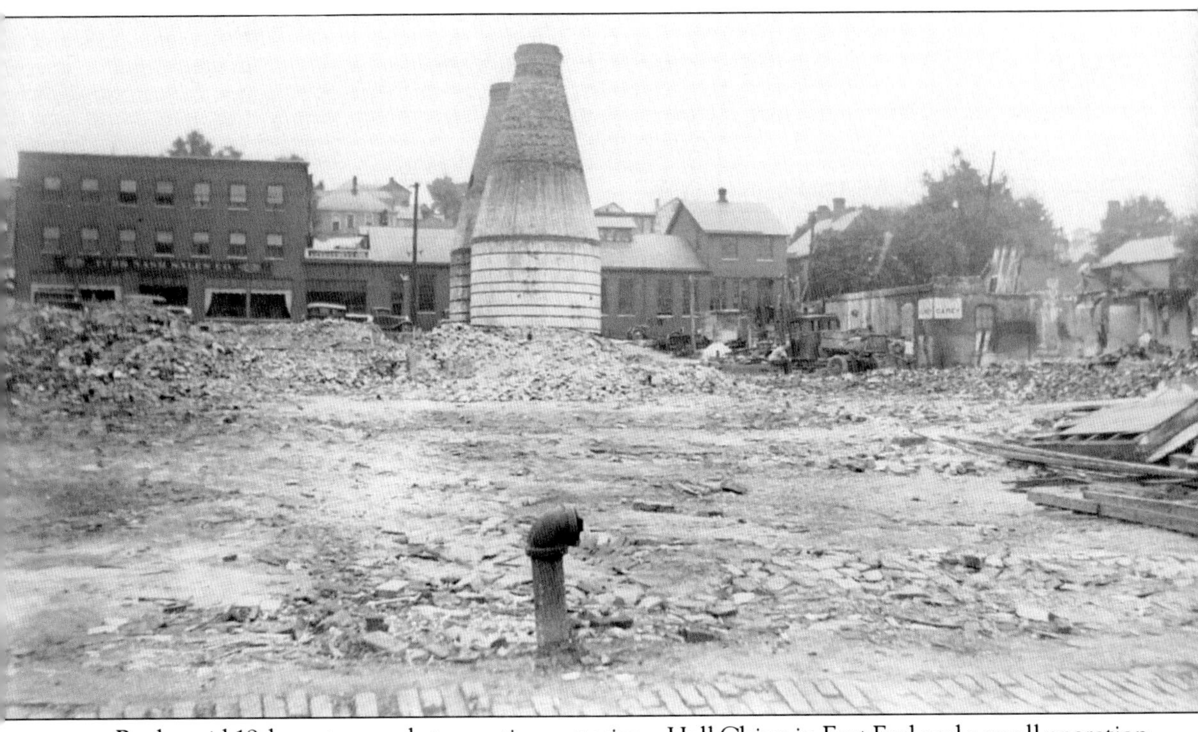

By the mid-19th century, only two active potteries—Hall China in East End and a small operation on Dresden Avenue called Pioneer Pottery—were left in East Liverpool. Some ancillary industries had also shut down. Sights like this, the teardown of a McNicol Pottery plant, were all too common, as was the sight of empty and decaying buildings. By 1970, barely 1,000 potters still lived in town, and many of those worked across the river at Homer Laughlin. Strip malls had begun to appear in nearby Calcutta, and downtown businesses began, one by one, to close down or move out. Tax levies were being turned down. Young families were moving to other places to find work. The city lost 8,000 in population between 1950 and 1980. It was time for East Liverpool to readjust, to come to terms with the fact there was very little industry left in the pottery capital of the nation. (East Liverpool Historical Society.)

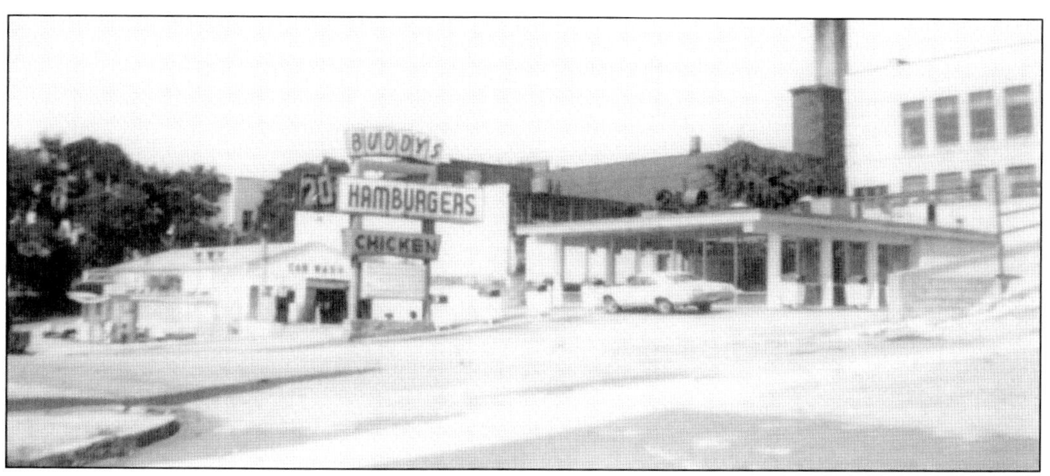

Buddy's Hamburgers, once a city landmark, started out at the corner of Third and College Streets in the 1970s, just behind Memorial Auditorium. Owned by city businessman Al Gloeckner, it was named for his son and was immediately popular with high school students. When the Route 11 freeway extension took many of the buildings on Second and Third Streets, Buddy's moved to Ninth Street and continued as a popular hangout. Another casualty of the Route 11 freeway extension was Naples Spaghetti House at 400 East Third Street, which is pictured below in 1970. (Both Inger Lloyd.)

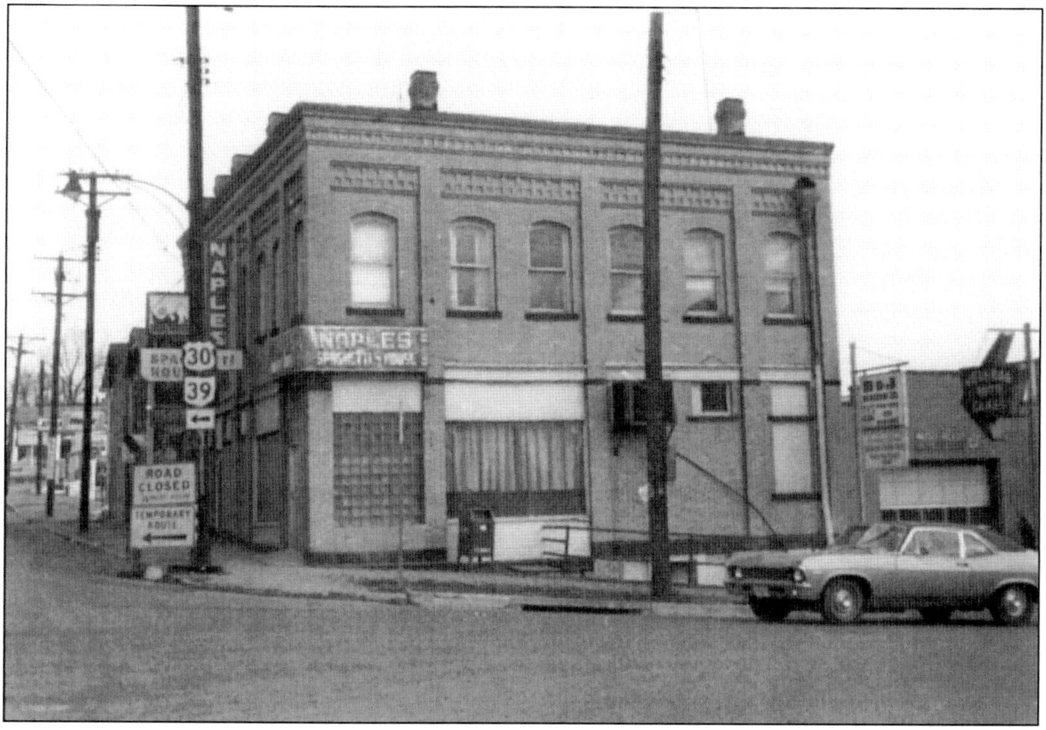

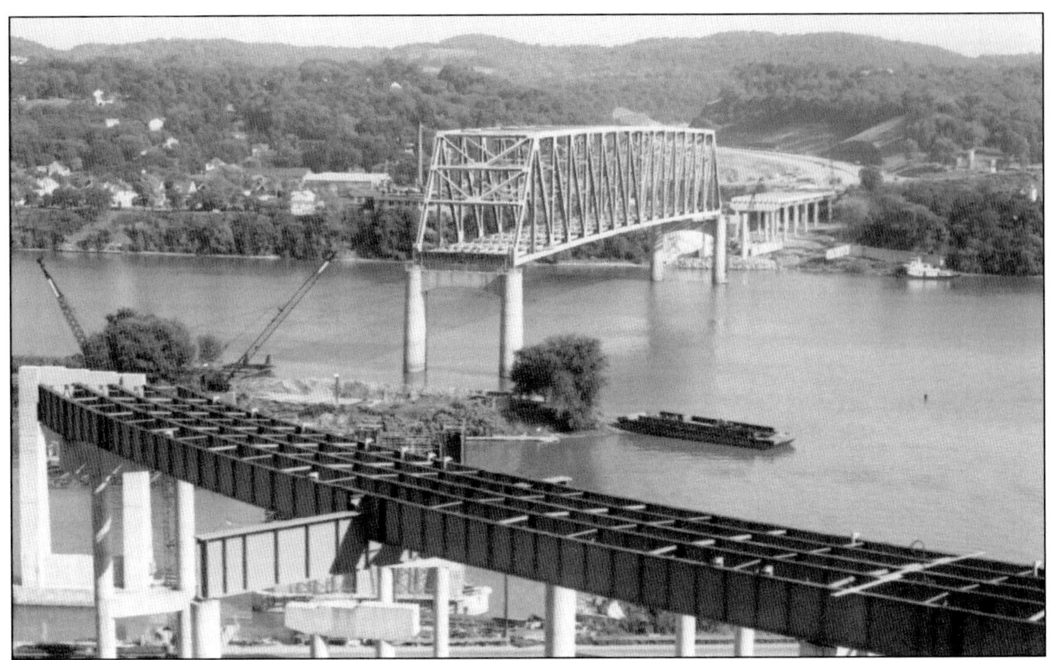

After "the old Chester Bridge that ain't," as locals called it, was torn down in 1969 following a 72-year lifespan, plans were immediately begun to replace it. The first piers were poured in 1971. It would take another six years for completion, during which time residents had to make do with the two-lane Newell toll bridge, causing frequent traffic congestion at both ends. Design changes, winter weather, and problems with material supply caused delays. Construction on bridge approaches was not begun until 1974. When completed in 1977, the bridge was 754 feet long—the largest Pratt truss bridge in North America. It was named for former West Virginia senator Jennings Randolph. Below, a 1950s view of East Fifth Street shows James Locke Jewelers, a city institution for 60 years, at right. The business continues today as Stevens Jewelers. (Both East Liverpool Historical Society.)

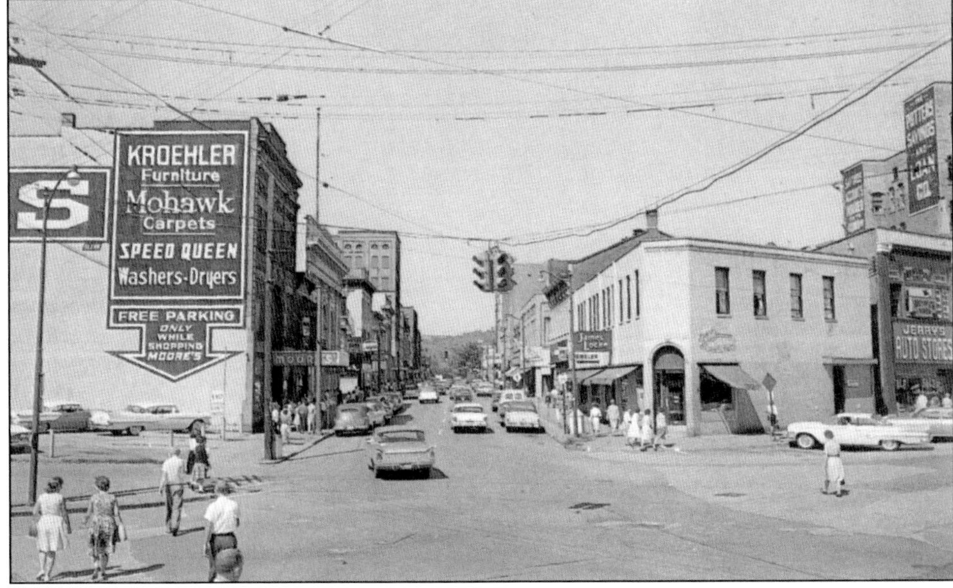

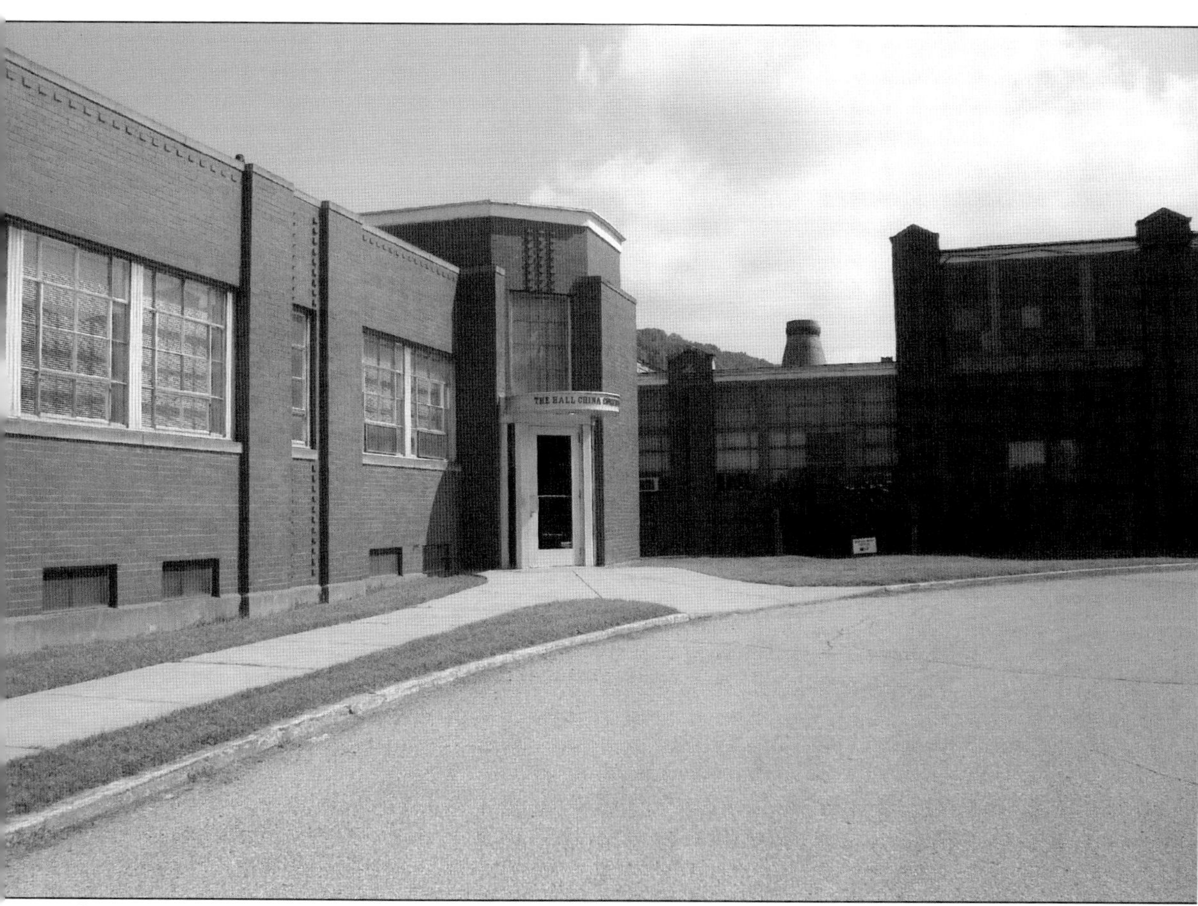

Robert T. Hall founded the Hall China Company in 1903 in the former East Liverpool Potteries plant at East Fourth and Walnut Streets. The firm thrived on the production of white dinnerware. During World War I, the company added the manufacture of chemical and laboratory porcelain to its production lines. During the Depression, the firm was able to prosper by delving into modern colors, shapes, and designs. The company expanded its teapot line, at one point producing 350 dozen teapots per day for the Lipton Tea Company. Hall's was the leading employer in town during the Depression years, with 815 workers in this new, more efficient plant in East End. By 1940, it was the only producer of tableware remaining in town. In 2010, the Homer Laughlin China Company acquired Hall China, which is still known for specialty dinnerware and unique teapots, including the popular Reagan teapot. (Author's collection.)

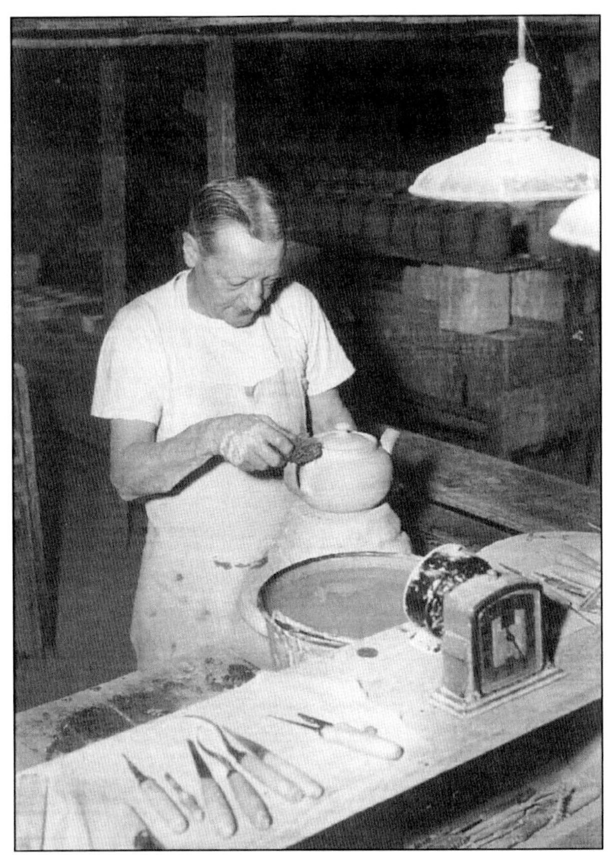

Wirtie W. Wilson, at left, worked for more than 75 years—most of the 20th century—as a caster at Hall China, according to his granddaughter Carolyn Nentwick. She says it was the only job he ever had, and he did it so well that every time he retired he was called back because no one could replace him. As a caster, he was responsible for cleaning ware after it came out of the molds but before it was sent for firing in a kiln. The photograph below shows another Hall's caster at work in 1970. (At left, Carolyn Wilson Nentwick; below, East Liverpool Historical Society.)

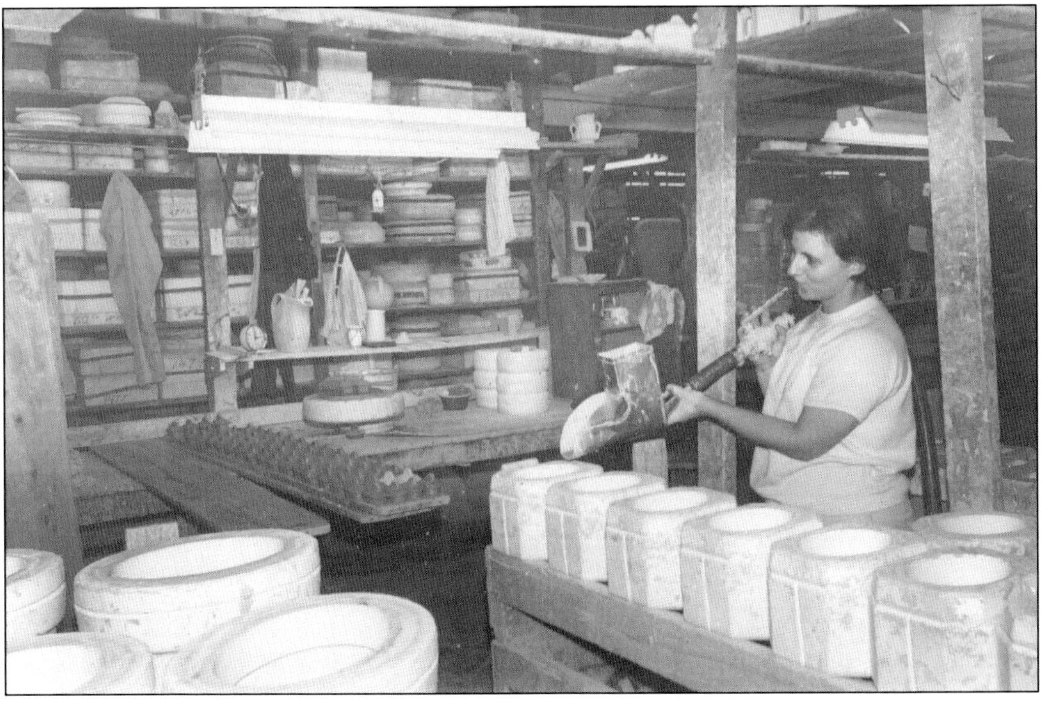

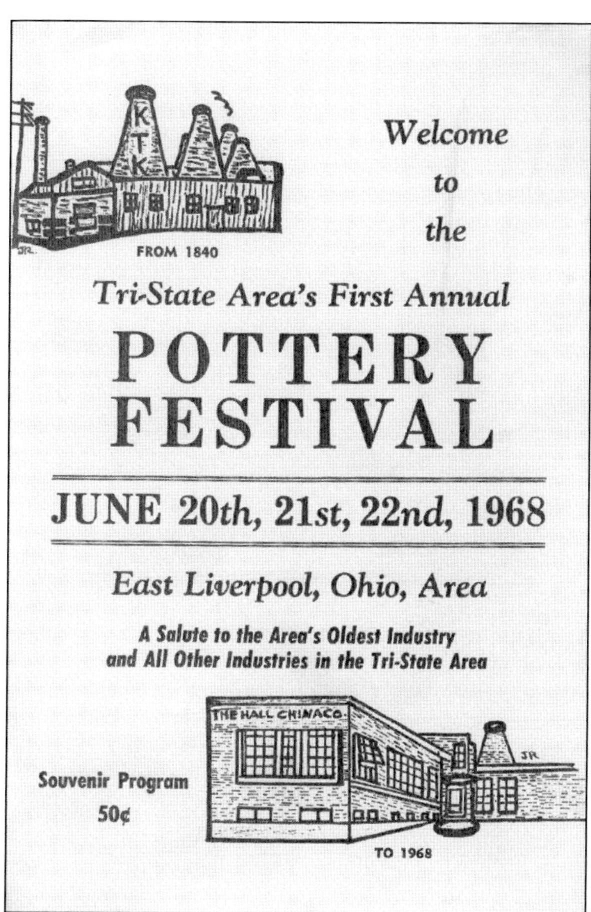

The Tri-State Area Pottery Festival, a summertime institution since 1968, has included such time-honored traditions as the National Doorknob Tossing Championship and the Pottery Olympics. In recent years, an auction for pottery collectibles has attracted plenty of interest. Additional events have included demonstrations of pottery decoration, window-decorating contests, a parade, fireworks, musical entertainment and contests, a beard-and-mustache contest, hamburger eat-off, rose show, photography and art exhibits, and of course a Pottery Festival queen. Pictured are the 1974 queen, Darlene Cain, her escort Tim Conley, and in the background festival official Cliff Conley. (At right, Keystone Printing; below, Phyllis Conley.)

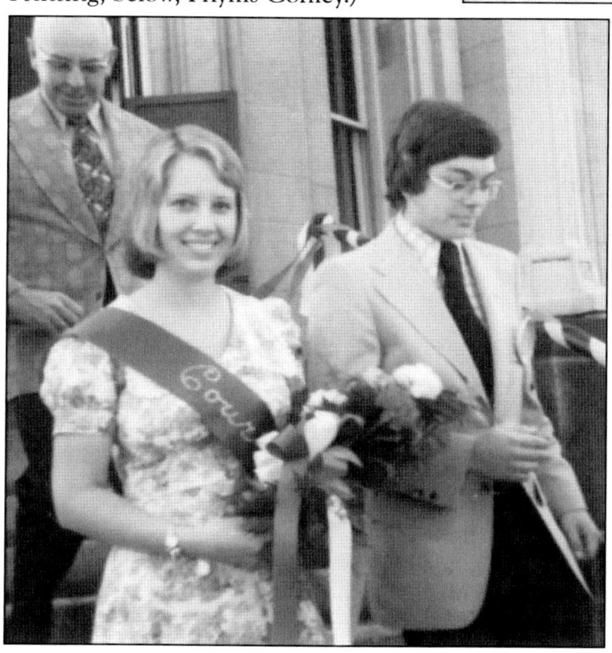

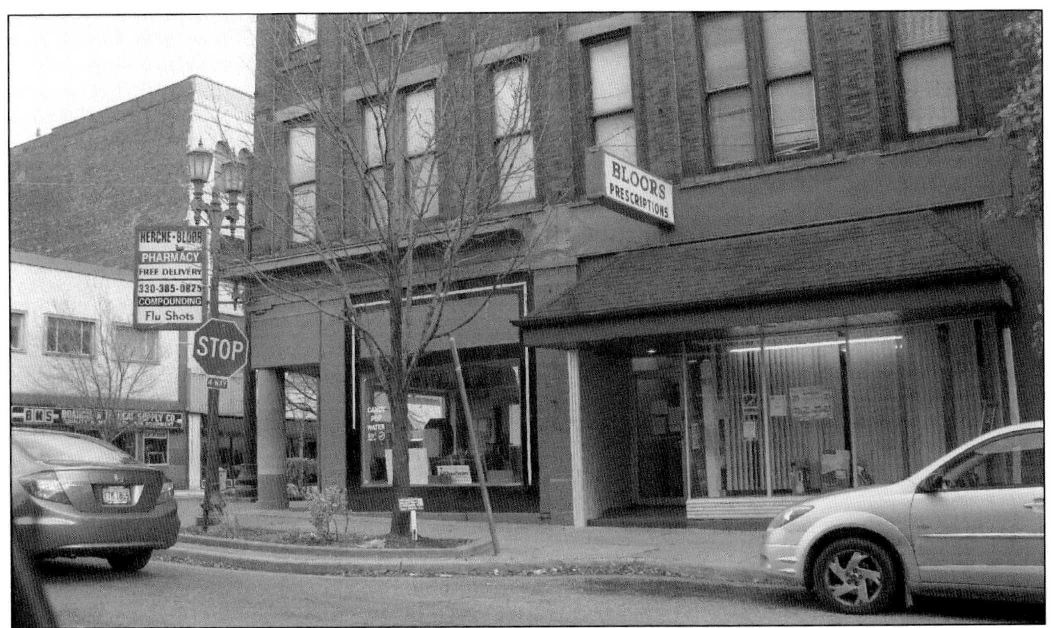

The Herche-Bloor Pharmacy on West Fifth Street, seen above, is a distillation of earlier drugstores in other locations. Bill Herche operated a downtown pharmacy. His nephew Clifford Comm worked there and eventually purchased the business. Comm's sons Cliff and Harry joined the family profession, and the three purchased the Bloor Pharmacy in the 1970s, renaming it Herche-Bloor Pharmacy. Tony DeCaria has owned the business since 1981. Below, Milligan Hardware has served residents since 1881, when T.V. Milligan Sr. bought a half interest, then a full interest, in Eagle Hardware on Fifth Street. The business moved to Smith Street in 1962. Arthur V. Doak joined the business around 1946, later marrying Milligan's great-granddaughter, Nancy Thompson, and purchasing the business in 1975. Arthur T. Doak has been president since 1985. (Above, author's collection; below, East Liverpool Historical Society.)

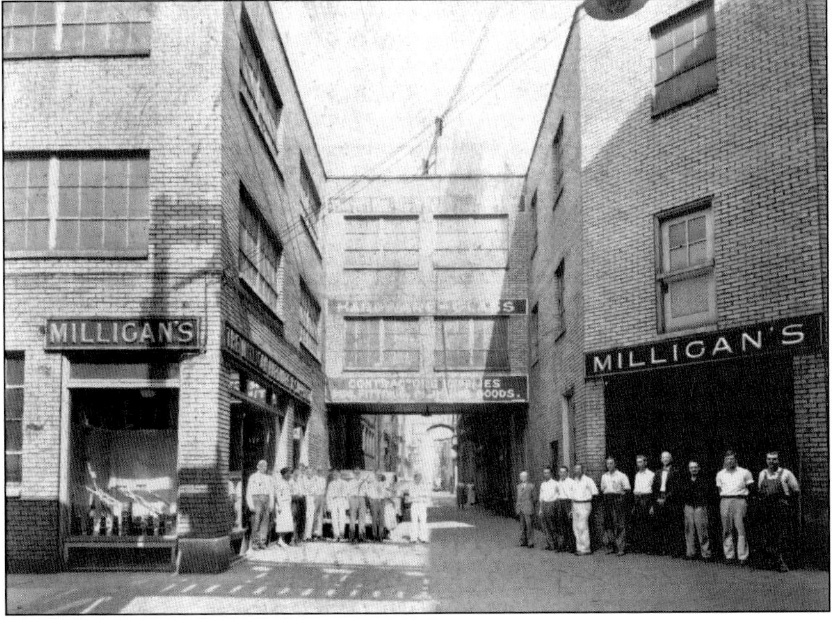

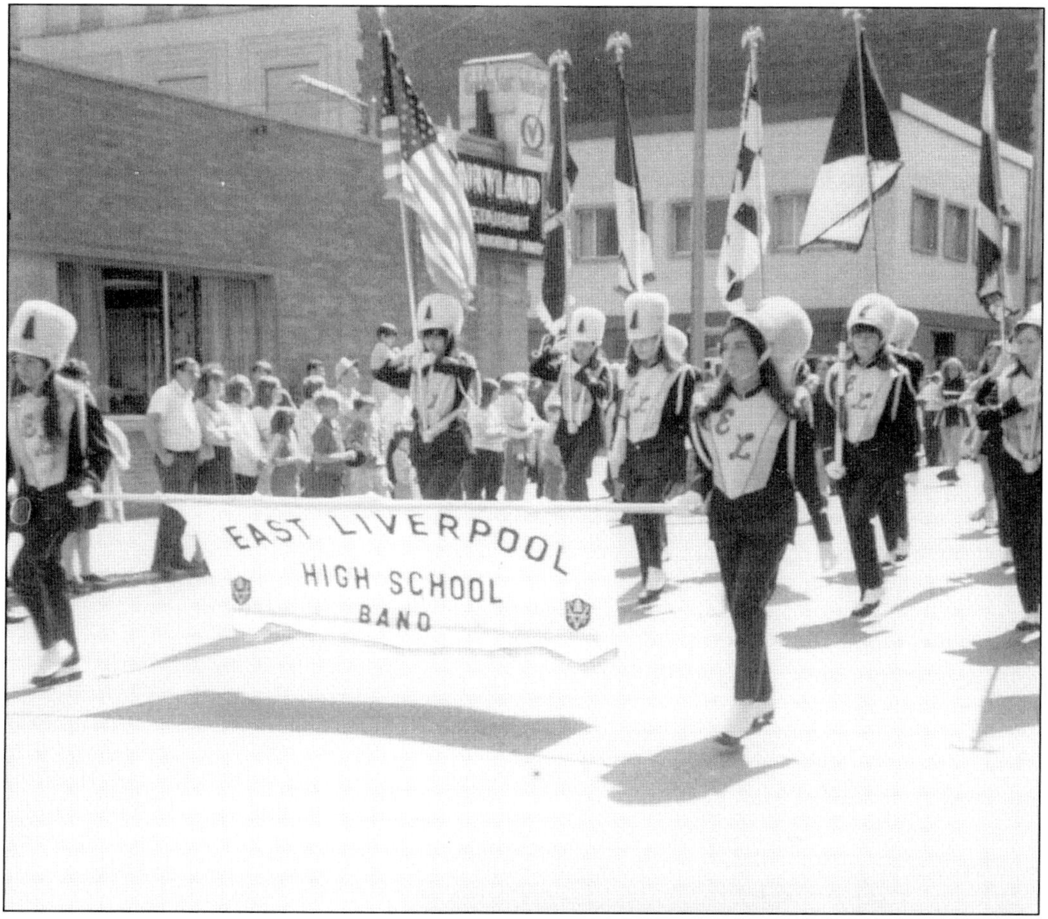

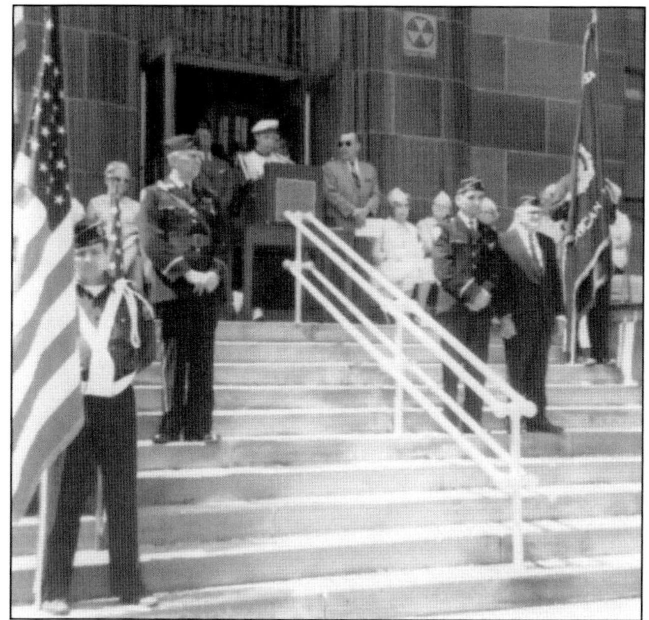

The 1970s and 1980s continued to be somber decades for East Liverpool. More than 1,000 locals lost their jobs when the Crucible Steel plant in nearby Midland closed in 1982. The population dropped again as young people continued to leave and more downtown businesses closed. Even with the slumps in business and lack of prospects in general, East Liverpudlians carried on with their lives and celebrations. The 1971 Memorial Day events in town included a parade featuring the East Liverpool High School Band, with band member John Conley reciting the Gettysburg Address on the steps of city hall. (Both Phyllis Conley.)

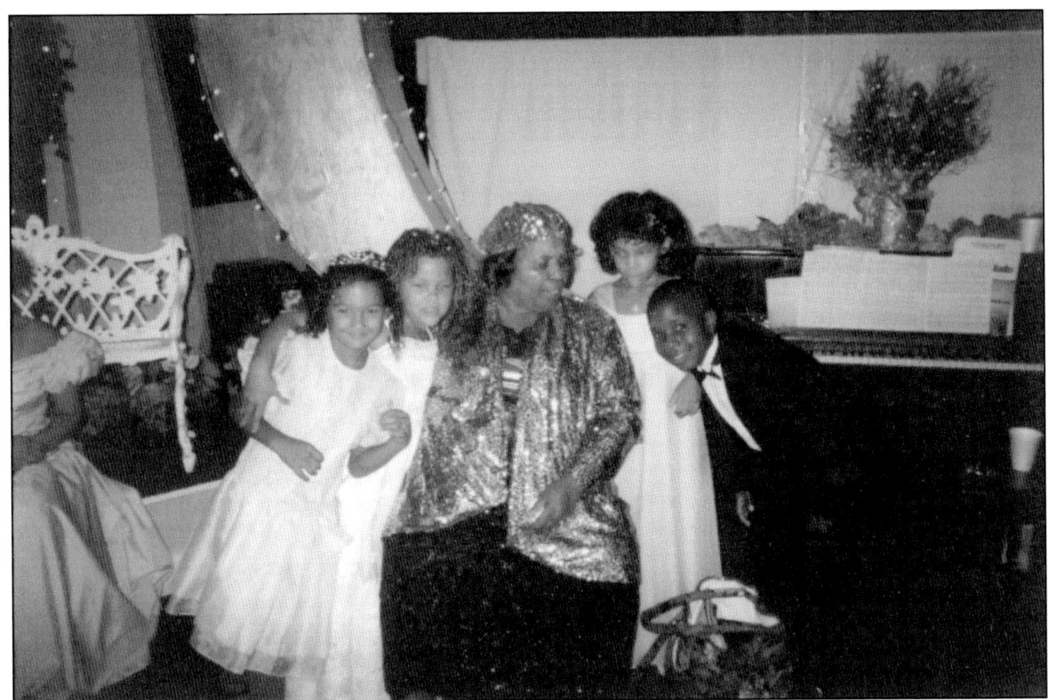

East End residents Elizabeth P. Carter, Ruth Kincaid, and Ann Johnston got together in 1965 to address the needs of the working poor, elderly, shut-ins, and youth in their neighborhoods. They formed the Tri-State Promoters Cultural and Creative Society, which quickly grew from a three-person project to a large network of social-service programs spread out in several buildings, run by dozens of volunteers, and funded by area donors. Above, Elizabeth Carter poses with, from left to right, an unidentified girl, Andrea Williams, Cierra Carter, and Nolan Harmon. Below, Richard and Elizabeth Carter share dessert at a Promoters dinner at the Point of Light Center. On August 15, 1990, Elizabeth was named George H.W. Bush's 222nd Point of Light, and in 1994 the work of the Tri-State Promoters was featured on *The Oprah Winfrey Show*. (Both Rick Carter.)

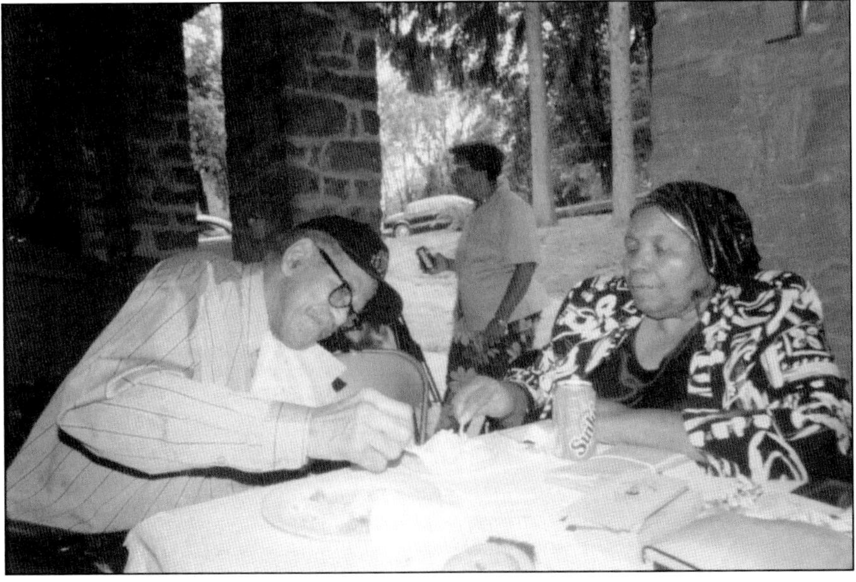

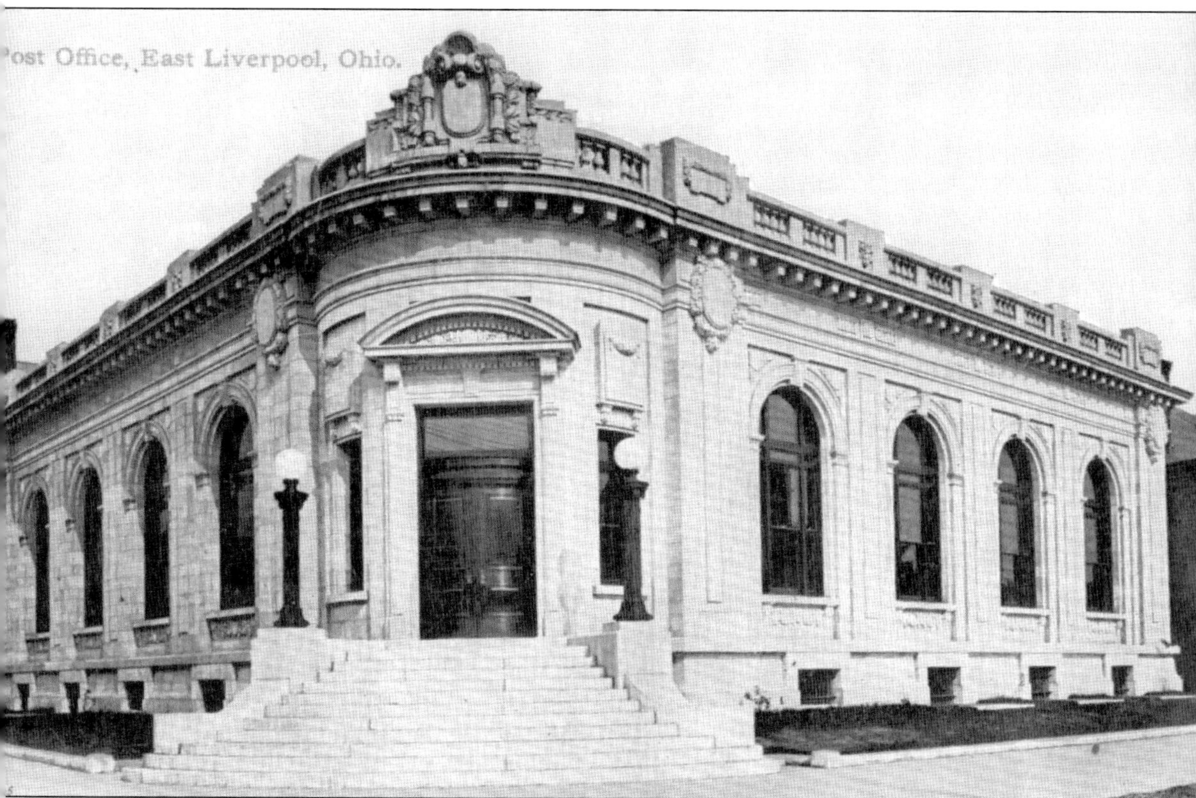

This imposing granite and limestone edifice at the corner of East Fifth Street and Broadway was built in 1909 on a lot purchased for $30,000 from William Brunt Sr. by the federal government for use as the city post office. The cost of construction was $100,000. In grand Beaux Arts style, the post office featured intricate domed ceilings, a marble and terrazzo floor, and wrought iron fixtures. In 1969, a smaller post office was built across town, and this facility was purchased by the State of Ohio for use as a museum. The Museum of Ceramics opened here in 1980, and it concentrates its collections on area pottery production between 1840 and 1930. The collection includes pottery machinery, thousands of pieces of locally made pottery, dioramas, photographs, document collections, and portraits of civic leaders and pottery owners. An auditorium offers a film on the pottery industry. Group and student tours, cultural and historical events, and children's activities are scheduled regularly. (Museum of Ceramics.)

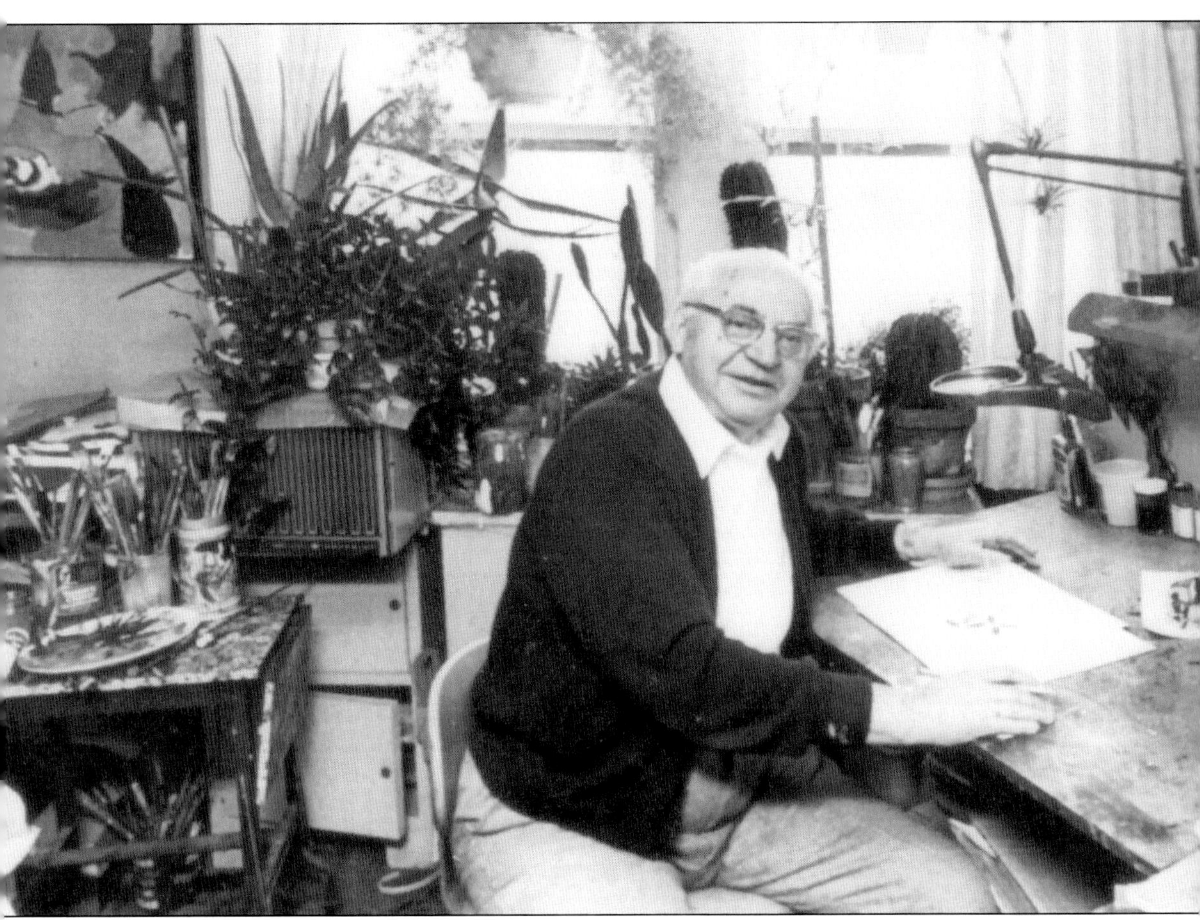

Hans Hacker first came to East Liverpool in 1932 as a representative of E. Wunderlich and Company of Germany, for which he was head designer. After immigrating here in the late 1930s, he became the art and technical director at Commercial Decal. He also painted hundreds of oils and watercolors of East Liverpool businesses, streets, and homes. For years, his renditions of city businesses were featured on plates and cups commemorating the annual Tri-State Pottery Festival. It was said of his paintings that one could "put them together like a jigsaw puzzle, lay them out, and have a city." Hacker was about 72 when this photograph was taken at the family home on Vine Street in the 1980s. His studio was a small alcove off the dining room overlooking the backyard. The East Liverpool Historical Society's Hans Hacker Archive Project, under the direction of Catherine S. Vodrey, has archived a collection of Hacker paintings available as a package with CD, DVD, and booklet at the Museum of Ceramics and from the historical society. (Peter Hacker.)

Nine

Divided We Fall, United We Stand

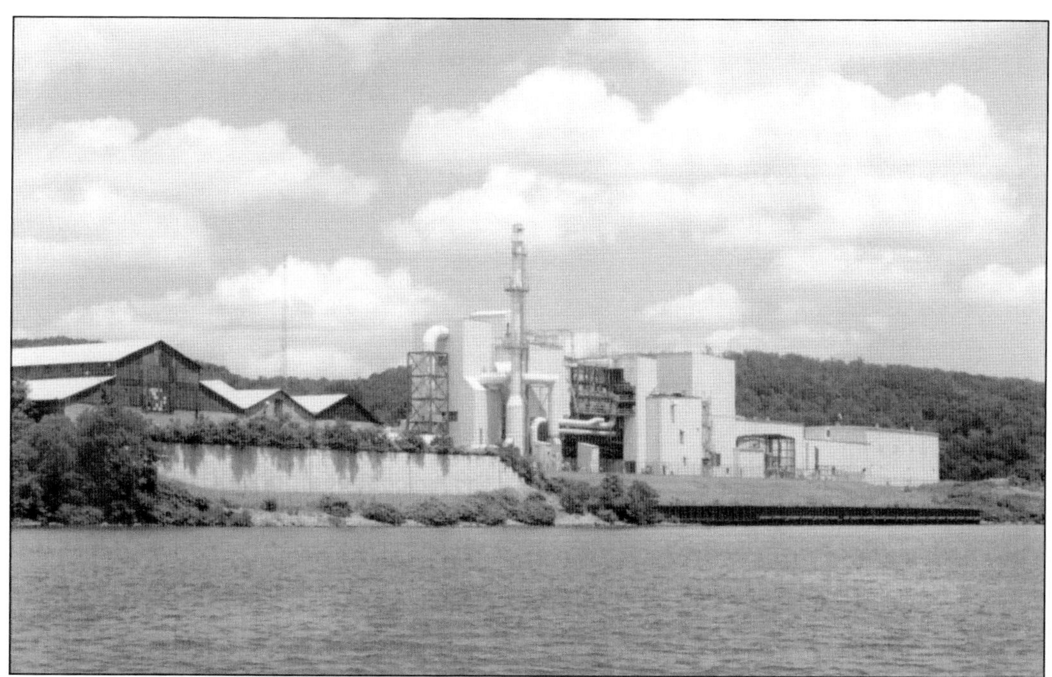

It should have been good news that a $90 million plant was to be built in East End, but to many Liverpudlians it was the worst news possible. In 1980, Waste Technologies Industries (WTI), a subsidiary of Von Roll of Switzerland, took a 20-year lease from the Columbiana County Port Authority to build a hazardous-waste incinerator 1,100 feet from East Elementary School. Parents and neighbors understandably had health concerns. (Alonzo Spencer.)

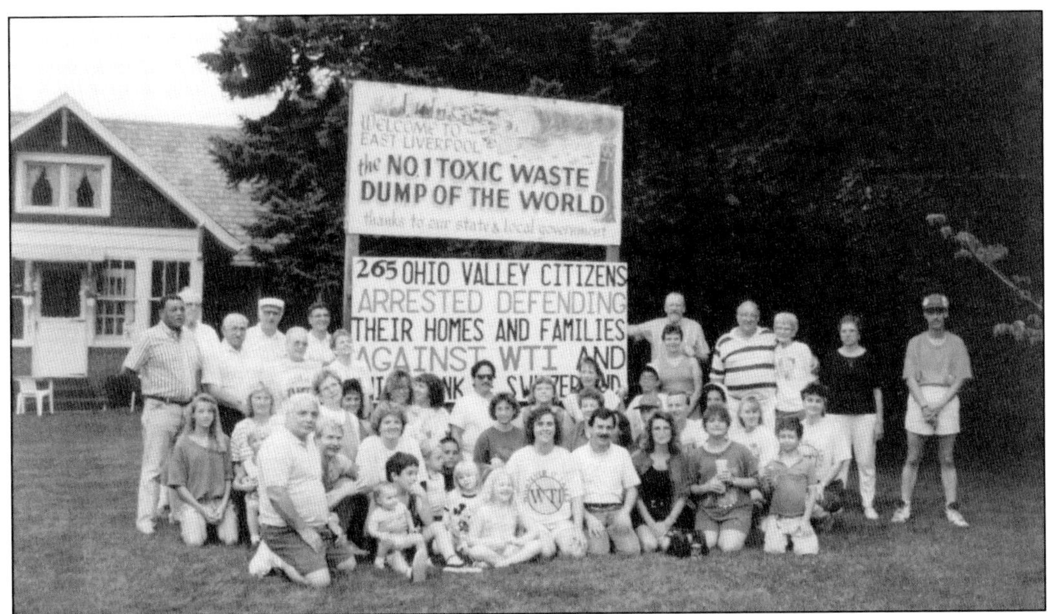

It did not take long for the proposed incinerator to polarize the community, and on both sides there were threats and name-calling. City council was divided 4-3 on WTI. The first protests were held in 1982 by the Save Our County group. The Ohio Hazardous Waste Facility Approval Board eventually issued a permit, and construction began amid vociferous opposition. The Tri-State Environmental Council formed in 1991 to continue protests over health concerns, while the Citizens for Progress promoted economic growth and employment. In 1997, the Ohio EPA issued a final permit. Protests lost momentum, though the fight continues. The incinerator, after two name changes, operates today as Heritage Thermal Services. Above, these signs stood prominently on a busy thoroughfare for years. Below, steadfast protester Alonzo Spencer takes a stand at the plant entrance. (Both Alonzo Spencer.)

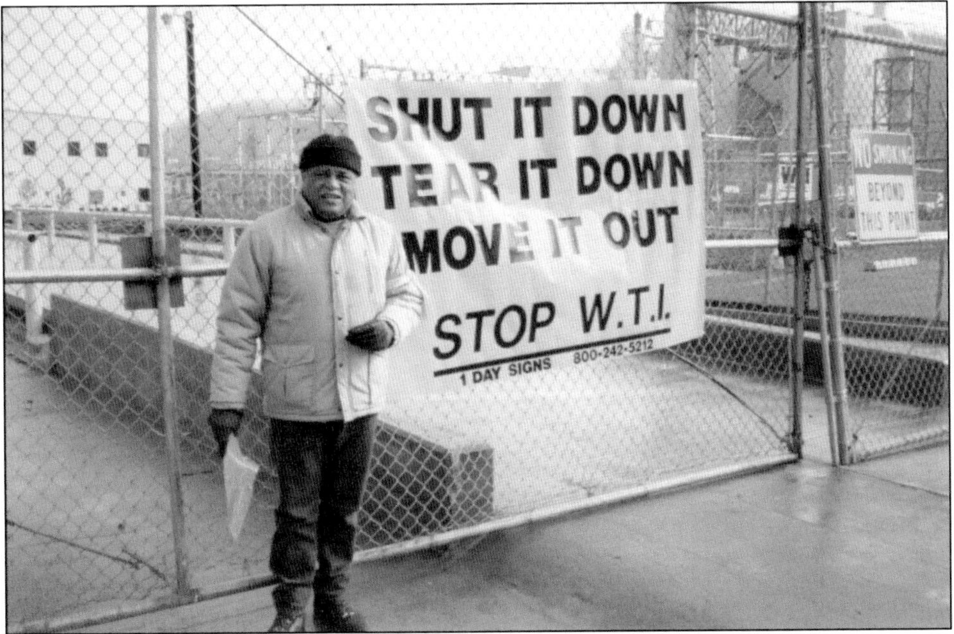

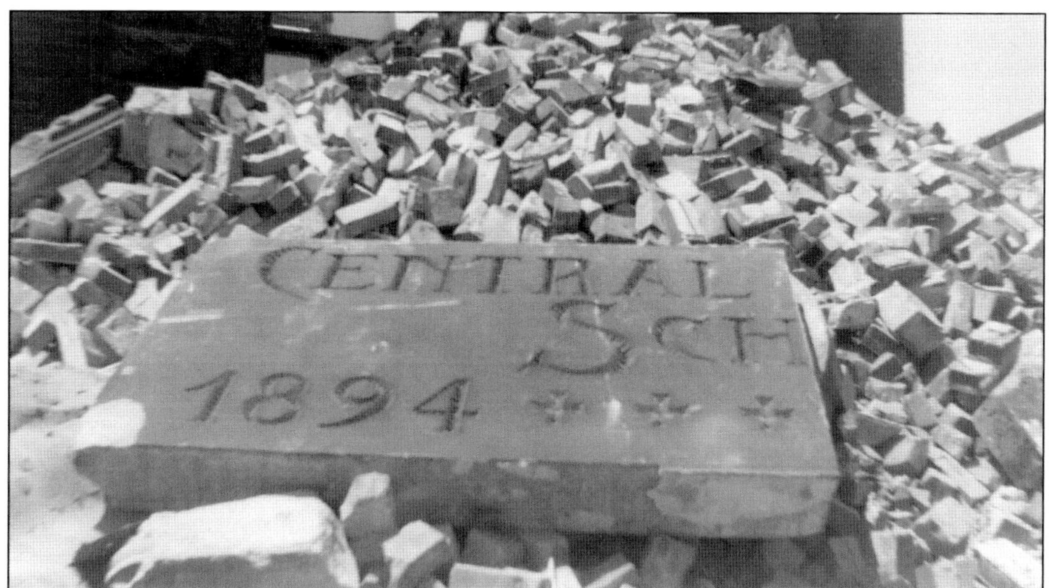

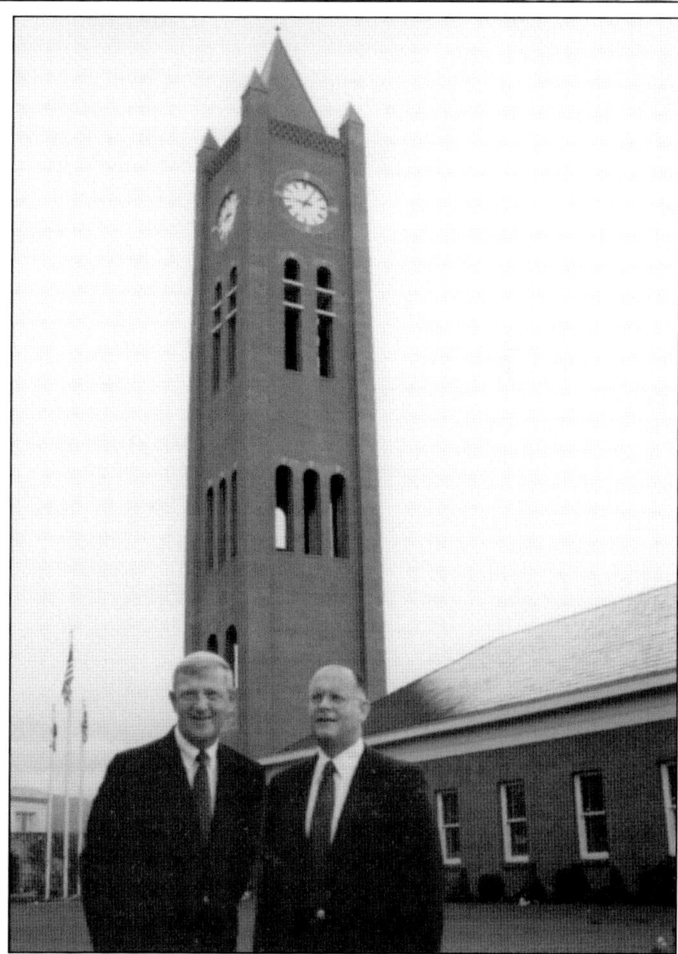

For past, present, and future students of East Liverpool High School, the somber photograph above evokes a wave of nostalgia and regret for Central School, a well-loved but vanished building torn down in 1969 or 1970. The best news Liverpudlians had heard for a while came in the late 1980s with the formation of an East Liverpool High School Alumni Association, spearheaded by Frank C. Dawson. A welcome tide of good feeling swept over the town, and with the enthusiastic outpouring of donations, plus generous volunteer labor, ground was broken during the first all-class reunion in 1987 for a museum that would include a rebuilt school clock tower, pictured at right with Lou Holtz (left) and Dawson (right). (Both East Liverpool High School Alumni Association.)

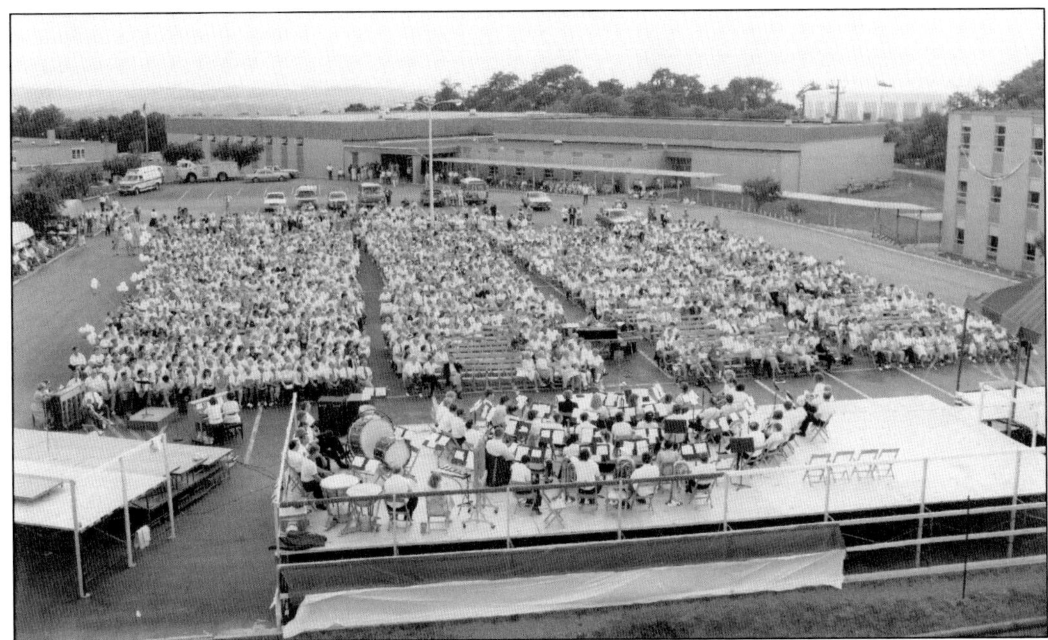

Thousands of ELHS alumni gathered at the new high school on Maine Boulevard over the Fourth of July weekend in 1987. ELH Student Alumni Association president Frank C. Dawson emceed the celebratory program that included the debut of a new anthem, "Let the Spirit Keep On Burning," written, scored, conducted, played, and sung by alumni. Downtown, there were museum tours, entertainment, banquets, and speeches. The newly formed alumni band, led by middle-aged majorettes with high-flying batons, marched in a circular parade that included every class. Banquet halls, lodges, and backyards filled up with individual class reunions, and revelers thronged the streets. Distinguished alumni were feted. There was even a high school dropout who roamed the town dressed as a bum, warning teens to stay in school. It was a celebration to end all celebrations in East Liverpool, a town that had not felt good about itself for many years. (Both Frank C. Dawson.)

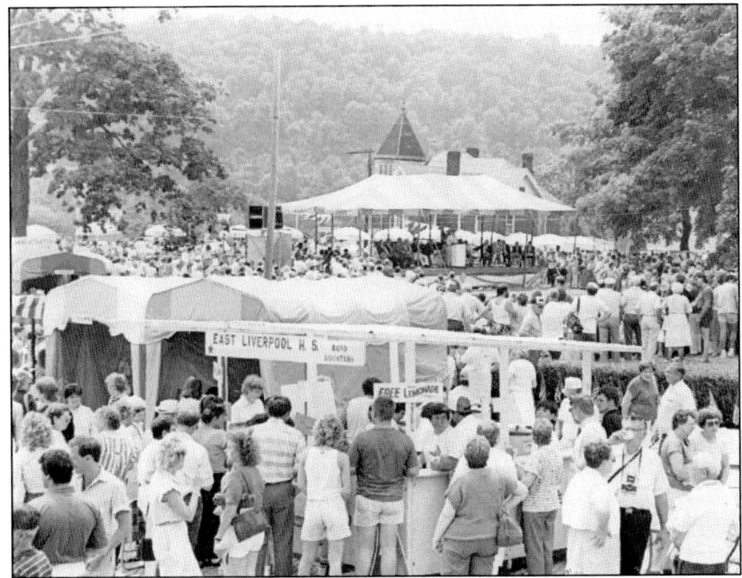

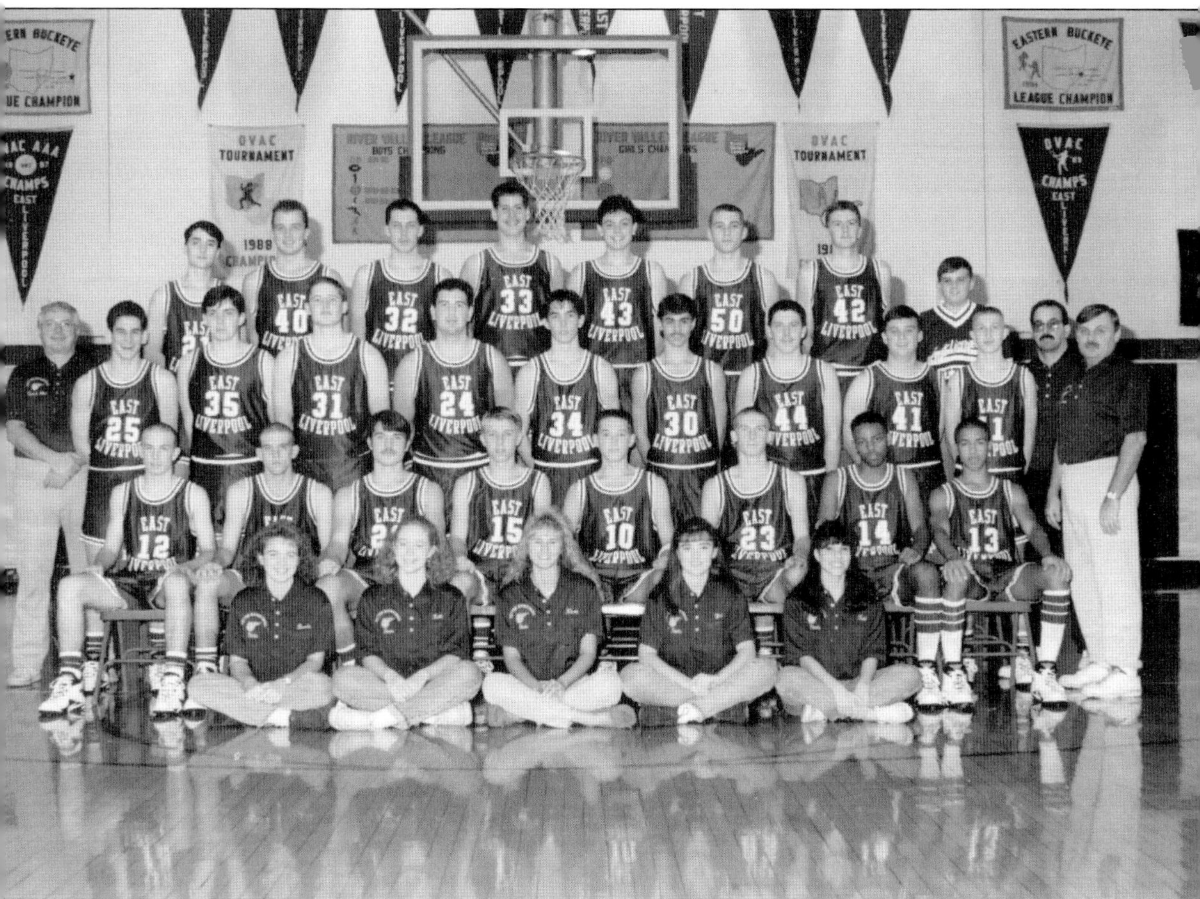

East Liverpool High School has a long and proud basketball history. The 1916 team, for instance, won a northern Ohio championship. This 1994 team had a 20-2 season, giving it up to Zanesville in sectionals. Pictured are, from left to right, (first row) statisticians Brenda Burns, Katie O'Hara, Nicole Michael, Holly Johnson, and Toni Amato; (second row) B.J. King, Fred Henderson, Ryan Cooper, Andy Swogger, Anson Weigand, Brett Bickar, B.J. Barrett, and John Scott; (third row) coach Nick Aloi, Mike Bosco, Joel Wolfe, Dave Hill, Ian Steffen, Rob Walgate, Ryan Pugliano, Eric Adkins, John Ash, Matt Bryan, coach Tony Branchetti, and assistant coach Gary Woods; (fourth row) Shawn Wilson, Kevin Mackey, Tim Adkins, Mark VanSickle, Steve Flores, Josh Martin, Dave Ward, and manager Josh Aikens. Flores would later, as a senior, set a school scoring record that would stand for eight years. (Andrea and Larry Adkins.)

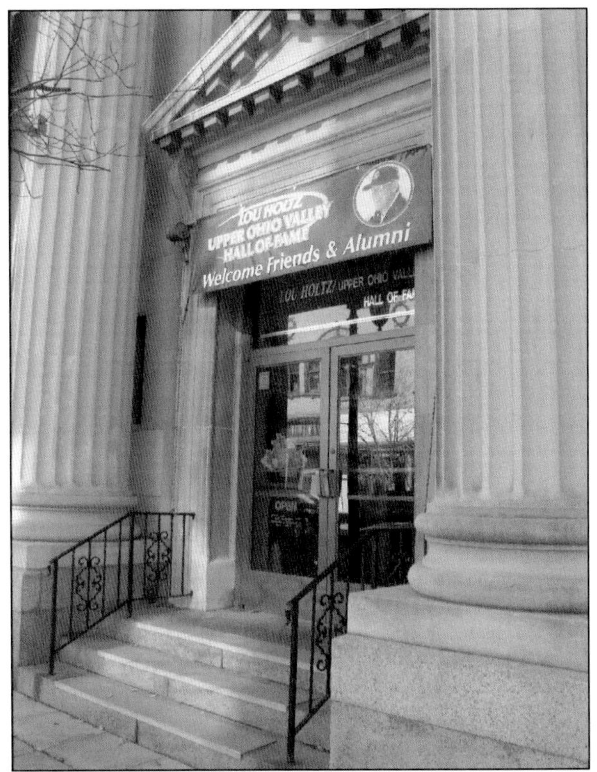

More good news came to East Liverpool courtesy of Frank Dawson in 1998 when he took an idea first proposed by business owner Pat Marshall and presented it to city native Lou Holtz, a well-known retired collegiate football coach. Marshall's idea had been to found a Lou Holtz museum in town. When Dawson and city native Dr. James Smith of New York approached Holtz with the idea, he agreed on the condition that the museum would celebrate the accomplishments of people of all fields in the upper Ohio Valley. The Lou Holtz/Upper Ohio Valley Hall of Fame opened in 1998 in the former First National Bank building on Fifth Street. Inside, the museum lives up to Holtz's vision by celebrating dozens of tristate-area people and preserving local history. (Both author's collection.)

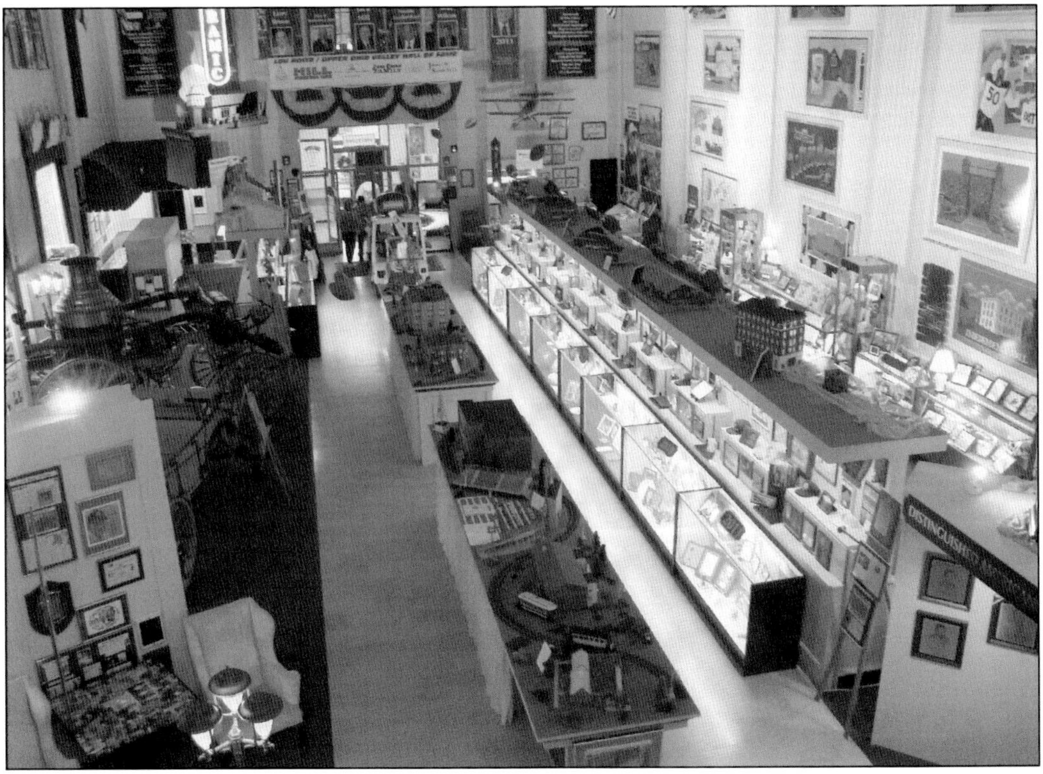

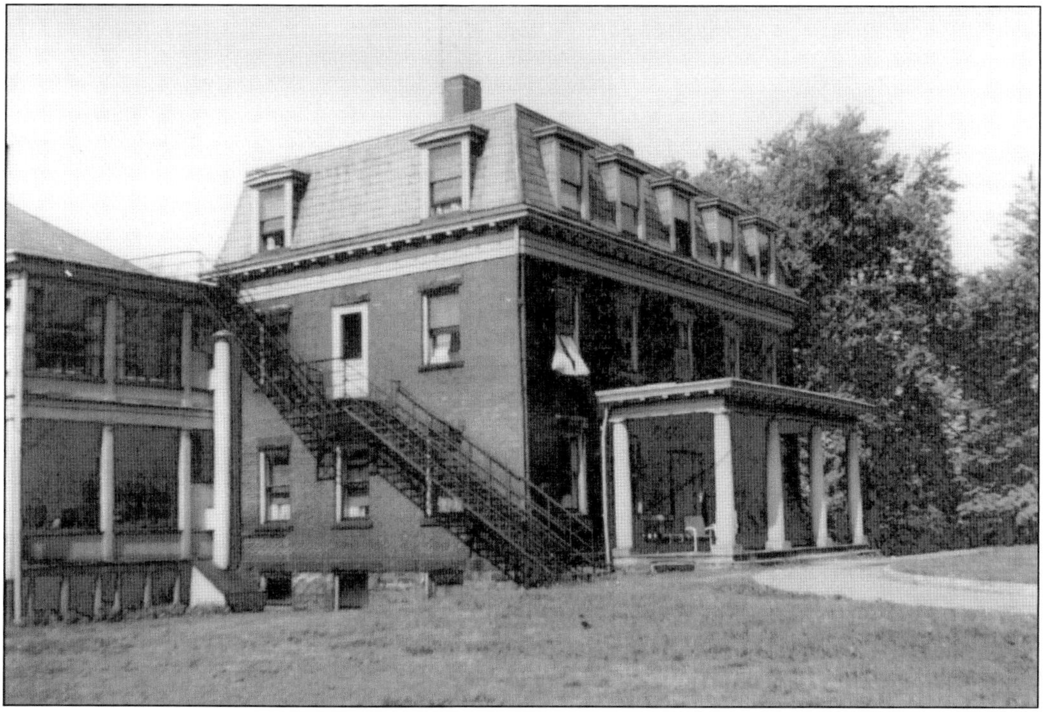

East Liverpool City Hospital, shown here in the original building in 1905, was constructed after a group of concerned city women formed the City Hospital Association in 1896. The first building had 52 ward beds and another 12 in private rooms. The hospital also operated a Training School of Nursing, and students cared for patients under supervision. The average stay in the early 20th century was 28 days. Additions were made to the hospital in 1911, 1931, 1954, 1964, 1966, 1977, 1990–1994, and 2005–2007. Today, the institution is owned by River Valley Health Partners and provides a full range of medical services. (Both River Valley Health Partners.)

Lorin Slates, pictured here, opened city landmark L&B Donuts on Market Street in 1938 with partner Bud Benson. Butch and Nancy Slates were the next owners before Fred Cain took over. Marta Schrieber owned the shop 22 years before selling to her niece Nicole Fitch, who had worked at the shop periodically since age 14. Fitch has expanded the business to include catering and a banquet hall. (Nicole Fitch.)

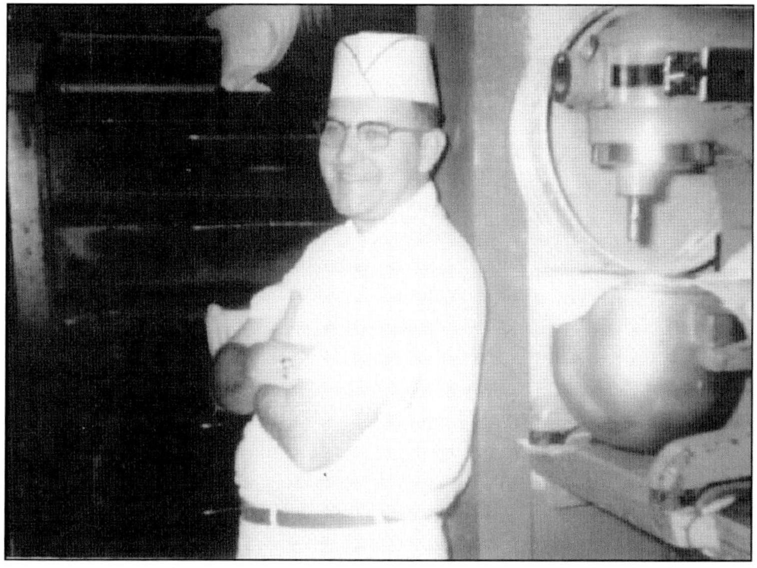

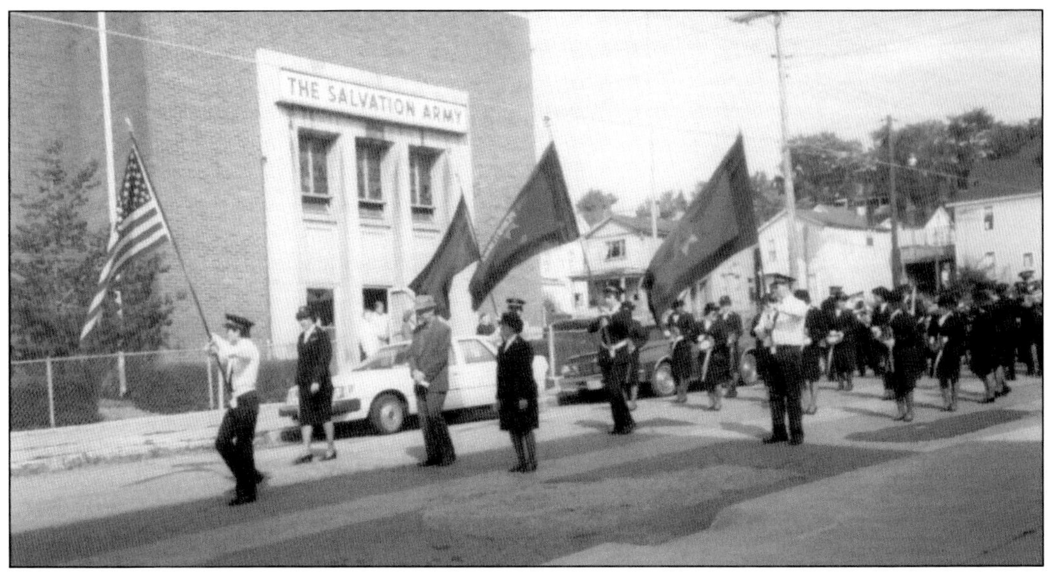

The East Liverpool Salvation Army Citadel on East Fourth Street celebrated its 125th year with programs and a parade through town in 2009. Across the street, its neighbor is the East Liverpool campus of Kent State University, housed in former city high school buildings and at the Mary Patterson building. KSU opened its first East Liverpool branch in 1959, but it soon closed because of low enrollment. After a Citizen's Committee for Higher Education petitioned Kent to reopen the branch, classes resumed in temporary quarters in 1965. By 1966, the branch was in full operation with 223 students. Today, KSU-EL offers eight associate degrees and three bachelor's degrees through traditional, online, and distance learning. (Above, Salvation Army; below, author's collection.)

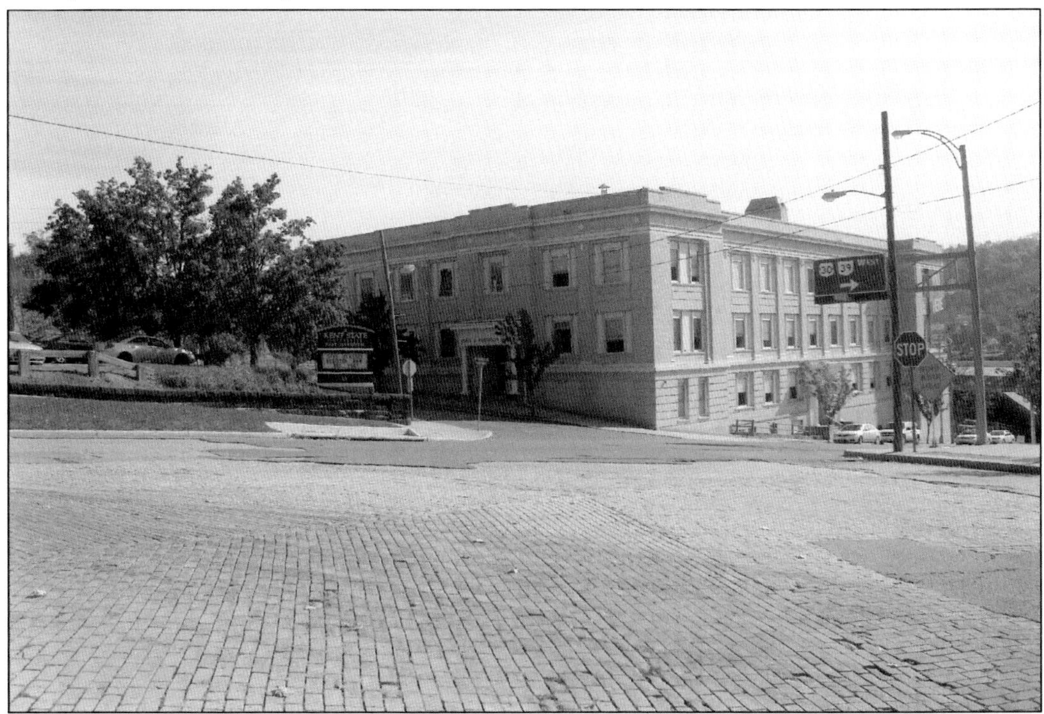

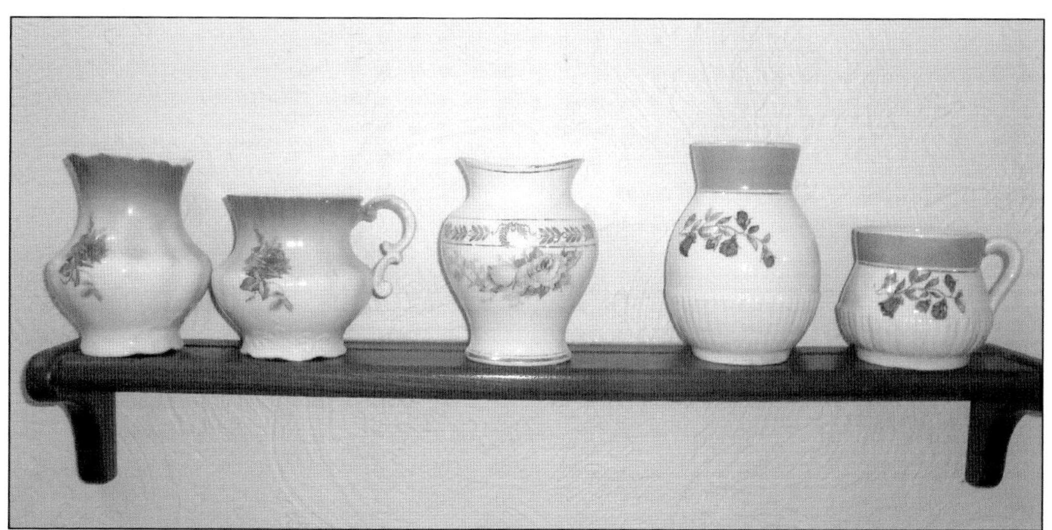

East Liverpudlians find unique ways to celebrate pottery heritage. Above is a collection of toothbrush holders. Officially known as brush vases, they were manufactured at area plants as part of toilet-ware sets. The two vases on the left are from the Goodwin Pottery, at center is a Homer Laughlin China Company vase, and the two on the right are from a Brunt pottery. Below, Java Jo House on Fifth Street preserves the 1900 home of pottery executive Francis Simmers, who was called "King of Sales" at Hall China. In 2006, Java Jo owner JoAnne Hissom Garcia and her husband, Ed, bought the rundown building, which had been empty for four years. After years of hard work and scrimping, they opened a coffee house in 2010. (Above, Phyllis Conley collection; below, author's collection.)

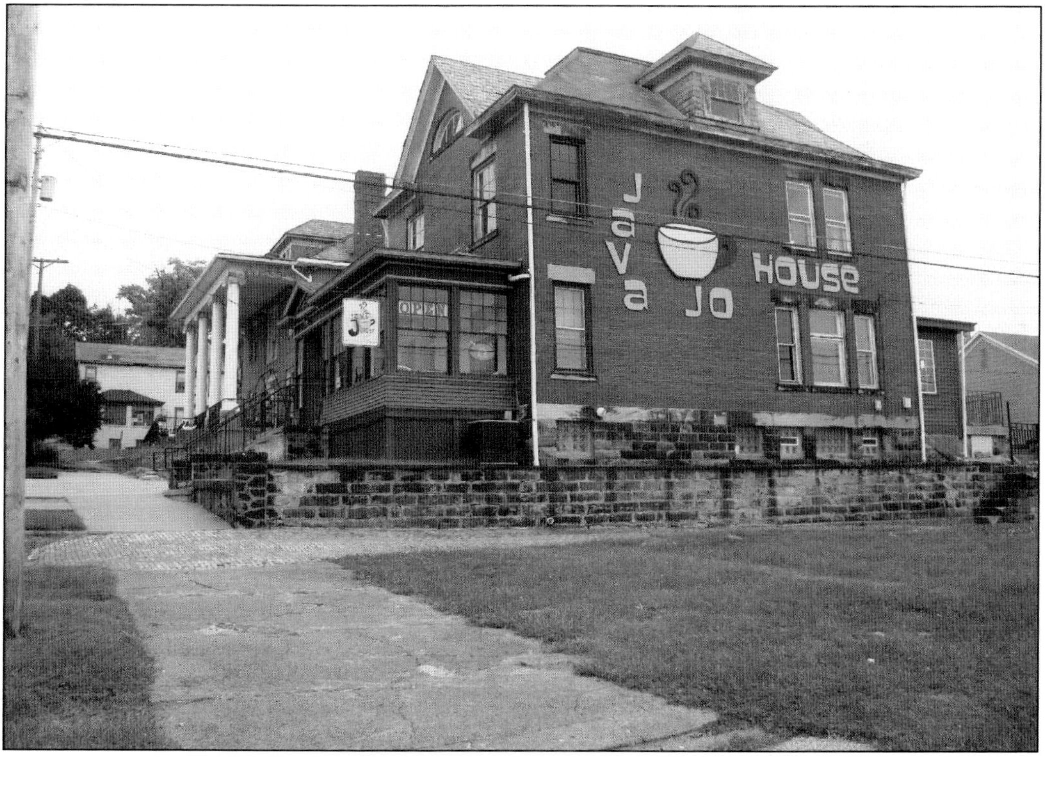

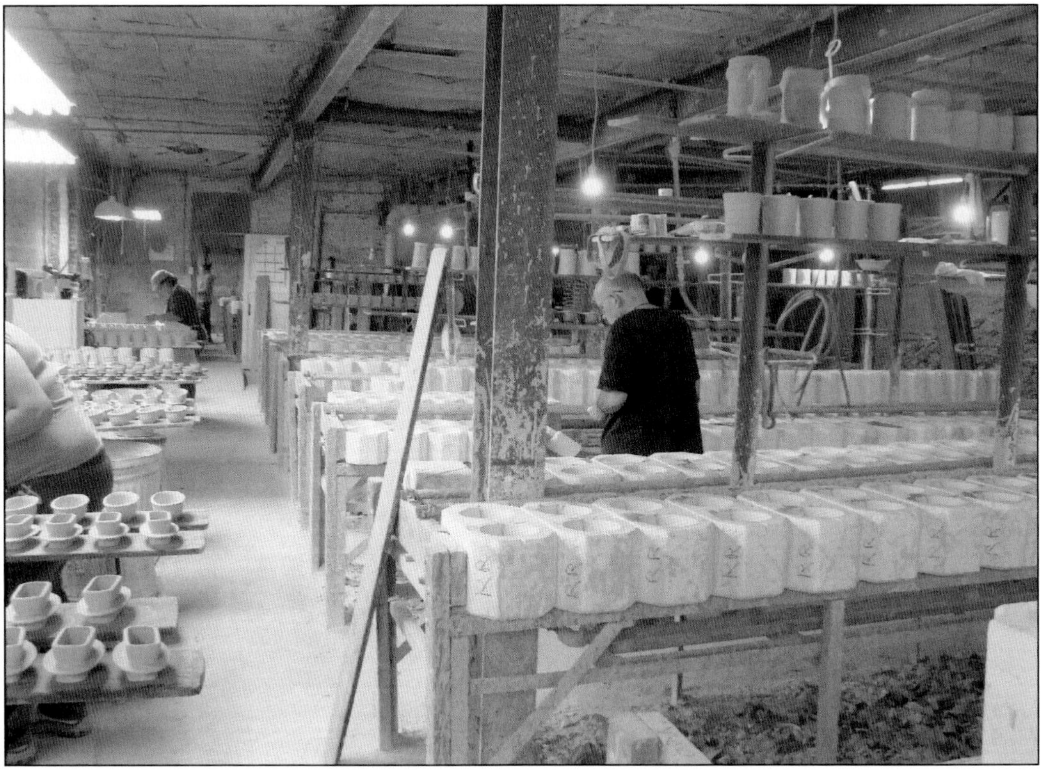

American Mug & Stein is a fairly recent addition to East Liverpool's pottery heritage. Known as Pioneer Pottery since the 1940s, when it was converted from a furniture factory, the Dresden Avenue business was owned by Bill and Arlene Bickle until 2009, when Clyde McClellan of Beaver, Pennsylvania, purchased and renamed it. Shortly after, the company was contacted by Hausenware, a ceramics distributor in Santa Rosa, California, representing Starbucks Coffee Company. The contract has been a foundation of the business ever since, says McClellan. Starbucks mugs made in East Liverpool are only sold in Seattle, Washington, according to McClellan, who notes that the small pottery operates in an old-fashioned way, each piece of ware being handled more than a dozen times. The 16 employees of American Mug & Stein mix clay, fill molds, finish green ware (above), and use a 250-cubic-foot shuttle kiln for firing (below). After the first firing, each piece is hand-dipped for glazing, then fired again. The company also manufactures coffee cups, mugs, steins, and butter dishes. (Both author's collection.)

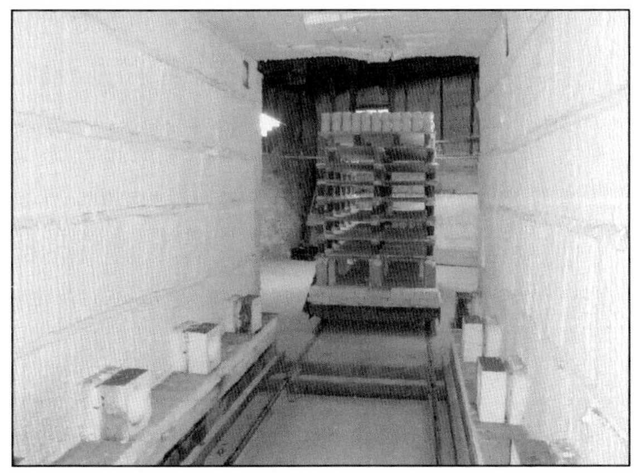

Bibliography

Barth, Harold B., *History of Columbiana County, Ohio.* Salem, MA: Higginson Book Company, 1997.

Brick and Clay Record, vol. 54. Windsor and Kenfield, 1919.

Gates, William C., *The City of Hills and Kilns*, East Liverpool, OH: East Liverpool Historical Society, 1984.

geosurvey.ohiodnr.gov

McCord, William B. *History of Columbiana County, Ohio and Representative Citizens.* Biographical Publishing Company, 1905.

www.amphilsoc.org

www.carnegie.lib.oh.us/potteries

www.eastliverpoolhistoricalsociety.org

www.heritage-wti.com

www.louholtzhalloffame.com

www.ohiohistorycentral.org

www.oplin.org

www.themuseumofceramics.org

Consistent with our mission to preserve history on a local level, this book was printed in South Carolina on American-made paper and manufactured entirely in the United States. Products carrying the accredited Forest Stewardship Council (FSC) label are printed on 100 percent FSC-certified paper.

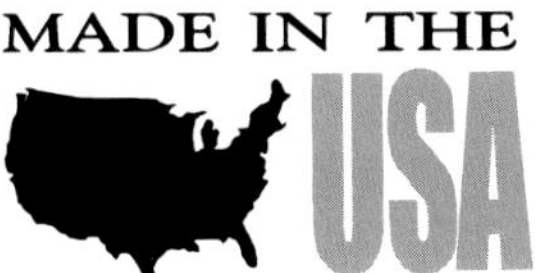